EURO-MEDITERRANEAN SECURITY

The International Political Economy of New Regionalisms Series

The International Political Economy of New Regionalisms Series presents innovative analyses of a range of novel regional relations and institutions. Going beyond established, formal, interstate economic organizations, this essential series provides informed interdisciplinary and international research and debate about myriad heterogeneous intermediate level interactions.

Reflective of its cosmopolitan and creative orientation, this series is developed by an international editorial team of established and emerging scholars in both the South and North. It reinforces ongoing networks of analysts in both academia and think-tanks as well as international agencies concerned with micro-, meso- and macro-level regionalisms.

Editorial Board

Timothy M. Shaw, University of London, UK
Isidro Morales, Universidad de las Américas - Puebla, Mexico
Maria Nzomo, University of Nairobi, Kenya
Nicola Phillips, University of Manchester, UK
Johan Saravanamuttu, Science University of Malaysia, Malaysia
Fredrik Söderbaum, Göteborgs Universitet, Sweden

Other Titles in the Series

Reconfigured Sovereignty
Thomas L. Ilgen

The New Regionalism in Africa
J. Andrew Grant and Fredrik Söderbaum

Comparative Regional Integration
Finn Laursen

Transnational Democracy in Critical and Comparative Perspective
Bruce Morrison

Euro-Mediterranean Security
A Search for Partnership

SVEN BISCOP
*The Royal Institute for International Relations,
Belgium*

LONDON AND NEW YORK

First published 2003 by Ashgate Publishing

Reissued 2018 by Routledge
2 Park Square, Milton Park, Abingdon, Oxon OX14 4RN
711 Third Avenue, New York, NY 10017, USA

Routledge is an imprint of the Taylor & Francis Group, an informa business

Copyright © Sven Biscop 2003

Sven Biscop has asserted his right under the Copyright, Designs and Patents Act, 1988, to be identified as author of this work.

All rights reserved. No part of this book may be reprinted or reproduced or utilised in any form or by any electronic, mechanical, or other means, now known or hereafter invented, including photocopying and recording, or in any information storage or retrieval system, without permission in writing from the publishers.

Notice:
Product or corporate names may be trademarks or registered trademarks, and are used only for identification and explanation without intent to infringe.

Publisher's Note
The publisher has gone to great lengths to ensure the quality of this reprint but points out that some imperfections in the original copies may be apparent.

Disclaimer
The publisher has made every effort to trace copyright holders and welcomes correspondence from those they have been unable to contact.

A Library of Congress record exists under LC control number: 2003052051

ISBN 13: 978-1-138-71398-7 (hbk)
ISBN 13: 978-1-138-71396-3 (pbk)
ISBN 13: 978-1-315-19798-2 (ebk)

Contents

List of Tables   *vi*
Preface   *vii*
Acknowledgements   *xiii*
List of Abbreviations   *xv*
Map of the Euro-Mediterranean Partnership   *xvii*

1	EU Interests and Mediterranean Security	1
2	The Euro-Mediterranean Partnership	23
3	EU Policy and Conflict in the Mediterranean	65
4	Building a Euro-Mediterranean Security Partnership	95
5	From Common Interests to Joint Actions	117

Bibliography   *127*
Index   *157*

List of Tables

1.1	Defence expenditure and armed forces in the Mediterranean in 1999	5
1.2	Ballistic missiles in the Mediterranean	7
1.3	Arms control agreements in the Mediterranean	8

Preface

The European Union is developing into a significant international actor in the field of security. In line with the overall objectives of the Common Foreign and Security Policy (CFSP) as included in the Treaty on European Union, the EU has now provided for itself an important role in the field of conflict prevention and crisis management. If the ambitious objectives regarding the creation of European capacities are achieved, *inter alia*, through the establishment of a military component for the CFSP, the European Security and Defence Policy (ESDP), the Union should emerge as a powerful international actor, possessing the whole range of policy instruments, from diplomatic and economic to military, to implement its CFSP.

Europe's ambitions to play a role in the field of international security are a result of fairly recent developments on the European continent. The end of the Cold War also saw the end of the stable and predictable security situation which, at least in Europe, had reigned for several decades. A new volatile security environment emerged, with the EU as a bloc of peace and stability amidst countries in the process of fundamental transformations. The Union's attention was immediately focussed on the Central and Eastern European countries which, after decades of seclusion, sought integration in the Western world. The EU acted as an 'exporter of stability': it provided, and still does, massive support for these countries' transition to democracy and the market economy and, hopefully, the welfare state, with membership of the Union as the ultimate objective. The eruption of a bloody conflict in Former Yugoslavia and the Union's inability to deal with it efficaciously, were a sad demonstration of the absolute need for Europe to develop a foreign and security policy suited to this new post-Cold War environment. The absence of structures to prevent or resolve the successive crises on the Balkans, the US' reluctance to intervene in what Washington deemed to be European problems, and the performance gap between European and American foreign and security policy very gradually convinced all Member States of the EU of the necessity to create the CFSP and later the ESDP. Several Member States, the Scandinavian countries e.g., are still hesitant regarding integration in these fields and both the CFSP and the ESDP yet retain an intergovernmental character, but they are fully developing.

Driven by the concerns of its Southern Member States, the EU gradually began to devote more attention to its Southern periphery as well. During the Cold War the focus of security policy had been continental Europe. The Mediterranean was merely a side-show to this central stage of East-West confrontation and Western security policy towards the region was completely dominated by the US. Now security in the Mediterranean has attained a higher profile and new security issues have become apparent. The Union became aware of its important interests in the area, hence the need for a security policy towards the region, if only because of geographic proximity. This prompted the EU in 1995 to launch the Euro-Mediterranean Partnership (EMP) with twelve Mediterranean countries. The Partnership includes an ambitious security dimension. At the same time as developing a new role in the fields of conflict prevention and crisis management, the Union is also manifesting itself in a region in which until a few years ago it played a very limited part, certainly in the politico-military field. One should not forget though that historically Europe has always been very much present in the Mediterranean, even to the point of dominating it. Until the Second World War France and the UK and, to a lesser extent, Spain and Italy, controlled most of the countries that are now the Union's Mediterranean partners and their influence based on that legacy is important still. In this sense the Union is only renewing its participation in the dynamics of the Mediterranean, but this time its policies are founded on a spirit of partnership and cooperation instead of imperialist designs. The Mediterranean today is a very unstable area however, a region troubled by persisting conflicts and disputes. The conflict in the Middle East is of course the most prominent of these, but Greek-Turkish tensions, the Cyprus issue, the violence in Algeria and the matter of the Western Sahara are equally threatening to peace and stability. While the Mediterranean during several periods in history functioned as a bridge, it is nowadays more often perceived as the frontier line between the West and the Arab world. More often than not the latter is seen as a source of security threats. A closer look however reveals interests which are common to both shores of the Mediterranean. The cooperative approach to security advocated by the EMP is an attempt to do away with the idea of the Mediterranean as a frontier and to make it once again into a crossroads of ideas.

This book is based on the thesis on the basis of which on 24 May 2002 I obtained the doctorate in political sciences from Ghent University (Belgium). Its object is the security policy of the EU towards the Mediterranean from 1 November 1993 until April 2003, when the final version of the manuscript was completed.

Piles of literature have been written on the definition of 'the Mediterranean'. There are in fact as many definitions as there are authors, varying from limited ones that include only the littoral states, to very broad definitions that include the Gulf region or even the Caucasus and Central Asia. Actually, depending on the issues under consideration, all of these definitions can be defended. As the object of my research is EU policy, I use the notion 'Mediterranean' as it is understood by the Union itself in its policy documents regarding the area: the twelve partner countries plus Libya, the remaining littoral state, which is already associated with the Partnership and which is universally recognized as a necessary future member. 'Euro-Mediterranean' refers then to the EU and its twelve partners combined. I will thus look at the Mediterranean in the context of the EMP, which is the Union's main policy framework with regard to the region. Rather than assessing EU policies towards the different countries and sub-regions separately, I will attempt to frame them in the overall objectives of the Partnership. Although they border the Mediterranean Sea, the Balkans are therefore excluded from this book, because by the EU they are dealt with in a completely separate policy framework, which is much closer to the Union's Central and Eastern European policy. The Gulf region, the Caucasus and Central Asia have been excluded for the same reason. Apart from any structural impact on the CFSP and Euro-Mediterranean relations, neither Afghanistan nor Iraq is covered – surely plenty of other, more qualified authors will devote their skills to these countries.

There is an ongoing debate on the question whether the Mediterranean really constitutes a region and whether it would not be closer to reality on the ground to deal with sub-regions, such as the Aegean, the Middle East and the Maghreb. The creation of the EMP does imply the existence of a Euro-Mediterranean community however, be it strong or weak, and therefore justifies an approach looking at the Mediterranean as a whole.

Just like the notion 'Mediterranean', 'security', the condition of being protected from or not exposed to danger and the feeling or perception of freedom from danger, is a very broad and flexible concept. A comprehensive approach to security is in order: security is the sum of political, economic, social, ecologic and cultural as well as military factors. Security therefore cannot be achieved by just security policy, i.e. by politico-military measures alone. Security requires the application of a whole range of policies, *inter alia*, external trade, development cooperation, environmental policy, police, justice and intelligence cooperation, immigration policy, foreign policy and also security policy. An actor which does not take this into account is bound to fail.

However, I have focused my own research on just one of these dimensions of security: 'traditional' or 'hard' security. In other words, I have limited the object of the book to security policy, to the politico-military aspects of conflict prevention and crisis management, because in the context of Euro-Mediterranean relations these of late have received rather limited attention. The need for a comprehensive approach and the difficulty of 'hard' security cooperation in the Mediterranean should not lead us into ignoring the importance of the politico-military dimension in a region that is still conflict-prone. The book thus concentrates on the 'hard' security aspects of the first basket of the EMP, the political and security partnership, but these are always seen as part of a broad, comprehensive approach to security. By themselves, Union policies in the fields of democratization, economic support, dialogue between cultures and other 'soft' security areas, although they do contribute to long-term conflict prevention, are not the subject of this book. Nor are post-conflict peace-building and issues that in my opinion are unjustly 'securitized', i.e. issues that are dealt with in the context of 'hard' security by several Western authors and policy-makers, because they are felt to pose a threat to the West, but that really should be the object of economic and social policy and development cooperation; migration is the most notable example.

One of the most important topics within the politico-military dimension of security is the development of confidence and security-building measures (CSBMs). Again, different definitions exist, even different terms, such as confidence-building measures (CBMs) and, in the context of the EMP, partnership-building measures (PBMs). I use the notion CSBMs as it is understood by the OSCE: provisions for the exchange and verification of information and mechanisms for cooperation regarding armed forces and military activities, with the aim of promoting mutual trust (OSCE, 2000, pp.120–22). The term PBMs is reserved for measures in the other fields covered by the EMP.

The starting date of 1 November 1993 has been chosen because it is the day of the commencement of the Maastricht Treaty and thus of the CFSP, which is the Union's foreign policy framework. The nature of the CFSP is therefore an important factor affecting the Union's Mediterranean policy. Apart from brief historical notes, the period before 1993 is not covered extensively, in order to avoid having to deal with the previous and now defunct foreign policy structure: European Political Cooperation (EPC). The limited nature of EPC had a severe effect on Europe's foreign policy, but, though interesting from a historical perspective, this is not relevant to current EU policy.

Having defined the object, the underlying hypothesis of my research is that in spite of the eye-catching diversity existing within the Euro-Mediterranean region, the EU and its twelve Mediterranean partners share important political, economic and other interests. Or, to put it differently, that the Mediterranean is in fact a *mare nostrum*, not of the EU, but of all twenty-seven partner countries. This fact necessitates a common Euro-Mediterranean security policy in order to preserve these joint interests, which at the same time provide the foundation on which a common policy can be established. Looking at the Mediterranean through the lens of EU policy, which is indeed the object of this book, might be considered a eurocentric approach, but the basic hypothesis is that shared interests by both shores of the Mediterranean outweigh the differences between North and South and therefore demand and make possible a truly Euro-Mediterranean policy: from common interests to joint actions.

Starting from this hypothesis, the objective of the book is threefold:

- to establish which are the interests of the Union in the Mediterranean and to which extent these are shared by its Mediterranean partners, in order to assess whether they are able to serve as the foundation of a common Euro-Mediterranean security policy, and to define which should be the objectives of such a policy, in order to safeguard the interests of the Union and its partners;
- to analyze the Union's Mediterranean security policy and to assess its efficacy. The basic methodology of policy analysis is applied, i.e. extracting from policy documents and from actions on the ground the objectives of the Union, the instruments applied to achieve them and the means (financial, personnel etc.) devoted to that end. Then follows the assessment of the efficacy of this policy, i.e. determining to what extent the policy objectives have been achieved and have safeguarded the Union's interests, and determining which factors explain the success or failure of a given policy;
- to formulate recommendations for the optimisation of the Union's Mediterranean security policy, in the framework of a comprehensive approach to security.

Chapter 1 thus starts with an analysis of the Union's interests in the area and an assessment of how these are affected by the major issues determining security in the Mediterranean, in order to establish what the objectives of a Euro-Mediterranean security policy should be, taking into account the interests which the EU and the Mediterranean countries have in common. The ensuing chapters then present an analysis of EU security policy towards the Mediterranean. First the security dimension of the EMP is looked at, which constitutes the general framework for Union policy and addresses region-wide security issues (chapter 2). The Mediterranean Dialogue of WEU, the organization which constituted the Union's military arm until the EU assumed the task of crisis management itself, is covered here as well. Then follows an analysis of Union policy with regard to specific disputes and conflicts in the different sub-regions of the Mediterranean: the Eastern Mediterranean, the Middle East and North Africa (chapter 3). This chapter also offers suggestions for an active EU conflict resolution policy. In chapter 4 an attempt is then made to formulate recommendations for the optimisation of the Union's Mediterranean security policy; the ultimate outcome should be an equitable and efficacious Euro-Mediterranean security partnership. Chapter 5 summarizes the main findings and recommendations.

I have not written a theoretical work. True to the spirit of my original academic education in public management, I have concentrated on the analysis of actual policy and on the attempt to arrive at policy recommendations which can be of use to policy-makers in the field. As I already made clear in the definition of the object of this book, I have avoided discussions on concepts, nor have I attempted to explain EU policy or the emergence of the EMP by theoretical models. I have rather concentrated on the interests of the Union and its partners, on the effects of Union policy and on the factors explaining its success or failure. I have tried though to put these in the context of the comprehensive approach to security, the further elaboration of which is the subject of my current research.

Because of the diversity and complexity of the region, the Mediterranean and European policy towards it proved to be a fascinating research object, equally so because the EMP is a fairly recent initiative and therefore still developing. The same goes for the CFSP, and for the ESDP and the Union's role in the fields of conflict prevention and crisis management in particular. In the more Northern Member States of the EU especially and certainly in Belgium, the number of academics dealing with the Mediterranean is limited. But it was leaving trodden paths and discovering a new subject that created the drive that is necessary to write a doctoral thesis and to wrestle through the less glamorous aspects of research. Part of that challenge also was that following publication of a book on the development of the bodies and mechanisms of the Union's security and defence policy (Biscop, 2000), I was eager to see how the Union managed its new role in these fields in actual practice, in this case with regard to the Mediterranean. Researching a subject of current world affairs presents difficulties of its own: the situation on the ground changes daily, and each change has to be taken into account. This is certainly the case with regard to the Middle East peace process, not to mention of course the tremendous impact of '11 September' and, in the final stages of revision, the Iraqi crisis. It is sometimes difficult to find primary sources on diplomatic and other actions that are taking place behind the closed doors and that only become fully clear with the passing of time. Likewise the number of academic publications about current events is smaller; often press reports are the only available source.

But on the other hand it is so much more interesting to closely follow ongoing developments, to contribute to the academic debate about them and, on the basis of one's research, to join in the broader debate among politicians, officials, journalists and public opinion. I can only hope that my own small contribution, and notably the suggestions for ways to optimize EU policy, will be of some relevance to policy-makers and thus to the people of the Euro-Mediterranean area. For if there is one important idea underlying my research, it is voluntarism: the idea that society can be changed for the better and that all of us, through our own work, can and should contribute to this. In this case, it is up to an activist EU to take the lead.

Sven Biscop

Acknowledgements

Firstly, I want to express my warmest thanks to Prof. Dr. Marc Cogen, who is responsible – or should I say, to blame? – for my choice of 'the academic profession'. Marc, who teaches international law at Ghent University, was the promoter of the thesis on the development of a European security and defence identity which I wrote to obtain my original degree in public management in 1998. It was his enthusiastic appeal to join him in his International and European Research Unit that convinced me to start the complex undertaking of writing a Ph.D. thesis – even though this implied joining the Law Faculty, something slightly less than evident for a graduate from the Faculty of Political and Social Sciences ... With one foot in both faculties I managed to keep upright though. It was also on Marc's suggestion that I chose the Mediterranean region as the object of my research and thus left the trodden paths of research on European security issues, to focus on an area which, in Belgium at least, receives far less attention. The combination of my public management education, my interest in the second pillar of the EU, particularly in its security and defence dimension, and the Mediterranean unveiled a very fascinating area of research.

With Marc's support I was lucky to obtain the Paul-Henri Spaak Ph.D. scholarship of the Fund for Scientific Research – Flanders (1999–2002), to which I thus owe all my gratitude. The support which I received from the Political and Social Sciences Faculty was instrumental in acquiring this positive response to my scholarship application. I particularly want to thank Prof. Dr. Rik Coolsaet, who was kind enough to act as referee for my application and who was always willing to provide his advice throughout my research. Having finished the Ph.D., I followed Rik to the Royal Institute for International Relations in Brussels, the think-tank of the Belgian Ministry of Foreign Affairs, where he became Director and I became research fellow of a new Security and Global Governance Department (2002). I would also like to thank Prof. Dr. Bob Van Hooland, who very graciously took me on as researcher in the public management department during the year between my graduation and the start of my scholarship (1998–1999), and who, even more generously, allowed me to spend all the time I needed on the preparation of my scholarship application and on the initial stages of research, which enabled me to make a head-start.

The best way to shape one's ideas is through interaction with fellow academics and others active in the same field. In this context I would like to mention the encouraging cooperation of the Belgian Army's Royal Defence College, notably Colonel Emiel Verstraelen, Director of its Centre for Defence Studies, and Lieutenant-Colonel Patrick Geysen, now working for the Belgian Military Representation to the EU, who through publication and lecturing opportunities provided ample occasions to test my views on an experienced military, diplomatic and political audience. Others whom I would have to mention are all the members of what one might rightfully call 'the Euro-Med community' among academics, whose previous research I could build on and who I had the opportunity to meet and talk with in the hallways, during meals and – of course – at night in the bar at several conferences. Their well-founded remarks and suggestions proved very encouraging.

At one of those many conferences I was very lucky to meet Professor Timothy Shaw, editor of the series of which this book is a part. I want to thank Tim and everyone at Ashgate for giving me the opportunity to publish this book and thus forcing me to rewrite my Ph.D. thesis into a – hopefully – more readable text. This book project was soon followed by other opportunities for cooperation with Tim, who really is one of the nicest colleagues I have ever met.

Two people that I cannot forget are my colleagues and fellow Ph.D. candidates in the International and European Research Unit, Samer Fares and Sharon Pardo. Both originating from the Mediterranean region – they are Palestinian and Israeli respectively and close friends at that – they were very interesting and interested interlocutors, with whom I spent many hours discussing the intricacies of Middle Eastern politics, introducing them meanwhile to the delicacies of the Belgian art of beer brewing. Not to be forgotten either is my close friend and intellectual sparring partner Elisabeth De Zutter, Ph.D. candidate in the Political Sciences Department, and probably the severest, and therefore most useful, critic of the product of my academic labour.

Finally, but most importantly, I thank the two people to whom I owe my name and all my good qualities (the bad ones I have acquired on my own): my parents, François Biscop and Flori Gillis. I thank them and my sister, Joke, for putting up with their son and brother, who is still living at home (though never there, for he is always off to some meeting or other) and, basically, for always being there to give help whenever asked something. And Dad, I'm sorry I was not laid out to become an engineer like you ...

List of Abbreviations

ACRS	Arms Control and Regional Security Working Group
AMU	Arab Maghreb Union
BTWC	Biological and Toxin Weapons Convention
CBMs	Confidence-building measures
CD	Conference on Disarmament
CEP	Civil Emergency Planning
CFE	Treaty on Conventional Armed Forces in Europe
CFSP	Common Foreign and Security Policy
CPC	Conflict Prevention Centre
CSBMs	Confidence and security-building measures
CSCE	Conference on Security and Cooperation in Europe
CSCM	Conference on Security and Cooperation in the Mediterranean
CTBT	Comprehensive Nuclear Test-Ban Treaty
CWC	Chemical Weapons Convention
DGP	High Level Senior Defence Group on Proliferation (NATO)
EEC	European Economic Community
EMP	Euro-Mediterranean Partnership
EP	European Parliament
EPC	European Political Cooperation
ESDP	European Security and Defence Policy
EU	European Union
EuroMeSCo	Euro-Mediterranean Study Commission
EUROFOR	Rapid Deployment Euroforce
EUROMARFOR	European Maritime Force
FAWEU	Forces Answerable to the Western European Union
FIS	Front Islamique du Salut
GCC	Gulf Cooperation Council
GDP	Gross Domestic Product
GMP	Global Mediterranean Policy
IAEA	International Atomic Energy Agency
ICC	International Criminal Court
ICJ	International Court of Justice
IFOR	Implementation Force
IMF	International Monetary Fund
KFOR	Kosovo Force
MCG	Mediterranean Cooperation Group
MEDA	Financial and technical measures to accompany the reform of social and economic structures in the Mediterranean non-member countries

MINURSO	United Nations Mission for the Referendum in Western Sahara
MTCR	Missile Technology Control Regime
NAC	North Atlantic Council
NATO	North Atlantic Treaty Organization
NPT	Non-Proliferation Treaty
NSG	Nuclear Suppliers Group
OAU	Organization of African Unity
OECD	Organization for Economic Cooperation and Development
OSCE	Organization for Security and Cooperation in Europe
PBMs	Partnership building measures
PKK	Kurdistan Workers' Party
PLO	Palestine Liberation Organization
POLISARIO	Frente Popular para la Liberación de Saguia el-Hamra y de Río de Oro
PSC	Political and Security Committee
RMP	Renovated or Redirected Mediterranean Policy
SADR	Sahrawi Arab Democratic Republic
SFOR	Stabilization Force
SIAF	Spanish-Italian Amphibious Force
TRNC	Turkish Republic of Northern Cyprus
UK	United Kingdom
UN	United Nations
UNFICYP	United Nations peacekeeping force in Cyprus
UNROCA	United Nations Register of Conventional Arms
US	United States
WEU	Western European Union
WMD	Weapons of mass destruction

Map of the Euro-Mediterranean Partnership

Source: Tim Van de Voorde, Free University of Brussels

Legend

- ▨ EU Member States
- ☐ Mediterranean Partners

Kilometers: 0 375 750 1,500 2,250 3,000

*To my sister Joke and her son, Jobbe Biscop,
11 February 2003*

Chapter 1

EU Interests and Mediterranean Security

Introduction

In order to discuss European security policy towards the Mediterranean, the general picture of security in the region must first be drawn. This chapter presents an overview of the main items on the Mediterranean security agenda and then goes on to assess how these affect the interests of the EU – interests which the EU turns out to have in common with its Mediterranean neighbours. This analysis allows for the objectives and the necessary components of EU security policy towards the region to be determined.

The Mediterranean Security Environment

Disputes over Territory and Resources

Although since the Gulf War there have been no major conflicts, stability in the Mediterranean remains highly precarious because of the large number of interrelated tensions in the area.

In the first place there are a number of 'conventional' disputes over territory and resources (Larrabee, Green, Lesser and Zanini, 1998, pp.11–12). In the Eastern Mediterranean the Cyprus issue remains a source of tension. Tensions over Cyprus are of course related to the general antagonism between Greece and Turkey, who still dispute the sovereignty over a number of islands in the Aegean, which in the past has led to several instances of nearly open conflict between these two members of NATO. Turkey also has troubled relations with the Arab countries, especially with Syria, notably since it concluded military cooperation agreements with Israel. Syria claims the Turkish province of Hatay,[1] while Turkey accuses Syria of supporting 'Kurdish separatism'. Syria plays an important role in the Middle East, demanding the return of the Golan Heights while still controlling Lebanon. Following the conclusion of the Oslo Accords considerable progress has been made in the relations between Israel and the Palestinian Authority, but a final settlement has still not been achieved and several sensitive issues (*inter alia* the status of Jerusalem, the return of Palestinian refugees, Israeli colonization) continue to haunt the peace process. The Arab-Israeli dispute is a central factor in Mediterranean security, for as long as it has remains unresolved and relations between Israel and the Arab countries have not been normalized, further cooperation towards the stabilization of the region is effectively blocked. In the Western Mediterranean the problem of the Western Sahara continues to create frictions between Morocco and Algeria, while relations between Libya and its neighbours remain strained even though the international isolation of the country is gradually coming to an end. Relations between Morocco and Spain are negatively influenced by the claims of the former on the enclaves of Ceuta and Melilla and the uninhabited island of Perejil, which was just recently put on the map when in the Summer of 2002 it was briefly occupied by Moroccan forces, a move which did succeed in putting off the dead season in the media for some time.

Another important source of potential conflict is the shortage of water in the region and the desertification problem. Already demand for water surpasses availability, while the rapid growth of the population aggravates the problem. The existence of territorial disputes increases the sensitivity of the water issue; states accuse each other of diverting water flows to their own benefit. To solve the problem requires international cooperation, but this is not easily achieved in a region prone to conflict and tensions (Braverman, 1995; Soffer, 1998). Environmental issues thus have an important impact on security in the Mediterranean. Pollution, desertification and other ecologic problems add a new dimension to the traditional struggle for scarce resources.

These tensions demonstrate that nationalism is a force to be reckoned with in the area, which has a major influence on the foreign policies of the Mediterranean countries. One of the causes of this is to be found in the domestic political situation of the states concerned (Lesser, 1997, p.2; Aliboni, 1999a, pp.5–8). The weakness or even absence of democracy and the poor economical situation of the majority of the population lead to a lack of support for the regimes and a low degree of legitimacy – tensions or alliances are between regimes rather than states. In order to distract attention away from internal problems and to achieve internal consensus on an alternative basis, governments tend to wage a nationalist foreign policy. Internal problems are easily blamed on outside influences and especially on the West. As religion is very important to the identity of the local populations, policies that are said to be aiming to guarantee the autonomy of their ethnic and religious culture in the world and to preserve it from foreign intrusion, combined with the aspiration of regional leadership, can easily mobilize the people and can reconcile religious, secular and even Westernized public opinion. Nationalist foreign policy thus serves a utilitarian purpose – more often than not it is evaluated in terms of its effects on domestic politics rather than as a policy field in its own right. Arab nationalism interacts with Israeli nationalism, which is most visible with the extremist Israelis, whose exorbitant demands often block the peace process. Thus Israeli nationalism also contributes to the region's instability (Winrow, 2000, pp.26-7).

The causes of these tensions for the greater part predate the Cold War, during which some tensions were rendered more intractable through foreign intervention, while others were contained or attention was simply distracted away from them. The Mediterranean or 'the Southern flank' was a marginalized area. The main concern of both NATO and the Warsaw Pact was the centre of Europe; the disengagement of France from NATO further contributed to the marginalization of Mediterranean issues. NATO's primary objective in the Mediterranean was to prevent the Soviet navy from acquiring naval bases, so as to safeguard lines of communication and trade routes. Superpower competition in the area did lead to arms proliferation and a number of proxy wars. In the end US and Soviet patronage created a regional variant of the worldwide mutual deterrence between the two blocs, with Syria counterpoised to Israel (Anderson and Fenech, 1994, pp.11–13). With the end of the Cold War Russian support to its Allies has weakened. The US are now the sole superpower and the main promoter of the Middle East peace process. The end of the Cold War has not removed the roots of conflict however – the diminished Russian influence might even increase instability because local rulers no longer have to take into account Russian imperatives.

All this results in a very fragile regional equilibrium and a much-divided area, because nationalist policies create inter-state competition and lead to tensions. The Gulf War provided a clear illustration of intra-Arab divisions and demonstrated the lack of a regional leader or organization with the ability to settle matters of security (Marr, 1998, p.76).

Low Level of Regional Integration

Nationalist policies, the absence of a common security threat and competition for scarce resources have indeed resulted in a very low level of regional integration, especially in the field of security. The most important organizations in the region are a witness to this effect (Faria and De Vasconcelos, 1996, p.12).

Arab League One of the goals of the Arab League is to safeguard the independence and sovereignty of the Member States.[2] Its Charter prohibits any resort to force in order to resolve disputes between Member States and stipulates that the Council can mediate in all differences which threaten to lead to war. In case of aggression or threat of aggression, the Member State in question can demand the immediate convocation of the Council, which can determine, by unanimity, the measures necessary to repulse the aggression. There is however no real collective security commitment in the Charter.

In 1950, following the 1948 defeat by Israel, the Member States concluded the Joint Defence and Economic Cooperation Treaty. This stipulates that

> the Contracting States consider any (act of) armed aggression made against any one or more of them or their armed forces, to be directed against them all [and therefore] undertake to go without delay to the aid of the State or States against which such an act of aggression is made, and immediately to take, individually and collectively, all steps available, including the use of armed force, to repel the aggression and restore security and peace.

In order to implement these obligations a Joint Defence Council was created, consisting of Foreign and Defence Ministers and assisted by a Permanent Military Commission, composed of representatives of the General Staffs, which was to plan for military operations and stimulate cooperation between the armed forces of the Member States. In practice however Member States have proved themselves divided and unwilling to develop a common security strategy. The Military Commission reverted to a study role without there being much activity on the ground and the Arab League played only a minor role in conflict management in the Mediterranean. Security and defence thus remain the prerogative of the individual countries (Agata, 1994; Kerdoun, 1995, p.94).

Arab Maghreb Union In 1989 Algeria, Libya, Mauritania, Morocco and Tunisia created the AMU. Among its goals are the preservation of peace and the defence of the independence of the Member States. The founding treaty stipulates that any attack against a Member State is considered to be an attack against the other Member States, but it does not contain an obligation of mutual assistance, nor does it define the measures to be taken in the case of aggression. The Member States further commit themselves not to allow on their territory any activity or organization which is directed against the security, territorial integrity or the political system of a Member State and to abstain from joining a military or political pact or alliance with this purpose. This provision was obviously meant to cover the tensions between Morocco and Algeria over the Western Sahara and the latter's support to the Polisario Front. It is exactly this ongoing dispute however which, together with the crisis in Algeria and continuing tensions between Libya and other countries, led to the paralysis of the AMU, especially in the field of security. A Defence Council was established in 1990 to promote coordination of defence policies, but it met only once, that same year. Member States remain preoccupied with internal political issues and because of their differences continue to make foreign policy individually; no common strategy has been developed (Hamdouni, 1992; Kerdoun, 1995, pp.91–3; Sehimi, 2001, pp.89–90).

Organization of African Unity Algeria, Egypt, Libya, the Saharawi Arab Democratic Republic (Western Sahara)[3] and Tunisia are also members of the OAU. The Charter of this organization provides for the establishment of a Commission of Mediation, Conciliation and Arbitration and of a Defence Commission, but these have remained ineffective. Since the creation of the African Mechanism Apparatus for Preventing, Managing and Resolving African Crises in 1993 the OAU has been active in conflict prevention on the African continent, but given its limited membership in the region, it plays little or no part in the Mediterranean. The organization's main focus is on Sub-Sahara Africa. At the OAU's 36th summit in Lomé on 10–12 July 2000, the constitutive act of the African Union was adopted, which entered into force on 26 May 2001. In the security field, the ambitious goals of the African Union include the objective to 'defend the sovereignty, territorial integrity and independence of its Member States', and to 'promote peace, security, and stability on the continent'. To that end, the Member States agreed on a number of principles, *inter alia*, the establishment of a common defence policy; peaceful resolution of conflicts among Member States; prohibition of the use of force or threat to use force among Member States; non-interference in internal affairs; the right of the Union to intervene in a Member State in grave circumstances, such as war crimes, genocide and crimes against humanity; peaceful co-existence of Member States and their right to live in peace and security; and the right to request intervention from the Union in order to restore peace and security. It remains to be seen however whether the Member States will be able and willing to meet these far-reaching commitments. Conditions on the African continent are such that time does not seem to be ripe yet for an all-embracing regional integration project such as the African Union.

Limited integration Whereas in Europe there are institutional frameworks for conflict management and confidence-building, the Southern shore of the Mediterranean completely lacks effective common security structures. The absence of an efficacious regional security organization means that there is a lack of regular consultation on issues of foreign and security policy, which otherwise could attenuate tensions in the region and lead to security cooperation. In combination with the game of rapidly shifting alliances this also means that third parties, such as the EU, often lack a dependable interlocutor and have difficulties to form a coherent policy towards the region. The low level of regional integration constitutes a political gap between both shores of the Mediterranean.

Defence Expenditure and Proliferation

The continuing instability and repeated conflicts in the region since 1945 have led to a regional arms race, hence a very high level of defence expenditure.

Table 1.1 Defence expenditure and armed forces in the Mediterranean in 1999

Country	Def. exp. (billion euro)	Def. exp. (per cent GDP)	Armed forces	Soldiers per 1000 inhabit.
Algeria	3.1	6.6	124000	4.1
Egypt	3.0	3.4	448000	7.2
Israel	8.9	8.9	172000	27.8
Jordan	0.6	7.8	103000	20.1
Lebanon	0.6	3.6	63570	14.6
Libya	1.5	4.3	76000	11.9
Morocco	1.8	5.1	198500	6.5
Pal. Auth.[a]	0.5	14.3	35000	11.7
Syria	1.9	4.9	316000	18.7
Tunisia	0.4	1.9	35000	3.7
Turkey	10.1	5.4	609700	9.2
Cyprus[b]	0.5	5.7	10000	11.4
Malta	0.03	0.9	2140	5.6

[a] Since it has no armed forces, figures for the PA represent its paramilitary forces.
[b] Figures for Cyprus do not take into account foreign troops on the island.

Source: adapted from International Institute for Strategic Studies (2000).

When compared with data about the EU, the figures in table 1.1 reveal the Mediterranean's unusually high degree of militarization. For the EU as a whole, defence expenditure represents only about 2.1 per cent of the GDP. With a total of just over one and a half million men under arms, the Union counts only 4.7 soldiers per thousand inhabitants. Figures are especially high for the countries of the Middle East and the Eastern Mediterranean, where inter-state tensions are highest. For the Maghreb countries, figures are much closer to the EU average. In spite of the global decline in arms sales, defence budgets in the region have remained very high or have even increased. The main supplier of weapons and equipment are the US; their share amounts to about half of the regional arms purchases. The UK comes second with about 30 per cent, while France and Russia supply most of the remainder.

The most worrying aspect of this regional arms race is the proliferation of weapons of mass destruction (WMD): nuclear, chemical and biological weapons (Cordesman, 1999; Lesser and Tellis, 1996).

Although it has never been officially admitted, Israeli possession of nuclear weapons and an autonomous production capacity is almost certain, giving it de facto nuclear status. It is reputed to have about a hundred warheads and the same number of ballistic missiles. The development of the Jericho III would increase this to intercontinental range. A number of its combat aircraft can also be equipped with atomic bombs. Considering its indefensible borders and lack of strategic depth, Israel has always seen nuclear deterrence as the only way to counter the 'existential threat' to the state posed by potential combinations of Arab forces. Its nuclear strategy has always been one of 'deliberate ambiguity': by not openly admitting possession of the much rumoured bomb, potential aggressors are purposely left into the dark as to possible retaliation, which forces them to take into account a worst-case scenario and thus discourages attack (Duval, 1998).

Algeria has two research reactors, the first one supplied by Argentina, the second one built secretly with Chinese support. Only after this was exposed, in 1991, and under heavy pressure from the US, did Algeria confirm this and accede to the Non-Proliferation Treaty (NPT), thus opening its installations to inspections by the International Atomic Energy Agency (IAEA). There are indications that the programme was continued, supposedly putting Algeria in a position to produce weapons grade plutonium should it decide to acquire nuclear weapons. Reports indicate that Algeria has been active in the underground nuclear trade; it was suspected of transferring uranium dioxide to Iran and of accepting natural uranium from Iraq. In spite of Algeria's repeated assertions to the contrary since its accession to the NPT, NATO's High Level Senior Defence Group on Proliferation (DGP) puts Algeria in the category of countries with the 'suspected intent' of acquiring nuclear weapons.

True to his troublesome reputation, Colonel Gaddafi publicly called on the Arab states to acquire nuclear weapons on at least two occasions, but until now Libya itself has not had any success in this field. An attempt to buy nuclear weapons from China in the 1970s failed. Libya possesses a research reactor, supplied by the former Soviet Union, which operates under IAEA safeguards, and continues to send nuclear scientists abroad for training. For the DGP Libya too falls into the 'suspected intent' category.

Other countries in the region are not seen as having any military nuclear aspirations, although some have limited civil nuclear programmes. Several states possess chemical and biological weapons however. Egypt, Israel, Libya and Syria are all known to have extensive programmes for the production of chemical weapons; Algeria's civil industry probably has the capacity to produce them, but there is no organized effort to this end. Syria has a biological weapons programme, while Israel could start up production at short notice. The DGP considers Libya as having the intention to produce biological weapons, but reports indicate that it has only reached the early stages of research. In combination with the spread of ballistic missiles, as shown in table 1.2, which are easily convertible to non-conventional payloads, the proliferation of WMD is a major security issue in the region.

Table 1.2 Ballistic missiles in the Mediterranean

Country	Missile	Range (km)	Current state
Egypt	Scud-100	600	in development
	Badr200/Vector	850–1000	eliminated
Israel	Jericho I (YA-1)	480	in service
	Jericho II (YA-3)	1450	in service
	Shavit	7500	in service
Libya	Al-Fatah	950	in development
Syria	Scud-C	600	in service
	M-9	600	on order

Source: adapted from Boniface (2000, p.180).

The causes of proliferation in the Mediterranean are diverse (Lesser and Tellis, 1996, pp.5–18; Weidenfeld, Janning and Behrendt, 1997, pp.8–11). During the Cold War the Southern littoral states could obtain strategic weight by aligning themselves with either of the two superpowers or by playing a prominent part in the non-aligned movement. Now possession of WMD and missiles is seen as an alternative way to obtain status and prestige and to ensure attention by the West, which is indeed guaranteed given Western concerns about proliferation. US action against Iraq because of the alleged possession of WMD might constitute a counter-argument, but then again the case of North Korea seems to demonstrate the increased bargaining power that WMD bring with them. The Arab states also regard possession of WMD as proof of their technological capacity. For the Southern states modernization of the military is an essential element of national independence and a means for asserting national sovereignty.

Proliferation is further motivated by regional security concerns. In the framework of South-South tensions, acquisition of WMD is linked to strategic competition and the regional military balance. Algerian, Egyptian and Syrian WMD programmes e.g. clearly serve to support these countries' aspirations for leadership in the Eastern or Western Mediterranean. Mistrust and uncertainty about the intentions of neighbour countries lead to a vicious circle: states acquire WMD as a safeguard to possible hostile intentions from their neighbours, who in turn see this as a ground to increase their own defence capacity and so on – the classic security dilemma. The Arab states also justify the build-up of a deterrent of their own by referring to Israel's nuclear capacity and its refusal to sign the NPT, which is a key factor in encouraging them to seek equivalent WMD. Acquisition of WMD is seen as a force multiplier and therefore a much more cost-effective way of achieving these goals than modernization of the conventional armed forces. Still, the financial burden of the development of WMD is very heavy. The heavy cost associated with acquiring or developing such weapons means that less resources are available for much-needed economic and social policies. Libyan programmes are closely tied to confrontation with the West. Other countries as well do not fail to appreciate the potential impact of a deterrent capacity on Western policy, notably on the possibility of Western intervention on the Southern shore of the Mediterranean. Finally, the fact that, especially since the end of the Cold War, WMD technology is readily available, overtly or clandestinely, is another factor explaining proliferation.

Although most countries in the region are party to them, as shown in table 1.3, the major arms control agreements have not been able to curb proliferation (Cordesman, 2000, pp.16–24).

Table 1.3 Arms control agreements in the Mediterranean

Country	Geneva Protocol	NPT	BTWC	CWC	Pelindaba Treaty	CTBT
Algeria	R	R	-	R	R	S
Egypt	R	R	S	-	S	S
Israel	R	-	-	S	n/a	S
Jordan	R	R	R	R	n/a	R
Lebanon	R	R	R	-	n/a	-
Libya	R	R	R	-	S	-
Morocco	R	R	S	R	S	R
Pal.Auth.*	n/a	n/a	n/a	n/a	n/a	n/a
Syria	R	R	S	-	n/a	-
Tunisia	R	R	R	R	S	S
Turkey	R	R	R	R	n/a	R
Cyprus	R	R	R	R	n/a	S
Malta	R	R	R	R	n/a	S

R ratified
S signed
n/a not applicable
* Since formally it is not a state, the Palestinian Authority cannot ratify these agreements.

Source: adapted from FIRST Database (http://first.sipri.org).

The NPT, which prohibits nuclear weapons states from transferring nuclear weapons to non-nuclear states or assisting or encouraging them to acquire or manufacture such weapons, has been the most successful treaty. Only Israel is not party to it, but no other states in the region have acquired nuclear weapons. Dual-use technology and the spread of knowledge and material from the former Soviet Union increase proliferation risks, but this can probably be checked by tight controls by the IAEA and pressure from the West. The EU itself has created an extensive regime for the control of exports of dual-use items and technology. The 1996 Pelindaba Treaty foresees a nuclear-free zone in Africa by forbidding research, development, manufacture, stationing and testing of nuclear explosive devices as well as attacks on nuclear installations and dumping of radioactive material. It has yet to enter into force however, and of course it covers only part of the Mediterranean area. The Comprehensive Nuclear Test-Ban Treaty (CTBT; 1996) prohibits the carrying out of any nuclear weapon test explosion or any other nuclear explosion but it too has not yet entered into force.

The 1925 Geneva Protocol prohibits the use of asphyxiating, poisonous or other gases and of bacteriological methods of warfare, but on most states it is only binding with respect to other states party to the treaty, and it does not prohibit production of such weapons. The Biological and Toxin Weapons Convention (BTWC; 1975) prohibits the development, production, stockpiling and acquisition of microbial agents or toxins of types or quantities that have no justification for peaceful purposes and delivery means designed to use such substances in armed conflict. Existing stocks were to be destroyed within nine months after the entry into force. The convention lacks a verification regime however, while here too dual-use technology increases the danger of proliferation. The Chemical Weapons Convention (CWC), which entered into force in 1997, provides analogous stipulations on chemical weapons and does include a verification regime to be implemented by the Organization for the Prohibition of Chemical Weapons. Several of the most significant states in the region are not party to it however, notably Syria, Egypt and Libya.

Other arrangements for arms control and disarmament have had a very limited appeal in the Mediterranean. The Conference on Disarmament (CD), the permanent multilateral negotiating forum for disarmament associated with the UN, has seven members from the region: Algeria, Egypt, Israel, Morocco, Syria, Tunisia and Turkey. Cooperation with the UN Register of Conventional Arms (UNROCA), which registers imports and exports of seven categories of weapons[4] in order to increase transparency, is limited. The major reason for this lack of compliance is Arab insistence on the inclusion of WMD in the register. Regimes seeking to control the spread of technology and essential materials for the production of WMD have been joined by just a handful of Mediterranean countries. The Nuclear Suppliers Group (NSG), which surveys nuclear materials and technology that can be used for military purposes, and the Australian Group, dealing with chemical and biological weapons, count only Cyprus and Turkey among its members. The Zangger Committee, which is active in the same field as the NSG, the Missile Technology Control Regime (MTCR), aiming to prevent the proliferation of delivery vehicles for WMD, and the Wassenaar Arrangement, promoting transparency in transfers of conventional arms and dual-use goods, have only been joined by Turkey (Daguzan, 2000a, pp.96–103).

Mutual distrust and a lack of confidence in compliance by neighbour countries are the main obstacles to disarmament and confidence and security-building measures in the region.

Islamism and Authoritarianism

An important factor in the Mediterranean region is islamism: groups 'seeking to increase Islam's role in society and politics, usually with the goal of an Islamic state'.[5] In essence this is the assertion of a separate identity and a call for cultural independence. The secular nationalism which has been practised by the Arab regimes since independence is seen as a continuation of Western dominance by means of values instead of by more direct ways, which is why a return to indigenous values is called for in order to achieve true independence. Often it is not simply a matter of rejecting Western or 'modern' values though, but rather also of 'cultural re-appropriation' of often universal values, of integrating these in local culture (Agha, 1994, pp.242–3; Burgat, 1996, p.41).

The term 'islamism' distinguishes between Islam as a religion, which in itself has not suddenly become political or radical, and groups with a political agenda who, justly or not, refer to Islam to legitimize their actions. Variously described as 'fundamentalism', 'integrism', 'political Islam', 'radical Islam' etc., the broad term 'islamism', unlike others, allows for the inclusion of all tendencies, ranging from moderates seeking to achieve their aims by acting within the political system, to extremists who do not hesitate to use violence. These aims may be as different as increasing the influence of Islam on the existing regime, overthrowing the state, replacing secular laws by the Shari'a or even establishing democracy. Islamism is not a uniform phenomenon: its outlook in the different countries of the region is defined by the circumstances to which it is a response.

The attractiveness of islamism is explained by several factors, of which religion is only a minor one (James, 1996; Naïr, 1995; Soltan, 1997). A major issue is a sort of 'Arab identity crisis'. After a perceived 'golden age' of Arab culture under islamic rule, followed the oppressive Ottoman empire and then colonization by the rich and technologically advanced West, which continues to spread its values over the world. The failure of pan-Arabism to achieve Arab unity, as witnessed by the lack of regional integration among the Arab countries, and the successive defeats at the hands of Israel further strengthened this sense of inferiority to the West (Lewis, 2002).

The adoption of secular ideologies by the Arab regimes after independence is perceived to have failed. Nationalist governments, whether associated with the West or with the Soviet Union ('Arab socialism'), did not succeed in creating a healthy economy, in establishing an efficacious state apparatus and, most importantly, in providing for the people, thus disappointing those who had fought for independence against the colonizers. This led to the belief that, except in the field of science and technology, Arabs have little to learn from the West and should therefore revert to islamic values as foundation of the state. The military defeat of 1967 was further proof of the failure of the modernizing ideology of the Arab elite. The 'success' of the 1979 Iranian revolution provided further inspiration. At the same time islamist movements provided alternatives for the state's shortcomings by organizing social services themselves, based on the mosques.

Because of their poor performance in the economic and social field the governing regimes have lost legitimacy. Economic problems, massive unemployment and high birth rates have combined to create huge poverty. Widespread corruption, the lack of democratic institutions and severe repression of any opposition have further eroded the regimes' basis. In these circumstances people are easily tempted by movements which seem to offer an alternative way. Ironically, oppression of secular opposition movements and the impossibility to express needs through regular political channels might have cleared the way for islamism. The often draconian repression of islamists, moderates and extremists alike, only serves to strengthen people in their determination or leads to radicalization and an escalation of violence. Governing elites are often more sympathetic to the West than the population, which confronts the West with the dilemma of whether it can support governments which lack democratic legitimacy, but the continuation in power of which ensures stability, while alternatives are uncertain.

Terrorism

Terrorism is much abundant in the Mediterranean. The Israeli-Palestinian conflict in particular has generated a large number of terrorist acts, while in the Arab countries a number of opposition movements, islamist ones and others, have reverted to terrorism as a way of achieving their objectives. Most terrorism is domestic: it is committed by groups that want to force concessions or policy changes from the government or that want to overthrow the state as such and replace it with another political system. Terrorism can also be directed against Western influence. Several states in the region, e.g. Syria and Libya, are reputed to support terrorist groups in other countries to further their own agendas. Terrorism is often linked to international crime with terrorist activities being financed by drugs smuggling etc. (Joffé, 2000; Wilkinson, 1997).

Socio-Economic Conditions

The Mediterranean is characterized by the existence of a wide economic gap between the rich, industrialized North and an impoverished South. For example, the EU accounts for more than fifteen per cent of world trade, while the other countries of the Euro-Mediterranean Partnership barely reach three per cent. GNP per capita varies from over 20000 euro in France to about 600 euro in Egypt. The Southern countries have become increasingly dependent upon the EU: more than half of their trade is with the Union, but this constitutes a mere four per cent of total EU trade. Intra-Southern trade is very limited: it accounts for only about ten per cent of the trade of the Southern countries. The South needs the EU for its markets, its technology, its investors etc. This relation of dependence in itself creates tensions between North and South (Ben Ali, 1996, pp.49–51; Joffé, 1996a).

In most Southern countries the economy is to a large degree controlled by the state, the often authoritarian nature of which extends into the economic field. Government policies focussing on autarky have failed to attract foreign investors and to realize the necessary modernization. Productivity of capital is very low and the scale of production is below optimum size, resulting in low volume production of goods at uncompetitive prices. Unduly high military spending has consumed resources which could have been put to much better use elsewhere. Other economic problems are a lack of diversification in the industry, limited private enterprise and an underdeveloped service sector (Niblock, 1996).

The demographic evolution aggravates these economic problems. The economy cannot keep up with the rapid growth of the population; growth rates are up to 7 per cent annually. It is estimated that by 2025 the population on the Southern shore of the Mediterranean will have risen to 350 million – from 184 million in 1988 – as opposed to 325 million in the EU. The number of people younger than 15 will then have reached some 30 per cent of the population. This demographic pressure creates severe economic and social strains. Already official unemployment figures are as high as 25 per cent, while social security provisions are very limited at best, and these figures do not take into account underemployment: people with jobs which do not earn them sufficient income to sustain their families. In order just to keep unemployment at this already very high level, given the growth of the population, the GDP should grow with over ten per cent annually, something which the Southern Mediterranean countries obviously cannot achieve. In combination with the undemocratic character of most Southern states the result will be an increase in domestic instability and further de-legitimization of existing regimes, while the Western countries fear mass migration to the North, as young people flee their home countries with the hope of finding better fortune elsewhere.

The EU's Interests in the Mediterranean

Politico-Military Issues

The Southern littoral states of the Mediterranean do not pose a direct military threat to the European Union; the possibility of a direct attack on the Union as a whole or on anyone of its Member States can be practically ruled out (Algieri, 1996, p.193).

Proliferation WMD proliferation however does have a profound impact on Mediterranean security (Cornish, Van Ham and Krause, 1996; Snyder, 1996). Southern Europe is already within the reach of certain WMD delivery vehicles. Fears of Europe coming under threat were fed by the experience of Scud missile attacks on Israel and Saudi Arabia during the Gulf War. Contrary to certain – mostly American – theorists, a direct attack is highly unlikely however, as no country has the means to mount a full scale offensive and to pose any serious threat to Europe, while use of WMD would imply the risk of massive retaliation, by conventional means or otherwise.[6] But the main argument is, quite simply, that, considering the economic interdependence between both shores of the Mediterranean, it is hard to imagine which country would not damage its own interests by an act of aggression against Europe. Also for the time being and although they are increasing, WMD capacities remain limited. Estimates on the future development vary, but one can suppose that no serious threat will materialize in the short or even medium term (10–15 years), considering the technological difficulties of constructing long-range weapons, which states in the region, apart from Israel, cannot overcome on their own.[7] In 1986, following the US raid on Tripoli, Libya did fire two Scud missiles at the US Coast Guard facility on the Italian island of Lampedusa, but this only served to further strengthen the international isolation of the country.

Proliferation could increase drastically by the spread of nuclear technology and material from the former Soviet Union and by the further spread of missile technology from e.g. China or North Korea. Even then however, unless nuclear weapons were acquired, Mediterranean states would not pose a significant threat to Europe, as this would require far too large a number of missiles, given the limited destructive power of conventional missiles or even of missiles armed with chemical or biological payloads. And of course the risk of retaliation by the superior Western forces remains. Only ballistic missiles with nuclear warheads would be a major security issue with far-reaching implications for the security situation in the Mediterranean and for Euro-Mediterranean relations. If next to Israel another Mediterranean state would acquire nuclear weapons, this would greatly affect the balance of power in the region. The consequences for the Middle East peace process would be difficult to predict, but cannot be underestimated. It is exactly therefore that any state suspected of acquiring a nuclear capacity would expose itself to the possibility of a pre-emptive strike by any of the potential victims, like the destruction of Iraqi nuclear installations at Tuwaitha by an Israeli attack in 1981. But the main argument against the Mediterranean posing a direct military threat to the EU would still remain valid: since economic relations with and support from the Union are vitally important to all of them, one can hardly think of a situation in which it would be in the interest of any Mediterranean state to consider an act of aggression against Europe.

Acquisition of nuclear weapons by one of the Arab states would certainly increase South-South tensions. Indeed rather than being a direct threat to Europe, proliferation of WMD creates much more immediate risks among the Mediterranean states themselves. There would probably be less hesitation to use WMD in a South-South conflict – mutual distrust and heavy tensions might even lead to pre-emptive use. WMD, including nuclear weapons, do lend themselves to tactical uses. Several countries have used chemical or biological weapons and ballistic missiles in the past. The human consequences of South-South conflicts would thus be much worse. Proliferation, especially of nuclear weapons, could also dangerously disturb the regional equilibrium. A state with large conventional forces backed by the threat of nuclear force could seriously hope to obtain regional hegemony by military means. Because of geographical proximity use of WMD on the Southern shore of the Mediterranean might produce negative effects for the EU (El-Sayed, 2000a, p.135; Müller, 2001, p.2).

The threat of WMD might be used successfully by a regime to influence European policy, e.g. to dissuade the EU from installing a sanctions regime or from intervening. In the case of intervention in the region European military forces might have to face adversaries armed with WMD, which would certainly impact upon the planning of any operation. During the Gulf War e.g. there was a risk of Iraqi forces using chemical or biological weapons against the Allied forces. In view of the increasing unwillingness of Western governments to risk human casualties, Western policies would certainly be affected by the threat of WMD. For the purpose of this form of 'deterrence', possession of WMD thus has a distinct advantage for the Southern states (Mey, 2000, pp.73–4).

Islamism Like proliferation, islamism does not pose a direct threat to Europe either. Moderate islamist movements acting within the political system should be regarded as just one political actor among others, even when one does not agree with their programme. Extremist islamism however, when reverting to violence, can lead to serious internal unrest and destabilisation of existing regimes. Ultimately this can end in open civil war, which effectively happened in Algeria, and which implies a large risk of spill-over into the neighbouring countries. Western countries fear that in such cases large numbers of refugees will try to reach Europe, which is considered worrying because of the internal political consequences this might cause, notably the further rise of right-wing extremism. It is also feared that if extremist islamists would succeed in overthrowing a regime, they might establish an anti-Western state. Such a regime might cut off relations with the West, which could seriously hamper the Union's Euro-Mediterranean project. The emergence of an extremist regime might endanger the Middle East peace process. It is further feared that such a state would be a safe-haven for terrorist groupings from the whole of the region. On the other hand countries like Saudi Arabia and a number of other Gulf states already have systems of government based on the Shari'a, but they are still considered to be allies of the West (Carpenter, 1999, pp.70–72).

Islamism is not a monolithic movement, nor is there a central leadership. Islamist movements in different countries, although often in contact with each other, seldom share the same objectives or tactics and, above all, almost all have national agendas, which is why islamism is not a direct threat to the West. On the contrary, islamist groups often are in opposition to one another and have displayed a tendency to splinter. The West should not let itself be blinded by cultural differences and should be careful not to invent a new enemy after the fall of the Soviet Union. It should certainly not revive the historical Christian-Muslim strife along the lines of Samuel Huntington's 'clash of civilizations' theory. Statements like that of former NATO Secretary-General Willy Claes, that Islamism 'is at least as dangerous as communism was',[8] might be self-fulfilling prophecies, as they strain relations with the Arab countries and strengthen some islamists in their anti-

Western beliefs (Hoch, 1995, pp.280–282; Lamchichi, 1998, p.272; Mortimer, 1994, pp.106–8; Reissner, 1999, pp.24–7).⁹

This was the message spread by the EU after '11 September', which carried with it the danger of a spread of anti-Muslim sentiments and of making the fight against Islamist terrorism into a fight against the world of Islam as a whole. A speech by Italian Prime Minister Silvio Berlusconi, in which he stated that Western civilisation and Islam cannot be placed on the same level, but that the West is superior and therefore 'bound to occidentalize and conquer new people' was very fiercely condemned by the other European leaders.¹⁰ At an extraordinary meeting in Brussels on 22 September, the European Council

> categorically rejects any equation of groups of fanatical terrorists with the Arab and Muslim world [and] emphasises the need to combat any nationalist, racist and xenophobic drift.

Or, as the German Chancellor, Gerhard Schröder, put it at the ensuing press conference: 'This is not a fight against Islam, nor a fight against cultures, but a fight for culture'.¹¹

Terrorism Even when islamists or other movements revert to terrorist action, the risk for the EU remains limited. At several occasions terrorism has indeed been exported to Europe. Expatriate dissidents have been targeted by government agents or by members of rivalling movements, while government representatives have been attacked by terrorist groups. European or US citizens and installations in Europe or abroad have been attacked as well, mostly with the aim of influencing foreign policy, e.g. a pro-Israeli stance or support for a contested regime, or to achieve the release of imprisoned fellow terrorists. Geographical proximity and the presence of large Arab communities as a potential source of logistic support and recruitment make Europe the prime target for international terrorism emanating from the Mediterranean. But the importance of the international terrorist threat to Europe should not be exaggerated: in recent years by far the largest number of casualties fell victim to domestic European terrorists, such as the IRA or ETA. The fact remains that most armed movements have a domestic agenda and therefore do not target the EU. The danger of terrorism could grow much bigger if proliferation of WMD was extended to terrorist movements, but so far no group has ever used such weapons; anyhow the arguments against the possibility of them targeting Europe remain valid. This demonstrates the importance of non-proliferation policies and the need for strict controls (Joffé, 1996b; Pisano, 1997).

The terrorist attack on the US, destroying the World Trade Center in New York and badly damaging the Pentagon and killing thousands of people, caused a peak in the attention devoted to terrorism, but although terrorism was put high on the Union's agenda, the events should not lead to a fundamental reappraisal of the threat which it poses to the EU. '11 September' saw indeed an exceptional direct attack on a Western country. Without condoning the atrocities, one can safely assume that the US were specifically targeted and that the instigators, whatever their own agenda was, were able to recruit 'martyrs' for the suicide attacks because of American policies *vis-à-vis* the Middle East and the islamic countries. In the sense that it has a very different policy, notably with regard to the Palestinian question, but also because of its non-confrontational policies in general, the Union itself will therefore not be a target. It might become one because of its support for the US (*inter alia* through NATO), but this possibility seems quite remote, especially since the attack did not lead the EU to envisage fundamental policy changes. Things might have been different had the EU joined in a purely military scenario of retaliation, but this is not the case. On the contrary, the Union stressed the need to deal with the underlying causes which are the breeding-ground of extremism and terrorism, i.e. the persisting conflict in the Middle East and poor socio-economic conditions, and demanded very clear conditions before accepting to invoke the collective defence guarantee of Article 5 of the NATO Treaty. The Union recognized the legitimacy of the American retaliation against the Taliban regime in Afghanistan and the organization of Osama Bin Laden which began on 7 October 2001, on the condition that they were specifically directed against the suspected perpetrators of the attacks on the US and their accomplices, and provided indirect support. The main message the Union was spreading was still one of reconciliation and cooperation.

In 2003 again the EU as such did not support military action as a way of disarming Iraq and in February of that year France, Germany and Belgium blocked US requests for NATO support for the military option. NATO authorized assistance to Turkey's defensive measures, but the other requests, *inter alia* use of airbases, replacement of US troops, naval protection of US passageways in the Mediterranean and a post-conflict NATO peace-keeping mission, were rejected, because they started from the assumption that military action would take place anyway, something which at that time Paris, Berlin and Brussels were not willing to condone. One does perceive an increased threat to the US presence in Europe though and to Member States that join the US in military action against EU policy. By all means terrorism therefore is an issue to be taken into account by a European security policy for the Mediterranean, but without letting it dominate the Euro-Mediterranean agenda.

Military threats. Reviewing the politico-military dimension of security in the Mediterranean, one must conclude that there is little or no direct military security threat to the EU originating from the region. Tensions in the area mostly are between or within the Southern states, so here lies the immediate danger of conflict. A South-South conflict could threaten EU citizens living on the Southern shore of the Mediterranean however, which might necessitate a European intervention in order to guarantee their security. In a worst case scenario a South-South conflict might even spill over into EU Member States; geographic proximity in itself increases the risk of escalation (Ragionieri, 1997, p.421). More importantly there are of course issues such as the Cyprus question which directly involve Member States and therefore do imply a – albeit limited – military risk.

Economic Interests

The main economic interest of the EU in the Mediterranean region lies in the supply of oil and gas. In the first place the Union is a major consumer of – primarily – gas emanating from the Mediterranean itself. One third of gas imports for the EU as a whole originate in the Maghreb, but figures for the Southern Member States of the Union are much higher. E.g. Algeria accounts for about 70 per cent of Spain's gas supplies. Gas is delivered through an extensive network of pipelines, such as the Trans-Med and Trans-Maghreb Pipelines connecting Algeria to Italy and the Iberian Peninsula respectively. Thus supply is dependent on an expensive, fixed delivery structure. Furthermore gas, unlike oil, has remained a regional rather than a global market, which implies that there are few short-term opportunities for procurement elsewhere in the event of interruptions in the supply from the Mediterranean. The EU therefore has a major interest in maintaining stability in the Mediterranean so as not to endanger gas delivery, which could be jeopardized by internal or inter-state conflict (Lesser, 1999a, p.218).

On the other hand oil and gas represent about 80 per cent of total Mediterranean exports to the EU and even up to 95 per cent for individual countries such as Algeria and Libya, which means that the exporting countries are as much dependent on the EU as *vice versa*. It is estimated that 96 per cent of all petrol and gas exports will go to Europe. Because of this interdependence, Northern and Southern states have a clear common interest in maintaining stability. Further development of Mediterranean energy resources encourages Euro-Mediterranean cooperation and offers important opportunities for the economic and social development of the Mediterranean states, thus also furthering internal stability (Calabrese, 1997, pp.90–91; Keramane, 2000; Khader, 1997a).

The Mediterranean is an essential passageway for oil and gas produced in other regions of the world. Oil from the Gulf is shipped across the Mediterranean, while major new pipelines are envisaged to transport oil and gas from Central Asia and the Caucasus to the West. Because of this and other important traffic it is in the interest of the EU to ensure that freedom of navigation in the Mediterranean is in no way impaired by instability in the region. Therefore in a broader context, stability in the Mediterranean, because of the way this region is linked to the Gulf – by geographical proximity, shared impact of the Middle East peace process, transport of oil etc. – is also a prerequisite for the protection of European interests in the Gulf and its huge supplies of oil (Aliboni, 1999b). In effect the main concern when it comes to energy security is not the quantity of supply – the supply side can easily meet demand – but the danger of an interruption of the transport of energy, be it through pipelines or by sea (Chatelus, 2000, pp.130–131).

Furthermore, the Mediterranean states are a market for the Member States of the EU. Main European export products are equipment (30–35 per cent), manufactured goods (15–20 per cent), agricultural products (11–15 per cent) and chemical products (7–9 per cent). Export of agricultural products has been rising because of the growing inability of most Arab countries to provide for their own needs. Although today the relative importance of the Mediterranean as a market to the EU is limited, it has considerable potential once the economic situation of the

Mediterranean states improves. Estimates indicate that each 10000 euro of GDP in the Mediterranean states generates approximately 1300 euro worth of EU exports (Khader, 1996a, p.12).

So instead of being a source of threats to the EU, the Mediterranean in the first place is an area of common economic interests and therefore security ought to be a common concern of countries on both shores.

Of course, it ought to be mentioned that there is another objective underlying the EU's economic policy towards the Mediterranean: slowing down migration. Ever since the European countries closed their borders for labour migration and extreme right-wing parties started to gain votes by drawing the card of xenophobia, (especially illegal) migration from the South to the North is seen more and more as a security issue. By improving the economic situation in the South, the EU therefore also hopes to tackle the causes of migration.

Finally, one can also discern a common ecologic interest between both shores of the Mediterranean. Shortage of water is directly linked to disputes and the potential for conflict. In a broader sense, pollution threatens countries on both shores. So in the environmental field as well cooperation is called for in order to avert a common threat.[12]

Political Issues

Among the objectives of the CFSP as mentioned in Article 11 of the Treaty on European Union, are the preservation of peace, the strengthening of international security, the promotion of international cooperation and the development and consolidation of democracy, the rule of law and respect for human rights and fundamental freedoms. At the Cologne European Council (June 1999) it was decided that the EU should have an autonomous capacity for crisis management, in order to be able to launch and conduct military operations in response to international crises. The Member States thus entrusted the Union with new tasks in the field of conflict prevention and crisis management, which it took over from the WEU. The Helsinki European Council of December 1999 adopted a concrete plan to realize the required operational capacity: the European Security and Defence Policy (ESDP). By 2003 a rapid reaction force of 60000 men, deployable within sixty days and sustainable for at least a year, ought to be operational ('the headline goal'). The Union is also in the process of creating a capacity for civil crisis management. New structures were set up within the Union's second pillar, to allow for the monitoring of international developments, and for the planning and implementation of military and non-military responses to international crises: the Political and Security Committee (PSC), the Military Committee and the Military Staff. The Göteborg European Council (15–16 June 2001) adopted the EU Programme for the prevention of violent conflicts, which makes conflict prevention into one of the priorities of the CFSP, to be integrated in all dimensions of the Union's foreign relations. At the Laeken European Council (14–15 December 2001) the ESDP was declared partly operational, i.e. able to conduct some crisis management operations. With the reinforcement of the CFSP and the construction of the ESDP, the Union is on the way to playing a much bigger role in conflict prevention and crisis management.

What the Union now needs is a 'security concept'. A security concept is a policy-making tool that, starting from the interests, outlines the long-term overall objectives that are to be achieved and the basic categories of instruments that are to be applied to that end. It is a strategy that serves as a reference framework for day-to-day policy-making in a rapidly evolving and increasingly complex international environment.[13] Because of globalisation, Europe's interests are inseparably linked to the stability of its interactions with other actors worldwide. This interdependency implies that events anywhere in the world can have an immediate impact on Europe. In effect therefore, the security of Europe is dependent on the stability of the international system as such, which is why a security concept must set global objectives.

But at the same time the Union does have a specific responsibility towards its periphery, i.e. Central and Eastern Europe and the Mediterranean: here its interests are more directly at stake, while the direct impact on the Union of factors of insecurity originating there will be greater. The Union's inability to handle the successive crises in the Balkans, with its poor military performance in the air campaign over Kosovo as a sad highlight, was the main cause prompting the strengthening of the CFSP and the creation of the ESDP. Now that it is equipped, or going to be, with the necessary instruments to deal with them, the Union can no longer allow crises in its backyard to escalate, nor can it persist in relying on the US to solve them. As the international actor with the necessary instruments and means at hand, the EU is responsible for stability in – at least – its periphery according to the self-proclaimed goals of the CFSP. The idea itself of European integration, which is inspired by respect for human rights and democratic values and which was taken up because of the desire to establish a durable peace, does not allow for disinterest in other regions and implies international solidarity.

This is also a matter of credibility for the CFSP and for the EU as a whole. The Union should live up to the expectations which the creation of the CFSP and the ESDP have engendered and should wage a foreign policy which corresponds to its economic weight. As a major donor to the Mediterranean in general and to the Middle East peace process in particular, the EU should assure that its voice is heard on the political stage as well, so as to make certain that its own interests are not neglected. Otherwise its credibility as an international actor will be severely undermined.

Certainly in the Middle East, if not in the Mediterranean as a whole, the US have for decades been the dominant player in the politico-military field, notably claiming a monopoly on all but the economic aspects of the Middle East peace process. Of course the US and Europe have common interests in the Mediterranean, mainly concerning oil, but a number of divergences are visible. The Americans mostly see the Mediterranean as part of a larger picture: to the US its prime importance lies in the security of their access to the oil reserves in the Middle East and the Gulf. For the US the Mediterranean constitutes the base for power-projection to the Gulf. This was evidenced during the Gulf War, when over 90 per cent of the military forces involved arrived from or through the

Mediterranean (Fröhlich, 2000, pp.59–60). Other US objectives in the region are the maintenance of its strategic and political interests in Israel and the prevention of anti-American Arab groupings in the area. So for the US the Mediterranean is more 'a means to an end', whereas the EU, because of geographical proximity and close economic ties, has much more direct interests in the Mediterranean as such. Besides, American policymakers think more in terms of the Gulf and the Middle East, with North Africa as a minor subset of the latter, rather than viewing the Mediterranean in its entirety (Fenech, 1997, pp.160–161; Latter, 1991, p.9; Lesser, 1999a, pp.212–3).

So EU and US policies *vis-à-vis* the Mediterranean have different accents. Whereas the EU attaches more importance to the maintenance of good-neighbourly relations and close economic links, the US, who do not have such immediate interests in the region, have put on a more aggressive stance, often against the will of their European Allies. Prominent examples are the repeated military actions against Libya or the 1996 Iran-Libya Sanctions Act, which prohibits all trade, American and non-American, with these countries (Marr, 1998, pp.82–4). In order to assure that attention is paid to European interests, the EU should therefore develop a Mediterranean policy of its own covering all dimensions of security.

A Mediterranean Security Policy for the EU

The EU does not have to fear a direct military threat from the Mediterranean. Economic problems, notably the poverty of the majority of the population, and the lack of democratic institutions, leading to de-legitimization of existing regimes and internal instability, constitute the major source of instability in the region. In order to meet the demands posed by this security environment, the Union clearly needs a comprehensive security concept, which combines all of its external policies into a broad and integrated framework, of which security policy (the politico-military field) is only one aspect, on the same height as the other external policies (i.e. external trade, development cooperation, environmental policy, police, justice and intelligence cooperation, immigration policy, foreign policy). Both at the global and at the regional, Euro-Mediterranean level, these policies work towards priority 'global public goods' (security, the rule of law, welfare, sustainable development, the environment), the lack of which creates instability. Each of these policies operates according to its own rationale and dynamic, so 'securitization' or 'militarization' of EU external policies is avoided. At the same time, setting a positive, objective-based agenda, rather than a negative, threat-based one, enhances the legitimacy of EU external action and avoids alienating others. Comprehensive security thus amounts to a permanent and structural policy of long-term conflict prevention by working on all dimensions of international stability, in an integrated way and through multilateral cooperation and partnership. Coercion is only reverted to as an instrument of last resort. The common economic interests of both shores provide the basis on which a comprehensive partnership can be founded.

But the need for a comprehensive approach should not lead the EU into ignoring the politico-military dimension (or 'hard' security). The EU does need a

Mediterranean security policy, as part of a comprehensive Euro-Mediterranean project, for its contribution is essential in order to attain the following objectives:

- to ensure that the Union continues to remain free from direct military threats like it is today;
- to resolve the ongoing conflicts and disputes in the Mediterranean, which hinder closer North-South and South-South cooperation in all fields of international relations;
- to prevent South-South conflicts, which might lead to spill-over into a Member State of the Union, which could jeopardize the security of EU citizens living abroad and which could endanger EU economic interests.

A security policy implies the development of a set of Euro-Mediterranean policy instruments:

- the promotion of confidence and security building measures, in order to prevent conflict. In the still unstable and highly militarized Mediterranean, political differences can easily lead to the use of military means. The EU should therefore give special attention to non-proliferation, arms control and disarmament;
- assisting the Southern Mediterranean countries in finding peaceful solutions to existing and to possible future conflicts, including the development of Euro-Mediterranean arrangements for preventive diplomacy, for peaceful settlement of disputes and for humanitarian, peacekeeping and peace enforcement operations.

So the EU's security policy should contribute both to long-term conflict prevention and to short-term crisis management, along with the other external policies of the Union. The development of the CFSP and the ESDP should enable EU policy-making in the politico-military field which in the Mediterranean cannot be ignored.

Notes

1 France gave the Syrian City of Alexandretta (Iskanderun in Turkish) and the surrounding area to Turkey in 1939 in order to guarantee its neutrality, a fact which has never been accepted by Syria.
2 The Arab League, founded in 1945, has twenty-two members: Algeria, Bahrain, the Comoros, Djibouti, Egypt, Iraq, Jordan, Kuwait, Lebanon, Libya, Mauritania, Morocco, Oman, Palestine, Qatar, Saudi Arabia, Somalia, Sudan, Syria, Tunisia, the United Arab Emirates and Yemen.
3 Polisario's government-in-exile, proclaimed in 1976, was seated as an OAU member in 1984.
4 Battle tanks, armoured combat vehicles, large calibre artillery systems, combat aircraft, attack helicopters, missiles and missile launchers and warships.
5 Definition by Fred Halliday quoted by James (1996, p.5).

6   American observers on the other hand talk of a 'surprisingly muted (at least in Europe) concern about the ever-increasing reach of missiles deployed in the European periphery' (Lesser, 2000b, pp.2–3).
7   In fact most states still operate on the basis of late 1940s Scud technology, which is very similar to the German V2 missile of World War II.
8   Quoted by Carpenter (1999, p.80).
9   Or as Michel Vauzelle, chairman of the Commission for Foreign Affairs of the French Assemblée Nationale, put it in 1991 already: 'la notion de menace du Sud est une sottise absolue [...] évoquer le danger du Sud est une faute morale: on le crée en en parlant' (Ravenel, 1991, p.6).
10 Belgian Foreign Minister Louis Michel, shedding the veil of diplomatic language, qualified Berlusconi's statements as 'almost barbaric, stupid and unacceptable' *Europe*, 22 September 2001.
11 Conclusions and plan of action of the extraordinary European Council meeting on 21 September 2001.
12 A number of international instruments exist in this field, apart from the actions taken in the framework of the Euro-Mediterranean Partnership, e.g. the 1976 Convention for the protection of the Mediterranean Sea against pollution and its related protocols.
13 In fact the discussion on the objectives of the ESDP should have preceded the creation of the decision-making structures and the military capacity, because how these are shaped depends on the aims which they are meant to achieve (e.g. the geographical scope in which it is expected to operate determines the composition of the rapid reaction force). In practice however the means were decided upon first, because on this a consensus could quite easily be found among the Member States in the aftermath of the Kosovo operation, while it was feared that starting with the debate on a strategic concept would lead to endless discussions and thus the long-time postponement of a reinforcement of the Union's security dimension.

Chapter 2

The Euro-Mediterranean Partnership

Introduction

The framework within which the EU makes its Mediterranean security policy is the EMP. This chapter analyzes the development of Europe's Mediterranean policy, and its politico-military dimension in particular, an evolution which was driven by the growing awareness of the European interests in the Mediterranean described in chapter 1. Then follows a detailed analysis of the politico-military aspects of the Barcelona Conference, where the EMP was founded, and of all follow-up conferences, in order to determine the causes of the Partnership's failure to realize its ambitious security policy objectives.

The Origins of Europe's Mediterranean Policy

From Global to Renovated Mediterranean Policy

From its very beginning the EEC had close relations with a number of Mediterranean countries. Morocco and Tunisia had only gained independence from France in 1956 and retained a special relationship with their former colonizer, which was confirmed in the Rome Treaty. Algeria at that time was still a French colony and as such was among the first countries to receive funds in the framework of EEC development cooperation. The Community lacked a clear Mediterranean strategy however. As other Mediterranean countries as well demanded arrangements for their relations with the EEC, a number of bilateral agreements of different types were concluded. Because of their strategic importance in the context of the Cold War NATO-members Greece (1962) and Turkey (1963) were offered comprehensive association agreements which included the prospect of Community membership. Similar agreements were concluded with Malta (1970) and Cyprus (1972) on the same grounds. Much more limited commercial agreements were granted to Morocco and Tunisia (1969), who were of much less strategic importance, and to Israel (1964), Lebanon (1965), Spain (1971) and Egypt and Portugal (1972). In the absence of a global view on the whole of the region, relations with the Mediterranean developed pragmatically, depending upon European interests in the individual Mediterranean states and the degree of influence of the latter on the EEC or on specific Member States. This resulted in a very complex mosaic of widely differing agreements (Gomez, 1998, pp.134–5; Jünemann, 1999, pp.37–8; Pierros, Meunier and Abrams, 1999, pp.49–81).

In order to end the disorderly character of Mediterranean relations, at the 1972 Paris Summit (19–21 October) the EEC announced the Global Mediterranean Policy (GMP). This covered all Southern littoral states and Jordan, with whom new bilateral cooperation agreements were concluded, with the aim of facilitating free flow of industrial goods, while customs duties for a number of agricultural products were lowered. The agreements were accompanied by renewable financial protocols providing for loans and grants from the Community budget. It was explicitly stated that the GMP did not apply to Greece and Turkey, the earlier association agreements remaining in force, while with economically more advanced Israel an agreement on free trade in industrial goods was signed. Libya stayed outside this network of agreements: its King, Idriss Sanoussi, was closer to the UK than to the EEC and then in 1969 Gadaffi came to power, which would lead to Libya's alienation from the West. The GMP arrangements were modified in 1986 to take into account the accession of Spain and Portugal to the EEC; certain products were put under specific regimes to protect the exports of these countries.

The GMP was strongly advocated by France, which wished to preserve the close relations with now decolonized North Africa, while the accession of the UK in 1973, which had a longstanding tradition of involvement in the Middle East, stimulated closer ties with that part of the Mediterranean (Waites and Stavridis, 1999, p.29). The creation of European Political Cooperation (EPC) in 1970, a mechanism for consultation on foreign affairs between the Member States of the EEC and the modest beginning of a European foreign policy, was a further incentive for an enhanced Mediterranean policy. Member States started to appreciate the importance of the Mediterranean to the Community, e.g. as a market for European products and as a major supplier of energy, which implied the need for stability in order to guarantee supply, as was emphasized by the 1973 Yom Kippur War and the subsequent oil crisis.

But in spite of the growing awareness of European security interests in the Mediterranean, the GMP essentially remained limited to economic issues and development cooperation. Economic support does serve stability, but success in the economic field was limited. The Community proved incapable of stemming the economic and social plight of the Mediterranean states, who were disappointed with the financial assistance and the degree of market access which they were granted. The GMP did not cover politico-military issues. The accession of Southern European countries to the EEC – Spain and Portugal and later Greece – strengthened the call for the addition of a security dimension to Euro-Mediterranean relations, because of these countries' closer contacts with the South, but at the same time also aggravated economic competition between the Northern and Southern shores and thus made relations more difficult. The 1973 war and oil crisis did lead to the Euro-Arab Dialogue between the Community and the Arab states of the Middle East, which primarily dealt with oil prices and the Middle East peace process. This dialogue continued intermittently until 1990 without achieving significant results. One could even say that the Euro-Arab Dialogue separated politico-military issues from the GMP and thus slowed down the emergence of a comprehensive Mediterranean policy including 'hard' security. Contrary to what the wording suggests, the GMP was still a network of bilateral agreements. It was only 'global' in so far as that, apart from Libya, it covered all the Mediterranean littoral states plus Jordan and increased uniformity in the Community's relations with these countries. The absence of other than economic issues and the lack of a multilateral framework made it difficult to speak of a truly global policy. The EEC still lacked a comprehensive strategy for the Mediterranean covering all dimensions of Euro-Mediterranean relations (Bretherton and Vogler, 1999, pp.153–4; Gautron, 1997, p.28; Piening, 1997, pp.72–4).

In the late 1980s the Community started to reconsider its relations with the Mediterranean. First of all it was clear that the current arrangements were unsatisfactory to the Mediterranean states, who feared the economic consequences of the Community's Southern enlargement. Their dissatisfaction was highlighted by Morocco's application for Community membership in 1987, in order to obtain better economic relations with the European countries (the application being rejected on the ground of Morocco not being a European country). Secondly and importantly, it was realized that the domestic economic and political problems of the Mediterranean states not only caused instability in the South, but could have consequences for European security as well, such as mass migration or uncertain supply of energy. The outbreak of riots in Algeria in 1988 and the emergence of an islamist opposition party, the Front Islamique du Salut (FIS), gave further impetus to the rethinking of the Community's Mediterranean policy. The Gulf War, which caused a radicalization of Arab public opinion, again underlined the inherent instability of the Mediterranean states and the need to address the grave socio-economic problems affecting them. With the end of the Cold War the Community renewed its relations with the countries of East and Central Europe, aiding them in the transformation to democracy and a market economy and thereby ensuring stability on the European continent. The Southern Member States of the EEC demanded that the Community should also play this role in its Southern periphery. The European Parliament too felt that the Community should ensure its 'geopolitical balance'.

In 1989 the Commission therefore proposed the Renovated or Redirected Mediterranean Policy (RMP). This initiative was prompted i.a. by the growing awareness of the importance of Mediterranean security issues to the Community, hence the need to broaden the scope of the almost exclusively economic Euro-Mediterranean relations. The Commission proposal explicitly stated that because of its geographical proximity the social and economic development of the Mediterranean is a 'fundamental security interest' for the Community (Gomez, 1998, pp.138–9; Marks, 1996, pp.10–11). The European Parliament as well in its call for a 'revamped' Mediterranean policy pointed to the fact that

> the political, social and economic stability of the EEC is dependent to a large extent on peace being achieved in this neighbouring region and on its gradual, harmonious development [and that] the Community should act as a stabilizing force between those groups of countries which are geographically close to it.

The EP specifically stressed the strategic importance of the Mediterranean to the Community's energy needs and the risk of social and economic crises leading to extremist Islamism or armed conflict. It therefore called for a global, multilateral dialogue which was to include politico-military issues and which was to create a climate of mutual trust.[1]

The RMP, which was launched in 1990, included a substantial increase of the financial assistance to the Mediterranean states, which was aimed more at structural readjustment, and a special aid package for Jordan, Egypt, Turkey, Israel and the Occupied Territories, to counter the consequences of the Gulf War. An important innovation when compared to the GMP was 'horizontal cooperation': multilateral aid programmes with the object of encouraging regional cooperation in fields of common interest, in order to increase regional integration among the Arab states, which was at a very low level. This was to serve as an example of multinational cooperation. The Mediterranean states were reluctant to share resources with their neighbour countries however and in the end not a single multilateral project was set up, while the RMP in itself remained bilateral in character. Again even enhanced financial support did not result in a substantial improvement of the economic situation in the Mediterranean states. More importantly the RMP, like its predecessor, retained an essentially economic and commercial focus, without a specific politico-military dimension. In spite of the explicit and repeated references to the Community's security interests when the RMP was initiated, the only innovation which it seemed to offer was an increase of the quantity of aid.

Proposals for Enhanced Euro-Mediterranean Relations

The failure of the GMP and RMP to resolve the socio-economic problems of the Mediterranean and their lack of a politico-military dimension prompted a number of proposals to organize Euro-Mediterranean relations along other lines. Most of these were put forward by the Community's Southern Member States, which wanted to try and convince the other EEC countries of the need for an enhanced role of the Community in the Mediterranean.

CSCM At the opening of the CSCE meeting in Palma de Mallorca (24 September 1990), Italy and Spain launched a far-reaching proposal to create a Conference on Security and Cooperation in the Mediterranean (CSCM), calling on Europe to assume primary responsibility in an area which is vital to its security and with which it has close historical ties. Mirroring the example of the CSCE, the CSCM was to comprise three baskets, with the following objectives: to safeguard security through arms control and the banning of WMD; to reduce the economic, social and demographic imbalances of the region; and to create understanding between societies through dialogue. Like its European counterpart, the CSCM was conceived as a process rather than as an organization. The CSCM would deal with all matters of security and would focus on confidence and security building measures (CSBMs) and crisis management (for which a centre was to be created). It was to include not only the EEC and the Mediterranean states, but also the Gulf countries, thus ranging 'from Mauritania to Iran' (Badini, 1995, pp.111–112; Fernández Ordóñez, 1990).

Seeking to build Euro-Mediterranean relations at three levels, political/security, economic and social/cultural, and thereby linking all dimensions of security, the CSCM constituted an innovative approach to Mediterranean policy. Ultimately it came to nothing however, because of the repercussions of the Gulf War, which strained relations between North and South, and the lack of progress in the Middle East peace process, which made successful negotiations in other fora dealing with security impossible. The CSCM met with opposition from the UK and the Netherlands and, what was a key factor in explaining its failure, from the US, which saw it as a threat to their dominant position in the peace process. France favoured a sub-regional approach based on cooperation with the Maghreb and therefore at the most adopted a 'non-negative' attitude, while Germany remained reticent as well. A number of Arab countries too felt that the CSCM drew attention away from the attempts to resolve the Arab-Israeli conflict, without offering concrete alternatives to settle security issues. The CSCM, though innovative, was just too grand a design for it to succeed (Echeverría, 1999a, pp.106–7; Gillespie, 1997a, pp.34–5).

An attempt to revive the CSCM proposal was made in 1992 when, at the invitation of the Spanish parliament, the Interparliamentary Union convened an interparliamentary CSCM in Malaga (15–20 June 1992). The conference was limited to parliamentarians from the Mediterranean littoral states, while the US, the UK and Russia (the three naval powers with an important presence in the Mediterranean) were given the status of 'associated participants', as were a number of international parliamentary assemblies (including the European Parliament) and the PLO. In protest to the participation of the latter, Israel and therefore also the US refused to take part; Algeria, which had dissolved its parliament, remained absent as well. In its final document the Conference recommended a number of measures reflecting the three baskets of the CSCM. The parliamentarians could indeed do nothing more than forward recommendations to the governments, who were not more willing to act than before, which is why the Interparliamentary Conference did not result in any concrete achievement. The Interparliamentary CSCM continues to hold regular meetings (Kerdoun, 1995, pp.142–51; Khader, 1997b, pp.59–60).

'5+5' In 1983, while on a visit in Morocco, French President François Mitterrand first proposed the creation of a new trans-Mediterranean dialogue in the Western Mediterranean with the aim of increasing cooperation between states on both shores through the exchange of views and concrete projects in the field of economic, social and cultural affairs. For France the Western Mediterranean was the principal peripheral zone; in the French view stability in the Mediterranean as a whole could only be achieved by starting to unite what Paris saw as the most stable countries of the region. Originally this '4+5 Dialogue' brought together four Southern Member States of the Community, France, Italy, Spain and Portugal; and Algeria, Libya, Mauritania, Morocco and Tunisia, who in 1989 founded the Arab Maghreb Union. This new international forum was seen as a vehicle for stability and an ideal channel to build cooperation with the Maghreb countries. Because of internal difficulties in France and because priority was given to the European integration, the first, informal '4+5' meeting did not take place until February 1988 in Marseille, followed by a second meeting in Tangiers in May 1989. Both dealt only with economic and financial issues and development cooperation (Calabrese, 1997, pp.96–7; Meyrede, 1999, pp.57–9).

On 10 October 1990 in Rome, a Ministerial Conference of the '4+5' (also attended by Malta) was held, which adopted a Declaration on Dialogue and Cooperation in the Western Mediterranean. This Ministerial Conference of the '4+5' was partly prompted by the impossibility of implementing the region-wide CSCM proposal, which by then was already apparent. Ministers engaged to construct an area of peace, cooperation and stability in the Western Mediterranean. To that end Ministers would meet at least annually to pursue a comprehensive dialogue including political, security, economic, cultural and ecological issues. A number of priority domains for action were defined in the field of economy, human resources and ecology. Ministers met a second time in Algiers on 27 October 1991, where Malta formally joined the now '5+5'; a representative of the European Commission was also present. In the resulting declaration Ministers expressed their conviction that an affirmation of democracy and human rights and of the Charter of the United Nations would contribute to stability and security in the region. A Political Committee consisting of officials from the Ministries of Foreign Affairs of the participating countries was created, to discuss political and security issues. A number of working groups were to initiate the implementation of projects in the priority areas. The next Ministerial meeting was planned in Tunisia in 1992.

The dialogue was paralyzed however by the outbreak of the Gulf War. Other factors which led to the ultimate failure of the '5+5' scheme were the domestic crisis in Algeria, friction between Morocco and Algeria over the Western Sahara and the international isolation of Libya following the embargo against the country. There were also disagreements among the participating Community Member States, with France advocating the sub-regional approach, while Italy and Spain, the initiators of the CSCM proposal, still looked for a global Mediterranean strategy, as they felt Mediterranean security to be indivisible. In spite of the intentions stated in the Ministerial declarations, the '5+5 Dialogue' failed to address security; no working groups were established, nor were any projects defined in this field. Again, as was the case with the successive Mediterranean policies of the EEC, security was only dealt with by way of the economy, while its politico-military dimension was mostly left untouched. The '5+5 Dialogue' was interrupted in 1992, because of the imposition of UN sanctions on Libya, and was suspended in 1999. The Dialogue was revived by a meeting of Foreign Ministers in Lisbon in January 2001. Its main role now seems to be a complementary one to the Euro-Mediterranean Partnership, to which it can contribute ideas and proposals. Unlike the Partnership, the '5+5 Dialogue' unites only part of the EU Member States and of the Mediterranean countries; it is thus a purely Mediterranean framework.

Mediterranean Forum Another scheme was the Mediterranean Forum, first mentioned by Egyptian President Hosni Mubarak in a speech to the European Parliament in November 1991 and soon supported by France. For Egypt, which was not included in the '5+5 Dialogue' or the AMU (to which it had in vain applied for accession), the Forum was a way to a bigger role in the Arab world and the Middle East peace process. French support for the initiative was driven by the aspiration to gain influence in the Middle East and by disappointment with the outcome of the '5+5'. The Forum took off with a meeting of Foreign Ministers in Alexandria on 3–4 July 1994. It now brings together eleven countries: France, Greece, Italy, Portugal, Spain, Malta, Algeria, Egypt, Morocco, Tunisia and Turkey. The Forum has an informal character; Ministers agreed that pending further agreement on the institutional structure it should be a flexible framework for cooperation. Like the CSCM the Forum comprises three baskets, on political, economic and cultural issues. Importantly, the Alexandria document called for coordination with the CFSP and the avoidance of duplication of EU objectives, ideas and resources. The actual achievements of the Forum have remained limited because of a lack of funds and because of disagreements among the participating states, notably on the enlargement of the Forum (with the European members opposing the inclusion of Libya, Arab members the inclusion of Israel and Turkey that of Cyprus) (Echeverría, 1997a, pp.62–3). From the beginning the informal character of the Forum made it more of a framework for preparatory talks rather than a performing organization. In fact the Forum was rendered more or less obsolete by the Euro-Mediterranean Partnership, negotiations on which were already underway during the creation of the Forum, which was pursued anyway because of the uncertain outcome of the negotiations on the Partnership at the time. The Forum still operates however, in a way similar to the '5+5 Dialogue': in a kind of ancillary relationship with the Euro-Mediterranean Partnership, as a place for exchanges of views on items on the agenda of the Partnership. Meetings are organized annually. Uniting only the Mediterranean Member States of the EU and a limited number of Southern Mediterranean countries, the Forum, rather than being an inter-regional organization, like the Partnership, is an exclusively Mediterranean club, just like the '5+5 Dialogue' (Aliboni, 1999e, pp.88–9; 2001, pp.2–4).

Mediterranean Council In 1992 Malta proposed yet another structure, the Mediterranean Council, as a framework for dialogue between both shores. Based on the example of the European Council this was to consist of a Ministerial Committee, a Parliamentary Assembly and a Secretariat. Membership was to be conditional on the acceptance of the Charter of the United Nations, respect for human rights and the rule of law and the establishment of representative institutions. This initiative received only a very limited response.

Ongoing efforts The advantage of all these schemes was that they allowed for more flexibility to discuss security, because they operated outside the formal Community framework. Before the creation of the CFSP there was little room for the Community Member States to discuss security: EPC only covered the technological and economic aspects of security, while the WEU was still very much a sleeping organization, which was not specifically linked to the Community. Proposals focussing on the Western Mediterranean had the advantage of being able to avoid discussions on sensitive and complex issues such as the Middle East peace process and the dispute between Greece and Turkey, while because they involved only a small group of countries attention could be focussed on matters of specific interest to them. But at the same time including only part of the Member States of the EEC and of the Mediterranean states tended to create divisions within the Community and hampered the generation of a new Community strategy for the Mediterranean as a whole and the security issues which it poses as such. Only proposals getting the full support of the Community as a whole can succeed, as the individual Southern Member States lack the means to make them work. The fact that all initiatives failed to create a sufficient organizational framework to effectively make policy and implement it and did not go beyond non-committing talks, is proof of this. It appears that only at the European level a sufficient organizational basis can be found to carry a forum for relations between Europe and other regions and, more importantly, to keep it going. A loose association of individual Member States lacks the persistence of effort to make this work. Besides, conditions for the creation of fora where Mediterranean security could be discussed were not favourable. The Gulf War in particular soured relations between the Northern and Southern shores of the Mediterranean, while the conflict in the Middle East, the international isolation of Libya and the continuing tensions over the Western Sahara fuelled differences among the Southern countries. As a consequence even those initiatives which took off with some success were eventually paralyzed (Masala, 2000b, p.163; Stivachis, 1999, pp.36–7; Tsardanidis, 1994, p.82).

During this period the Community itself continued to consider possible improvements to its Mediterranean policy. The 1991 Maastricht Treaty had created the CFSP. In a report to the Lisbon European Council (June 1992) the Commission identified the priority regions for action in the framework of the future CFSP. Among these were the Middle East and the Maghreb, which were both described as regions in which the Community has strong interests in terms of security but where stability is threatened. The Commission therefore advised that the Community should establish good-neighbourly relations with the countries of the area in order to

> avoid a deepening of the North-South gap in the region by favouring economic development and promoting full respect for human rights and fundamental freedoms and the development and consolidation of democracy and the rule of law.

The Commission report distinguished between the Maghreb and the Middle East, calling for specific joint actions to support the Middle East peace process, while advocating a further-reaching comprehensive partnership with the Maghreb.[2]

In its Declaration on Relations between Europe and the Maghreb the Lisbon European Council adopted the sub-regional option suggested by the Commission and envisaged the creation of 'a true Euro-Maghreb Partnership' in the political, economic, social and cultural fields. One of the reasons for this sub-regional approach was that it was felt that a breakthrough in the peace process was a necessary prerequisite before a similar initiative in the Middle East could be considered, while the Maghreb and the AMU seemed to offer much better prospects for cooperation and regional integration. In an EPC report to his Community colleagues Spanish Foreign Minister Francisco Fernández-Ordóñez described the Maghreb as 'a time-bomb which Europe, by means of a greater commitment of resources and a new approach to the region, might still be able to disarm' (Gillespie, 1997a, p.36). However, the crisis in Algeria, the embargo against Libya and the paralysis of the AMU soon made it evident that the Maghreb was further away from being an area of entente than had been thought. Besides, the sub-regional approach ignored region-wide issues such as proliferation, terrorism and regional integration, although the importance of these could actually be implied from the Commission report itself. The project of a Euro-Maghreb Partnership was thus never implemented. By providing for a global partnership including a political, social and cultural dimension, it did represent an important innovation of the traditionally economic focus of the Community's Mediterranean policy though. In this sense the pleas of the Community's Southern Member States and the different schemes for enhanced Euro-Mediterranean relations did have a significant influence on Community policy.

The Barcelona Conference

Preparation of the Conference

The comprehensive and multilateral approach to Euro-Mediterranean relations of the proposed Euro-Maghreb Partnership was retained in the ensuing new policy initiatives of the now European Union. The Corfu European Council (24–25 June 1994) tasked the Council and the Commission with evaluating the Mediterranean Policy of the EU and suggesting ways to strengthen it and stressed the value of 'jointly examining political, economic and social problems'.

This decision followed renewed pleas by the Union's Southern Member States, particularly France, Spain and Italy, for a greater European effort towards the Mediterranean, in order to ensure symmetry in the Union's external relations, considering the huge EU contribution to the countries of Central and Eastern Europe. The Southern Member States were supported by the driving role of the Commission. With the 'Europe Agreements' the EU created a framework to support the countries in its European periphery in their transformation to democracy and the market economy. During the 1990s almost all Central and Eastern European countries became candidates for accession. The EU thus functions as an 'exporter of stability' on the European continent. The Union's Southern Member States felt that the EU should assume a similar responsibility *vis-à-vis* its Mediterranean periphery. Unlike the other Member States, they were directly confronted with the emergence of 'new' security issues in the Mediterranean. Indeed, the main factor which also convinced the Northern Member States of the necessity of a global Mediterranean policy was the growing awareness of the impact of Mediterranean developments on the security of the whole of the Union. Whereas during the Cold War the focus of security policy was clearly on Central and Eastern Europe and the perceived threat of the Soviet Union, any direct military threat to the Union had now disappeared, to be replaced by a plethora of risks which were much less easy to identify or to predict and which emerged from a much wider geographical area. As a result of these developments Mediterranean security issues came much more to the forefront, which contributed to the making of a consensus between the Union's Northern and Southern Member States. There was also the wish for a greater political involvement, matching the Union's financial efforts in the region. As the main donor, the Union should make its voice be heard on the political stage as well (Barbé, 1996). The launching of the Middle East peace process at the 1991 Madrid Conference created the political conditions under which a new and enhanced Mediterranean initiative was possible.

In response to the demand for an enhanced Mediterranean policy, the Commission proposed the creation of a Euro-Mediterranean Partnership (EMP). Given the many areas of interdependence between North and South, a Mediterranean policy should be multi-dimensional. The Commission therefore suggested enhanced economic and financial cooperation and the creation of a Euro-Mediterranean zone of peace and stability. The latter was to be achieved through a 'close political dialogue based on respect for democracy, good governance and human rights', which would also include 'hard' security issues such as non-proliferation and CSBMs. A Euro-Mediterranean Conference, to be held in 1995, should decide on the guidelines for future relations.[3] The European Council of Essen (9–10 December 1994) endorsed the idea of the Partnership, considering that 'the Mediterranean represents a priority area of strategic importance for the European Union', and accepted the offer of the Spanish Presidency to organize a Euro-Mediterranean Ministerial Conference in the second half of 1995.

Participation in the Conference was limited to the Fifteen and the eleven Mediterranean countries which had signed agreements with the Union plus the Palestinian Authority: Cyprus, Malta, Turkey, Jordan, Syria, Lebanon, Israel, Egypt, Tunisia, Morocco and Algeria. The AMU had adopted a common position indicating that it wanted Libya to be included, but this was vetoed by the majority of EU Member States, particularly by France and the UK, because of the sanctions against the country. Eventually Libya withdrew its request to participate, describing the event as high treason and a conspiracy. The US request for full participation in the Conference was not granted either. This refusal can be interpreted as an expression of the desire of the EU, as an emerging international actor, to develop a policy of its own towards a region with which it has close ties; perhaps it might even be seen as a small 'act of rebellion' against the dominant position of the US in world politics in general and in the Middle East in particular. A number of observers were admitted to the Conference, such as Mauritania (a Member State of the AMU), the Arab League and the Gulf Cooperation Council (GCC), while other countries and organizations wishing to follow the debates, such as the US, Russia and the Central and Eastern European countries, could do so from a diplomatic tribune.

It was also feared though that a number of countries might not be willing to participate, which could seriously endanger the outcome of the Conference and block the Union's objective of creating a partnership encompassing the whole of the Mediterranean. Syria and Lebanon e.g. were reluctant to participate in a ministerial meeting together with Israel, fearing that the Conference would end up as a sort of 'Trojan horse' of the Middle East peace process. Morocco, with which an association agreement was being negotiated, feared that the multilateral framework which was now being envisaged would detract from what it considered to be its privileged bilateral relations with the EU. Therefore it was made explicit that the specificity of bilateral relations would be preserved within the multilateral process. In the end all Arab countries that were invited attended the Conference, mainly because of the potential benefits in the field of economic and financial cooperation and because the EMP was perceived as a way to counterbalance American dominance in the region (El-Sayed, 1999, pp.146–9).

The Barcelona Declaration (November 1995)

The Euro-Mediterranean conference was held in Barcelona on 27–28 November 1995. Participants were the Ministers of Foreign Affairs of the Fifteen, their counterparts from the twelve Mediterranean countries – except for the Palestinian Authority, which was represented by its President, Yasser Arafat – and the then Vice-President of the European Commission, Manuel Marin. The Conference adopted the Barcelona Declaration, establishing the EMP, which comprises three baskets.

The first is a Political and Security Partnership which aims at the establishment of 'a common area of peace and stability'. Expressing 'their conviction that the peace, stability and security of the Mediterranean region are a common asset', the signatories agreed 'to conduct a strengthened political dialogue at regular intervals' and subscribed to a number of high-flown principles:

- to act in accordance with international law, especially with the UN Charter and the Universal Declaration of Human Rights;
- to develop the rule of law and democracy, to further diversity and tolerance and respect for human rights and fundamental freedoms and to exchange information on these matters;
- to respect each other's sovereign equality and territorial integrity and the equal rights of peoples and their right to self-determination, to refrain from intervention in each other's internal affairs and to settle disputes by peaceful means;
- to strengthen cooperation in the fight against terrorism, organized crime and drug trafficking;
- to promote non-proliferation of WMD, arms control and disarmament, to 'refrain from developing military capacity beyond their legitimate defence requirements' and to pursue good-neighbourly relations and confidence-building measures, 'including the long term possibility of establishing a Euro-Mediterranean Pact'.

Second is an Economic and Financial Partnership to create 'an area of shared prosperity', aimed specifically at the 'acceleration of the pace of sustainable socio-economic development', 'improvement of living conditions [...], increase in employment level and reduction of the development gap in the [...] region' and 'encouragement of regional cooperation and integration'. This partnership 'will be based on the progressive establishment of a free trade area', economic cooperation and 'a substantial increase in the EU's financial assistance to its partners'. Finally there is a Partnership in Social, Cultural and Human Affairs aimed at the development of human resources, the promotion of understanding between cultures and exchanges between civil societies. The pledge to cooperate in the fight against terrorism, organized crime and drug trafficking was repeated in this basket.

The Declaration states that the Ministers of Foreign Affairs are to meet periodically to monitor the application of the Declaration and to define actions to achieve its objectives, while the various activities are to be followed by ad hoc meetings of Ministers, officials and experts. A Euro-Mediterranean Committee for the Barcelona Process, at senior-official level, consisting of the EU Troika and a representative of each Mediterranean partner, is to hold regular meetings to evaluate the process and prepare the meetings of the Foreign Ministers. The first meeting of the Euro-Mediterranean Committee took place on 16–17 April 1996 in Brussels. The Commission departments are to undertake the necessary preparatory and follow-up work. The next meeting of the Ministers of Foreign Affairs was scheduled for the first semester of 1997. To ensure follow-up to the Conference, a work programme listing the priority actions was annexed to the Declaration. In the field of security senior officials are to meet periodically, starting within the first quarter of 1996, to conduct a political dialogue which is to identify the means to implement the principles which were endorsed by the Declaration. The work programme further provided that foreign policy institutes would be encouraged to establish a network for cooperation, to become operational as of 1996.

With its three baskets the EMP mirrors the structure of the CSCE/OSCE and of the earlier CSCM and Euro-Maghreb Partnership proposals. The global or comprehensive approach to Mediterranean policy, i.e. the integration of the political and security, economic and social and human dimensions, was now formally adopted as the framework for future Euro-Mediterranean relations. The emergence of Mediterranean security issues with an impact on the EU and the comprehensive nature of security in the post-Cold War era, i.e. the inter-relation between the politico-military, economic and other dimensions of security, necessitate such an approach. The predominantly economic focus of the EU's Mediterranean policy was abandoned, although, understandably considering the years of experience in this field, the economic dimension was still the most elaborate. But for the first time since the creation of the EEC, a 'hard' security dimension was explicitly included in Europe's Mediterranean policy. In fact, in view of the limited development of the CFSP and of its security and defence component in particular at that time, one can say that the politico-military commitments entered into by the EU surpassed its capacities in that field, something which would later be made good by the creation of the ESDP (Spencer, 2001a, pp.14–15).

So the EMP offered three innovations:

- the inclusion of a politico-military dimension ('hard' security);
- the adoption of a comprehensive approach to security, integrating the politico-military dimension in a broader framework and combining instruments from the whole range of EU external policies;
- the adoption of a cooperative or partnership approach to security, aiming to achieve the security objectives by cooperating with the Mediterranean partners on the basis of joint interests instead of through a unilateral, threat-based European policy.

The development of the security dimension of Europe's Mediterranean policy is linked to the gradual establishment of a European foreign and security policy. These matters were outside the scope of the EEC. Later EPC covered foreign policy, but it could only deal with the economic and technological aspects of security, and, being a mechanism for consultation, it did not involve actual common policies. Only after the creation of the CFSP did the addition of a real security dimension to Europe's Mediterranean policy prove possible. Before, Europe lacked not only the institutions, instruments and procedures to make foreign and security policy, but also the experience and practice and the culture of working together on European policies in this field.

The EMP is multilateral in character, as a complement to the existing bilateral relations. The multilateral approach allows for more uniformity in relations with the Mediterranean partners and, more importantly, creates a forum to discuss region-wide issues which concern all 27 partners. It was provided that the bilateral relations would be enhanced by the conclusion of a new generation of free trade agreements, the Euro-Mediterranean Association Agreements. The Partnership further offers incentives for South-South cooperation, in order to meet the need for more integration in the area, with the EU serving as an example of successful regional integration (Fenech, 1997, p.169; Lannon, 1996, p.360).

Like the Helsinki Act of the CSCE the Barcelona Declaration is only politically binding. The political and security partnership, in which the 'hard' security issues are included, is a declaration of principles and not a ready-to-implement policy document: with the ultimate aim of achieving an area of peace and stability, the signatories committed themselves to a number of principles and broad objectives, which indicate the priority fields for further action. The instruments and means to achieve these objectives still had to be defined, by a political dialogue between the partners. The Barcelona Declaration, an example of a long term vision, is the strategic framework within which these further steps have to be taken and thus initiated a process of consultation and policy-making. The principles and broad objectives mentioned in the Declaration, although including some far-reaching commitments, e.g. the limit on the development of a military capacity, focus almost exclusively on conflict prevention. No provisions are included on possible cooperation on resolution of existing or future conflicts and on post-conflict peace-building. A major dimension of security policy is thus neglected. In this way, the principles and objectives of the Barcelona Declaration will not suffice to attain the three objectives which a Mediterranean security policy is to achieve in order to safeguard the Union's interests: keeping the EU free from military threats, preventing South-South conflicts and resolving ongoing conflicts.

Contrary to the much more detailed work programmes for the economic and social partnerships, the work programme for the political and security partnership only mentioned the time when the political dialogue should start, besides encouraging cooperation between foreign policy institutes in the partner countries. The inclusion of a follow-up mechanism was in itself a very significant improvement however, as it creates a dynamic and ensures constant attention, whereas before Mediterranean policy was to a large extent dependent on the willingness of the consecutive Presidencies to take initiatives. The EMP thus provides for an organizational framework which should enable the partner countries to engage in a process of common decision-making. In the text of the Declaration itself mention was made of the possibility of establishing a Euro-Mediterranean Pact, as proposed separately by France and Malta, with the aim of formalizing and deepening the political dialogue.

A drawback was the absence of Libya, a country which is very much involved in many of the region's security issues, making it hard to achieve global stability in the Mediterranean without its participation; including Libya proved to be a political impossibility however.

The political and security partnership, which clearly is the most innovative part of the Barcelona Declaration, did prove to be the hardest to reach agreement upon. Even after the end of the formal Conference sessions and in spite of further negotiations, three points of disagreement remained, opposing Israel to the Arab countries: the right of peoples to self-determination, non-proliferation of nuclear weapons and the fight against terrorism. In the end the Spanish Presidency presented the text as it was finally adopted in the form of an ultimatum, making it clear that any country which would not accept it would be held responsible for the failure of the Conference. By this forceful strategy, the Presidency was able to achieve the unanimous approval of the Declaration (Barbé, 1996, pp.39–40).

An important factor in allowing the participants to reach consensus on the political and security partnership was the separation of the Middle East peace process from the EMP, as outlined in the introductory part of the Declaration, where it is stated that

> this Euro-Mediterranean initiative is not intended to replace the other activities and initiatives undertaken in the interests of the peace, stability and development of the region, but that it will contribute to their success.

French proposals to include a formal commitment to a regional security structure were watered down by the Spanish Presidency because the inherent link with the Middle East peace process would seriously hinder negotiations. Although it meant limiting the scope of the political and security dimension of the EMP beforehand, the explicit and repeatedly emphasized intention not to discuss the peace process made progress in other fields possible – though as related above negotiations remained difficult. Attempts by Spanish Foreign Minister Javier Solana to bring together Israeli and Syrian representatives in the margin of the Conference to have peace talks were clearly rebuked by both parties, referring such discussions to other fora and other mediators (meaning the US). The Barcelona Conference was indeed historic for bringing together Israel and Syria in a multilateral framework, something in which no one had succeeded since the 1991 Madrid Conference (as Syria and Lebanon boycotted the subsequent multilateral track of the Middle East peace process). Exactly because the peace process is not discussed the EMP continues to be a meeting-place for countries which do not interact in other fora, which, especially in the absence of effective Southern Mediterranean security institutions, is a confidence-building measure in itself (Barbé, 1996, pp.38–9; Gomez, 1998, pp.145–6; Spencer, 1997, p.41). It was also clear that if it had not been for the breakthrough in the peace process in the period 1993–1995, the Barcelona Conference would have never succeeded. It was only in the aftermath of the Gulf War and the 'new world order' which was then envisaged and because a peace process for the Middle East was initiated in Madrid, that an ambitious project like the EMP could take off.

Still, the exclusion of the Middle East peace process – and actually of all other outstanding Mediterranean conflicts, such as the Cyprus issue or the Algerian crisis – from the EMP, creates a dilemma. Not discussing these sensitive matters allows the partners to avoid what would certainly be extremely difficult discussions and to reach consensus on other issues. But it is also clear that in the end a Mediterranean security policy cannot succeed in establishing an area of peace and stability if it continues to ignore existing conflicts. The vagueness of the work programme and the gaps in the set of principles and objectives reflect the difficulties in discussing politico-military issues between partners which are divided by tensions and conflict. That a consensus was finally found indicates that partner countries on both sides of the Mediterranean recognize the existence of common interests. One should ask however whether perhaps for the Arab countries the main reason for agreeing to the political and security partnership might not have been the benefits of the economic and financial partnership.

Nonetheless, considering the immense difficulties of bringing together the 27 partner countries to discuss security, let alone achieving any form of consensus, the declaration of principles in itself, especially because it includes 'hard' security, was a huge achievement and a major innovation, in spite of the drawbacks. The Declaration was indeed the potential starting point of a true EU security policy for the Mediterranean and also of Euro-Mediterranean security cooperation. Solana dubbed this 'the spirit of Barcelona': a spirit of openness and generosity leading to a climate of trust.

Organization and Finance of the EMP

The Euro-Mediterranean (or earlier) Association Agreements or, where these are still in the process of being negotiated, the earlier Cooperation Agreements constitute the bilateral track of the EMP.

The multilateral or regional track covers the three baskets of the Barcelona Declaration.

- The top steering body of the Barcelona Process are the Euro-Mediterranean Ministerial Conferences, which gather regularly at the level of Foreign

Ministers to monitor the implementation of the Declaration and to define the actions to be taken towards that end.
- Sectoral Ministers can also meet to discuss specific topics, but they have not done so in the framework of the political and security chapter.
- The Euro-Mediterranean Committee is responsible for the general management of the three baskets; it monitors the implementation of the Barcelona Declaration and of Ministers' decisions and prepares for the Ministerial Conferences and the other meetings of Ministers, senior officials and experts. The Committee, which meets on a quarterly basis at senior official level, is chaired by the EU Presidency and is composed of the EU Troika, the Mediterranean partners and representatives of the European Commission. The other Member States of the Union also participate, each being represented in the EU delegation, so as to make discussions less dependent on the composition of the Troika.
- Within each of the three baskets senior officials, experts and representatives of civil society meet to discuss specific items. In the political and security field meetings of senior officials of all partners (these are actually the same officials as those who sit in the Euro-Mediterranean Committee) are held quarterly to conduct a political and security dialogue, to manage the implementation of existing CSBMs and to prepare the Charter for Peace and Stability and further CSBMs. Other ad hoc meetings have been held, *inter alia* on terrorism and prevention of natural and manmade disasters.

Within the EU the political and security partnership is dealt with in the framework of the CFSP. The European Council has defined the Union's objectives concerning the EMP in a Common Strategy. Common strategies are implemented by the Council through joint actions and common positions, but in this case measures to implement the Barcelona Declaration have of course first to be negotiated with the Mediterranean partners in the different fora of the EMP, by the representatives of the EU (Presidency, Troika, officials). The Presidency is responsible for organizing the Euro-Mediterranean Ministerial Conferences and has a very important role, both in the EMP and within the EU, in that it determines the agenda of the Council, can initiate new actions and presides over the Euro-Mediterranean Committee.

The European Commission, more particularly the Commissioner for External Relations and the External Relations Directorate-General, is also very much involved in the political and security chapter. The Commission implements the actions as decided by the Foreign Ministers and, together with the other EU bodies, monitors the Barcelona Process and prepares further measures. In fact distinctions between the First and Second Pillars of the EU have been blurred where the Barcelona Process is concerned (Gomez, 1998, p.149; Monar, 1998, pp.54–6). In order to relieve the burden for the Secretariat-General of the Council and the administration of the Member States, within the EU implementation and follow-up of actions and preparation of new policies have been largely delegated to the Commission, which thus also deals with political and security issues. Following the Barcelona Conference it was the Commission that took the lead on a number of issues, such as the establishment of EuroMeSCo and the register of adherence to international conventions, initiatives which in spite of their security nature were not given the shape of CFSP joint actions and were therefore funded under the EC-Treaty, from the MEDA programme. MEDA, the EU's financial instrument for the implementation of the EMP, is managed by the Commission. For the period 1995–1999 MEDA accounted for over 3400 million euro; for the period 2000–2006 5350 million euro have been allocated to MEDA (Edwards and Philippart, 1997).

The organization of the EMP is asymmetric: while the Fifteen first coordinate their views within the EU before making proposals in the bodies of the EMP, the partner countries, in spite of some efforts at coordination, do not have such a mechanism and thus each approach the EMP individually, defending national views, an example of the limited level of regional integration among the partners.

The Follow-Up Conferences

The Malta Conference (April 1997)

The second Euro-Mediterranean Ministerial Conference was to be held in one of the partner countries. But the follow-up of the Barcelona Conference was clouded by a deterioration of the situation in the Middle East following the coming to power of Benjamin Netanyahu's Likud-government in Israel in May 1996. In September 1996 the Arab countries threatened to leave the EMP if Israel would not live up to its commitments concerning the Occupied Territories. Certain Arab countries, i.a. Syria and Lebanon, made it known that they would not participate in a conference in an Arab country in the presence of an Israeli delegation, which is why as a last resort Malta was chosen as venue. Indeed the Middle East peace process cast its shadow over the whole of the Conference, which took place in Valletta on 15–16 April 1997.

Although the Dutch Presidency believed it had received undertakings to the contrary, disagreement arose by Arab insistence on the inclusion of strong wording on the recent developments in the peace process in the preamble of the draft declaration, even before the political and security basket could be discussed. Consequently it proved impossible to find consensus on further measures which were proposed by the EU to implement the security basket of the Barcelona Declaration. Almost all proposals were vetoed by Syria and Lebanon, even though some Arab countries were willing to consider them (Edis, 1998, pp.98–101; Zaim, 1998, pp.32–6). Only the following CSBMs could be agreed upon:

- setting up a network of contact points for political and security issues;
- exchange of information on adherence to human rights treaties, which was completed by the time of the Malta Conference;
- exchange of information on membership of disarmament and arms control schemes and of instruments in the field of anti-terrorism; replies on both questionnaires were being awaited;

- convening of diplomatic seminars; diplomats from the 27 partner countries met twice in Malta, which resulted *inter alia* in the creation of the Euromed Internet Forum to distribute information on the EMP;
- establishment of the Euro-Mediterranean Study Commission (EuroMeSCo), a network of foreign policy institutes, established in 1996, grouping some 40 research institutes.

These measures were rather limited when compared to the ambitious objectives of the Barcelona Declaration. They still focussed exclusively on conflict prevention and avoided 'hard' military CSBMs, dealing instead with useful but rather obvious exchanges of information. Other measures which had been put forward by the senior officials were not retained by the Malta Conference; proposals included i.a. reporting of military expenditure, prior notification of military manoeuvres, exchange of expertise and Euro-Mediterranean arrangements on conflict prevention and crisis management, cooperation on peacekeeping, a Euro-Mediterranean conference on nuclear safety, a Middle East zone free of WMD and a network of defence institutes (Marquina, 2000a, pp.69–70; Spencer, 1999a, p.206). Apart from the measures which were approved, the participants only took

> note of the various activities that the senior officials have undertaken [...] encourage [them] to continue and deepen the political dialogue [...] [took] note of the work carried out [...] on confidence and security building measures, especially those already in operation or approved [...] They recognize that other measures [...] should be approved in a progressive way.

No time-table was agreed upon however, nor was there an indication of the priorities or general orientation of future measures.

The same went for the most important point on the agenda of the security basket, the elaboration of a Charter for Peace and Stability. Both France and Malta had originally proposed the conclusion of a Euro-Mediterranean Pact detailing the arrangements for a security dialogue as a framework for the implementation of the political and security partnership. Although quite soon the term 'pact' was dropped in favour of the less binding 'charter', senior officials had made considerable headway with the preparation of a draft. But on the issue of the Charter as well, no agreement could be found on the extensive proposals elaborated by the senior officials. On Malta participants just took 'note of the work of senior officials' and 'instruct them to continue the preparatory work [...] in order to submit an agreed text at a future Ministerial Meeting when political circumstances allow'. So although the Charter was not approved, the project as such was not abandoned (Tanner, 1996, pp.282–5).

In the end tensions rose so high that the partners could not even agree on the text of the conclusions before the end of the Conference; the text was finally adopted at a meeting of senior officials in Brussels on 6 May 1997.

Prior to the Conference, Member States had had difficulties agreeing on a common approach for the negotiations – a regular problem of the CFSP. The Dutch Presidency wanted to leave out the Middle East peace process altogether in order not to endanger the reaching of an agreement, while France held this to be impossible and preferred instead an openly critical attitude towards Israel. As a result of these disagreements the Presidency went into the negotiations with a very limited mandate. This was the first demonstration of the fact that the formal separation between the Partnership and the peace process would be very difficult to maintain. The crisis in the peace process effectively blocked the achievement of substantial progress in the EMP. On the other hand the continuing willingness of all partners, especially of Syria, Israel and the Palestinian Authority, to attend the meeting and engage in multilateral talks, in spite of the high tensions between them, indicated the great importance which they attached to the Barcelona Process and the Partnership's potential to serve as a security-building forum. Again the mere existence of the Partnership could be seen to be a CSBM, but this could not hide the fact that the Malta Conference had failed its objective of deepening and implementing the security basket of the EMP (Calleya, 1997, pp.3–13; Monar, 1999, pp.81–2).

The Ad Hoc Meeting in Palermo (June 1998)

On Malta it had been agreed to hold the next Ministerial Conference in Germany in the first half of 1999. Quite soon however there was talk of an additional conference at an earlier time in order to put the Barcelona process back on track after the failure of the Malta Conference. A number of factors necessitated, in the eyes of the Union's Southern Member States especially, a reinvigoration of the EMP. The Presidencies of three Southern Member States – France and Spain in 1995 and Italy in the first half of 1996 – during which the EMP had been launched, had been followed by those of three Northern countries: Ireland, the Netherlands and Luxemburg. As these countries maintained a very different focus in their foreign policies, they had given much less attention to Mediterranean issues. The scheduling of the opening of the accession process to the countries of Central and Eastern Europe for mid-1998 increased the Mediterranean states' fear of being marginalized in favour of the Union's European periphery. The UK, which had never been particularly active in the EMP and which held the Presidency from 1 January 1998, was now pressed to organize an extra ministerial meeting. At first a brief meeting in the margin of the General Affairs Council was proposed, but Italy succeeded in convincing the UK to convene a more significant separate ad hoc ministerial meeting, which took place in Palermo on 3–4 June 1998.

In order to avoid a repetition of what had happened on Malta, which might prove to be the final straw for the EMP, the UK adopted a different approach. The meeting was to be informal, without the need to produce formal conclusions or binding policy decisions, thus avoiding long negotiations on texts. Instead British Foreign Secretary Robin Cook summarized the outcome of the meeting in a Concluding Statement of his own. Developments in the Middle East peace process were to be discussed openly, but while maintaining the formal separation between the peace process and the EMP and without letting it overshadow the whole of the meeting. Indeed the Arab countries greatly appreciated the relevant paragraph in Cook's Concluding Statement, while Israel refrained from taking on too strong a position. 'Difficult' issues such as the Charter for Peace and Stability or terrorism were to be addressed properly.

As a result of this approach the Palermo meeting took place in a positive atmosphere. But at the same time the informal character of the meeting and the absence of discussions on concrete objectives and actions also made for very limited progress in the implementation and deepening of the EMP. CSBMs were now named 'partnership building measures', a term supposedly more acceptable to the Arab countries because it avoided the connotation of – the sensitive issue of – 'hard' security associated with CSBMs in the OSCE context.[4] The only new measure to become operational was the Euro-Med System of Prevention, Mitigation and Management of Natural and Man-made Disasters, providing for cooperation between the civil protection services of the partner countries. No other measures were agreed upon, nor was there any progress in establishing the Charter for Peace and Stability, except the agreement of a special ad hoc meeting of senior officials with the aim of making progress before the next Ministerial Meeting. Events in Algeria and renewed pressure from the partners for assistance with counter-terrorism put terrorism high on the agenda of the meeting. Here too a special meeting of senior officials was the only decision that was taken, as a first step to reconcile partner countries' views on the issue.

So although the Palermo meeting had a positive effect in that the participation of all partner countries was proof of their constant conviction of the usefulness of the EMP, it certainly did not constitute a fundamental revitalization of the Barcelona process, nor did it bring implementation of its political and security chapter much closer (Edis, 1998, pp.101–3; Youngs, 1999).

The Stuttgart Conference (April 1999)

The third Euro-Mediterranean Ministerial Conference took place as planned in Stuttgart on 15–16 April 1999. Senior officials had made considerable headway in drafting the Charter for Peace and Stability. An agreement was in place on the main guidelines and the philosophy of the project. Ministers could not reach agreement on its formal adoption however, so as Guidelines for Elaborating a Euro-Mediterranean Charter they only approved them as an informal working document, to be completed by the senior officials during additional ad hoc meetings by the next Ministerial Conference. This was programmed for the French Presidency in the second half of 2000. The completed Charter was to be 'approved formally by Ministers as soon as political circumstances allow', a reference to the obstruction of the political and security partnership caused by the conflict in the Middle East.

The Guidelines give a pivotal role to 'an enhanced political dialogue'. Regular consultations between Foreign Ministers and senior officials would form the basis for institutionalizing this dialogue, awaiting 'appropriate decision-making mechanisms reinforcing the existing institutional framework' to be included in the Charter; all decisions would be taken by consensus. The institutionalized political dialogue would thus be the policy-making entity in the political and security chapter. Because of its increased frequency and comprehensiveness, one could see it as the nucleus of early warning in the Mediterranean. The Guidelines further provide for the development of additional CSBMs, good-neighbourly relations, regional cooperation and preventive diplomacy in order to prevent tensions and crises. Very importantly, reference is made to crisis management and post-conflict rehabilitation, including Euro-Mediterranean cooperation in peacekeeping, thus leaving for the first time the exclusive emphasis on conflict prevention. In this field the wording of the Guidelines is very cautious, stating that such measures will be developed 'on a strictly voluntary and consensual basis [...] without interference with other institutions and bilateral efforts', taking into account the extreme sensitivity of the issue to the Arab partner countries. Ongoing disputes are excluded from the Charter: the Guidelines include the principle of 'non interference in the settlement of current conflicts'. The Charter is to be a politically, not a legally binding document, like the Barcelona Declaration itself.

At the Stuttgart Conference, Ministers did not agree upon any additional CSBMs, but instead 'acknowledged the difficulties which prevail and agreed to sustain and develop [existing] measures as well as identify and explore new areas of cooperation'. More particularly senior officials were again instructed to convene additional special meetings on the issue of terrorism. The Arab countries had urged the EU to allow Libya to participate in the conference as a full member, but the German Presidency only invited it as 'special guest' alongside Mauritania, the AMU and the Arab League. Ministers decided however that Libya would 'become a full member of the Barcelona Process as soon as the UN Security Council sanctions have been lifted and Libya has accepted the whole Barcelona acquis'. Following the Security Council decision to suspend part of the sanctions, because of indications that Libya renounced terrorism, the EU did lift its own restrictive measures, apart from the arms embargo. The inclusion of Libya in the EMP thus became a short term prospect.

Like the previous conferences the Stuttgart Conference did not succeed in implementing the political and security basket of the EMP. Once again partner countries were willing to continue the dialogue, but failed to adopt concrete actions.

The Common Strategy on the Mediterranean Region (June 2000)

On the European side of the Partnership, the European Council at the Santa Maria da Feira summit (19–20 June 2000) adopted a Common Strategy on the Mediterranean Region. The major objective of the Common Strategy is 'to make significant and measurable progress towards achieving the objectives of the Barcelona Declaration and its subsequent acquis'. It defines what actions ought to be taken in the view of the EU in order to implement the Barcelona Declaration. In its paragraphs dealing with political and security issues, the Common Strategy, expressing the strategic importance of stability in the Mediterranean to the EU and to Europe as a whole, repeats the objective of establishing a common area of peace and stability. To this end the political and security-related dialogue is to be strengthened at all levels, bilateral as well as multilateral, including the Charter for Peace and Stability, and further CSBMs are to be elaborated. Specific actions in the field of security are to be:

- regular consultations and 'timely information on initiatives that might be of concern to partners;

- reinforce cooperation in the fight against terrorism;
- establish arrangements for conflict prevention, crisis management and post-conflict rehabilitation, including the encouragement of the peaceful settlement of conflicts and disputes, including by judicial means;
- cooperate in addressing the problem of anti-personnel landmines;
- promote the ratification of all non-proliferation instruments, including the NPT, CWC, BTWC and CTBT, by all partner countries and establish a verifiable Middle East zone free of WMD.

In order to assure the follow-up of the Strategy, the Council was requested 'to ensure that each incoming Presidency presents [...] priorities for implementation of this Common Strategy' and 'to review and evaluate the Union's actions under this Strategy and to report to the European Council on progress towards its objectives not less than annually'. The Strategy deals with all the EU's relations with its Mediterranean partners and Libya, except for the bilateral relations with the Mediterranean candidates for membership, which are covered by the accession process.

The Common Strategy on the Mediterranean Region is only the third one adopted by the European Council, after the strategies on Russia (4 June 1999) and Ukraine (11 December 1999), which serves as an indication of the importance the EU attaches to its immediate periphery and to the Mediterranean in particular.[5]

In the Common Strategy the EU puts additional emphasis on a number of 'hard' security issues. Most of these were already included in the Barcelona Declaration, such as non-proliferation. The extra emphasis on terrorism can clearly be seen as a response to the repeated requests by the Mediterranean partners to devote more attention to this issue. The reference to the problem of anti-personnel landmines probably is a consequence of the importance which this issue acquired on the political agenda of the Union following its leading role in the conclusion of the Ottawa Convention; concerns expressed by the Southern partners would have played a role as well.[6] Most important is the fact that the EU expressly and formally includes cooperation on crisis management and post-conflict rehabilitation as major points on its Mediterranean agenda, thus strongly emphasizing a dimension of security policy which was absent from the Barcelona Declaration and which until then had only been dealt with in the informal Guidelines for Elaborating a Euro-Mediterranean Charter. In this context it is important to note that the Strategy takes into account recent developments in the Second Pillar, where it mentions that the EU will make use of the further elaboration of the ESDP to strengthen security cooperation with its Mediterranean partners. The gradual construction of a military dimension at the level of the EU creates possibilities for Euro-Mediterranean cooperation in this field.

The EU recognized the link between the achievement of the objectives of the Barcelona Declaration and the outcome of the peace process, stating that it

> is convinced that the successful conclusion of the Middle East peace process on all its tracks, and the resolution of other conflicts in the region, are important prerequisites for peace and stability in the Mediterranean.

The Common Strategy therefore sees a much more prominent role for the EU in the Middle East peace process, stipulating that 'the Union aspires to play its full part in bringing about stability and development in the Middle East'. But how the EU could contribute to the resolution of the conflict is not mentioned; it is just said that 'this Common Strategy will cover the EU's contribution to the consolidation of peace in the Middle East once a comprehensive peace settlement has been achieved'. No role in the settlement of the conflict is envisaged for the EMP, which is to come into the play only 'after peace has been achieved'.

The Common Strategy has the merit of clearly summing up the actions by which the EU means to achieve its broad objective of establishing an area of peace and stability and of including crisis management and post-conflict peace-building among them. But it is of course a unilateral document, binding upon the Member States of the EU only and in no way committing the Mediterranean partners, whose consent is still needed to bring implementation of the EMP any closer. It can be argued that the Common Strategy could have gone into much more detail. Most of the actions which it defines in the field of security are still rather broad. For example, no concrete measures are proposed to further cooperation in the fight against terrorism, nor are any options suggested for the establishment of arrangements for crisis management. The impact and the relevance of the Common Strategy would have been much greater if it had really elaborated the measures necessary – or a number of options – to realize the Mediterranean security objectives of the Union. In spite of the references to the Union's role in the Middle East peace process, the Strategy also does not address the causes of the failure to substantiate the political and security partnership, nor does it advance any solutions. So the Common Strategy does add to the list of fields in which the EU deems action necessary, but in the sense that it does not detail which actions should be taken, nor deals with possible ways of overcoming the obstacles to the implementation of the political and security partnership, its added value is limited. On the other hand the Strategy did come timely (Spencer, 2001b, pp.41–2). It highlighted anew the importance of the Mediterranean to the EU and assured policymakers' constant attention after a period in which events in the Balkans had led security policy to focus on the European continent and in which the political and security partnership had proved to be very cumbersome to implement.

In the partner countries the adoption of the Common Strategy, which is a CFSP and not an EC instrument, can be seen as an example of the Union's emphasis on the security dimension of the Barcelona Process (Whitman, 2001, p.11). But the move to include all aspects of Mediterranean policy into one CFSP framework document should be viewed in a positive light, as a precondition for the coordination of all dimensions of EU external policy, true to its comprehensive approach. Some Mediterranean observers reject the unilateral character of the Common Strategy, but this is of course unavoidable: as an EU policy decision, it is subject to EU decision-making procedures only. But that shows precisely what it is: a set of proposals which the EU wants to input into the Partnership, but which have then of course to be discussed with all partners.

The Marseille Conference (November 2000)

Prior to the fourth Euro-Mediterranean Ministerial Conference, the Commission drew up a report containing an evaluation of the Barcelona Process so far and recommendations for the future.[7] In the field of security the Commission appreciated the fact that the EMP is the only forum in which all partners, including Israel, Syria and Lebanon, continued to meet regardless of the evolution of the Middle East peace process. The Commission was also forced to note however that difficulties in the peace process had considerably slowed down the Barcelona process and had held back 'the willingness to cooperate more actively with neighbours', as the Commission rather euphemistically phrased it. The Commission further regretted that on certain issues the EMP had not led to 'a sufficiently frank and serious dialogue', mentioning, *inter alia*, terrorism, to which can easily be added military CSBMs, crisis management and post-conflict peace-building. Therefore the Commission called for a reinvigoration of the Barcelona Process. Within the political and security chapter this was to be primarily achieved by the adoption of the Charter for Peace and Stability. The existing ad hoc meetings of senior officials could then be converted into a regular and systematic dialogue on security and mechanisms for conflict prevention and crisis management could be created. The Commission also recommended to allow for a degree of flexibility in the EMP, so that a smaller number of partners could advance more quickly in adopting certain CSBMs if they so wished.

Unluckily the Conference, which took place on 15–16 November 2000, was preceded on 28 September by the outbreak of rapidly escalating violence between Israelis and Palestinians, which caused a severe crisis in the Middle East peace process. As a result of this for the first time in the short history of the EMP two partners, Syria and Lebanon, without much prior warning, refused to take part in the Conference. In his opening speech French Foreign Minister Hubert Védrine regretted their decision. While he admitted that the current situation was far from favourable to the negotiations, he expressed his conviction that the EMP was sufficiently important in itself for it to be continued in spite of the breakdown of the peace process. He also stressed that the development of the ESDP, which at that time was fully underway, was not in any way directed against third countries and that its primary area of focus would be Europe itself, the first time partners' doubts in this regard were addressed. Védrine stated that it was thus no cause for concern to the Mediterranean partners, which had already voiced their suspicions *vis-à-vis* the creation of a military dimension for the EU, fearing 'Western interventionism'. Circumstances in the Middle East did not permit any progress on the political and security chapter however, nor would any agreement without the participation of Syria and Lebanon have been workable. The non-participation of two partner countries also meant that the importance of the EMP as a CSBM in itself was very much reduced. Contrary to expectations, Libya on the other hand did participate in the Conference. Although at first it had declined the invitation to attend as a 'special guest', as at Stuttgart, and had stated that the goal of the conference would be 'to integrate Israel in the Mediterranean area', in the end Libya delegated the equivalent of its Minister of Foreign Affairs.[8]

In its Formal Conclusions the Presidency tried to save the Conference by emphasizing the importance of the fact that the Barcelona Process continued and that the existing CSBMs were maintained. But in reality the Marseille Conference was a failure. Ministers had to note the feeble results of the EMP in the field of security and the failure to adopt additional CSBMs. The adoption of the Euro-Mediterranean Charter for Peace and Stability had been expected at this conference; French President Jacques Chirac had even thought to convene a Euro-Mediterranean conference of Heads of State and Government to mark this solemn occasion. But, by now almost traditionally, the adoption of the Charter was once more postponed until circumstances permitted. As a poor substitute, but the maximum on which consensus could be found, Ministers called for a reinforcement of the political dialogue, without awaiting the adoption of the Charter, in order to clear up misunderstandings and reconcile the visions of the partner countries. To this end they mandated the senior officials to deepen the dialogue in a number of specified fields, *inter alia*, terrorism, and to broaden it so as to include issues such as disarmament and regional security developments. Ministers also suggested to study measures such as security of maritime transport in the Mediterranean and the fight against crime and drug trafficking. On a more general level Ministers underlined the necessity to reinforce the strategic role of the Euro-Mediterranean Committee as the main body for the stimulation, evaluation and follow-up of the Barcelona Process.

Once again developments in the Middle East peace process completely paralyzed the EMP. The first report from the Council on the implementation of the Common Strategy, when stating that 'all participants agreed that the Conference had given a fresh boost to the Barcelona Process', thus seemed to present a rather overoptimistic view of the situation, to say the least.[9]

The Brussels Conference (November 2001)

'11 September' led a number of European leaders to call for a reinvigoration of the EMP, in order, finally, to try and give substance to the security basket of the Partnership and also to give a clear signal that the EU still viewed the Mediterranean countries as partners for cooperation, with which to work jointly to establish peace and stability, rather than as potential enemies. The events did indeed carry with them the risk that henceforth relations with the Arab countries would be seen exclusively in the context of security threats. At the extraordinary meeting of the European Council on 21 September Commission President Romano Prodi emphasized that 'the Barcelona Process did not obtain the desired results and must be given a new impulse by strengthening and rethinking its structures and policies'.[10] A few days later a similar appeal was made by Spanish Prime Minister Jose Maria Aznar and Greek President Costis Stephanopoulos. Aznar, who announced that the EMP would be a priority for the upcoming Spanish Presidency, expressed the traditional view of the Union's Southern Members states, stating that

> the new international circumstances have placed the Mediterranean at the centre of international attention [...] the EU has a priority with its enlargement Eastwards but

must also understand that at all levels, economic, political, security, the whole Mediterranean is important and that the North-South dialogue is of primary importance at this time.[11]

On 25–26 October 2001 an extraordinary meeting of the Mediterranean Forum was convened in Agadir on the initiative of the King of Morocco, in order to assess the consequences of '11 September'. Exceptionally the EU was invited to participate, in the person of Belgian Foreign Minister Louis Michel. The exchange of views was concluded with what Greek Foreign Minister Georges Papandreou, presiding over the meeting, deemed 'an unequivocal condemnation of terrorism', but in fact the participants were unable to find agreement on a definition of terrorism.[12]

As was to be expected the Euro-Mediterranean Ministerial Conference, which took place as planned in Brussels on 5–6 November 2001, was completely dominated by the global campaign against terrorism and the need to find a breakthrough in the Middle East in order to rally the Arab countries behind it. Next to the Fifteen and the twelve Mediterranean partners, Libya, Mauritania and the AMU participated as observers. That Syria and Lebanon were present, while they had boycotted the previous summit, was seen as a signal of support for the attitude which the EU had adopted after '11 September', i.e. emphasizing the need to tackle the underlying causes of terrorism, notably the Middle East conflict.

Terrorism has always been a controversial issue in the EMP. The Arab states feel that the Fifteen devote far too little attention to this subject, which for them represents one of the major security concerns. Contrary to the European inclination to view the terrorism issue in the context of the EMP as a problem of export of terrorism to the EU, the Arab states see it as a primarily Southern security risk. Indeed studies indicate that 60 to 70 per cent of all terrorist acts committed worldwide occur in Arab countries. These therefore demand anti-terrorist measures focussing on the Mediterranean partners rather than on the EU. The ad hoc meetings on terrorism in the framework of the political and security chapter resulted in a number of proposals, such as exchange of information through the national sections of Interpol, creation of a database on terrorist activities, organizing expert meetings on the financing of terrorist groups and composing a catalogue of travel documents and legislation on the port of fire-arms of all partners. These measures have yet to be agreed upon by the Ministers however (Chikh, 1999, p.5; Perthes, 1999b, pp.3–4).

The EU has always been rather reluctant to push cooperation on terrorism in the framework of the EMP, which would imply the need to have first a sensitive discussion on the definition of terrorism. The Arab countries consider Israeli repression of the Palestinian struggle to be 'state terrorism' and they demand the extradition of a number of 'terrorists' residing in the EU, which are not always labelled as such by the countries who have granted them asylum; this is especially the case for the UK. On the other hand a number of Arab states refuse to refer to attacks against Israel as terrorist acts, claiming that these are legitimate acts in the struggle against occupation, and several Arab countries are accused of harbouring and supporting terrorist groups. The conflict in Algeria is another factor explaining the EU's reluctance. The Union has wanted to avoid being dragged into effective support of the military regime under the guise of the fight against terrorism when the Algerian regime is itself accused of atrocities.

These divisions emerged again at the Brussels Conference. Addressing the Conference, Yasser Arafat repeated his forceful condemnation of the attacks on the US and his willingness to participate in any international collective effort to counter terrorism, including, as he added, terrorism organized by an occupying state. Syrian Foreign Minister Farouq Al-Shara too, acting as spokesman for the Arab partners, appealed to the EU to combat Israel's 'state terrorism' as strongly as that carried out by political groups or religious sects.[13] In the end Ministers avoided the issue of the definition of terrorism and 'expressed their total condemnation of terrorism everywhere in the world and their solidarity with the peoples who are victims thereof'. They also emphasized the need to address the underlying causes of terrorism. Resolved to do away with the idea of a 'clash of civilizations', Ministers

> formally rejected as both dangerous and unfounded any equating of terrorism with the Arab and muslim world. In this connection the importance of the Barcelona Process as a relevant and recognized instrument for promoting a dialogue of equals between cultures and civilizations was recognized by all.

By way of concrete measures, Ministers undertook to rapidly implement Security Council Resolution 1373, aimed at eliminating all forms of support for terrorists, and 'to press ahead with the signing, ratification and implementation [...] of all the United Nations Conventions, in particular that of December 1999 for the suppression of the financing of terrorism'. Further, 'Ministers encouraged efforts to speed up the negotiations in the United Nations with the aim of drafting a general convention against terrorism'. On the main point however, i.e. the possibility of taking measures against terrorism within the EMP, no decisions were taken. The Ministers just 'asked the senior officials to continue their dialogue on terrorism matters by organising a third *ad hoc* meeting which should be held as quickly as possible'. Cooperation in the fight against terrorism cannot be established in the Partnership without first resolving the issue of the definition of terrorism.[14]

Next to terrorism, all of the attention went to the Middle East peace process and an Arafat-Peres meeting held in the margin of the Conference. For the first time though Ministers went beyond the obligatory phrases regarding the peace process and adopted an outspoken view as to the desired outcome of the negotiations, calling for a Palestinian state and safety for Israel. Apparently, in the aftermath of '11 September' and in view of the need to preserve close relations with the Mediterranean partners and advancing security cooperation, awareness had grown of the impossibility of maintaining the separation between the Partnership and the peace process.

But as was to be expected under the current circumstances, no progress could be achieved with regard to the political and security basket of the Partnership. Ministers simply 'confirmed the mandate given in Marseilles to the senior officials to continue and complete their work on the adoption of the Charter for Peace and Stability as soon as the situation allows'. They further instructed them to consolidate the CSBMs already in force and to gradually develop new measures and extend the political dialogue to new topics, such as regional trends regarding security and disarmament. This lack of progress contrasted sharply with the desire expressed by several of the Southern participants to finally actually implement all the decisions that have been taken. This concern had been raised at the Mediterranean Forum by Moroccan Foreign Minister Mohamed Bin Aissa, who deplored 'the lack of genuinely joint structures, operational efficiency, and a genuine regular strategic dialogue' and therefore called for a new strategy, 'as we can no longer be contented with false consensus, nor escape laboriously negotiated and unanimously accepted commitments'. Participants stated to count on the next formal Euro-Mediterranean summit to breath new life into the Barcelona Process.[15]

The Valencia Conference (April 2002)

Contrary to expectations, given the unresolved crisis in the Middle East, the Valencia Conference (22–23 April 2002) did achieve some major progress, thanks to the Spanish Presidency, although its success went almost completely unnoticed because of events in the Middle East. Convinced that in the aftermath of '11 September' the Barcelona process was 'more necessary than ever', but at the same time was in urgent need of revitalization, Ministers adopted the Valencia Action Plan. This was clearly a far more realistic assessment than that made by the Commission in its communication to prepare the Conference, which stated about the EMP that 'particularly since its reinvigoration in Marseilles, in 2000, it has been accompanied by strong political drive which has led to the achievement of ambitious and concrete progress' – just in which fields is not quite clear.[16]

In the political and security field, the Action Plan offered little concrete projects, though it did have the merit of indicating the direction which future action should take, notably the elaboration of 'a common language on defence and security', the development of mechanisms for preventive diplomacy and crisis management and the inclusion of the ESDP on the agenda of the political dialogue. One must doubt however whether the partner countries really were more willing than before to take action on these 'hard' security matters. The paragraph relating to terrorism is exemplary: Ministers reaffirmed the central role of the UN and the need to implement the relevant Security Council Resolutions, but could not agree on a substantial EMP action plan against terrorism.

The Conference's major achievement then lay in the organization of the Partnership, notably by strengthening the balance between the EU and the Mediterranean partners – the dominance of the EU in the EMP bodies was a constant source of complaint for the latter. Ministers now decided to introduce co-chairmanship, the principle of which was deemed to be 'consistent with the essence of the Partnership', and to examine ways for the restructuring of the Euro-Mediterranean Committee in order to ensure greater involvement of the partner countries. These measures should do a great deal for increasing the sense of 'co-ownership' of the EMP. Other important innovations were the establishment of a

Euro-Mediterranean Parliamentary Assembly and of an informal Euro-Med Working Group to hold meetings of like-minded Euro-Mediterranean countries whenever issues of relevance for the region are discussed, notably within the UN.

If carried through, the remarkable organizational decisions of the Valencia Conference, which equally remarkably attracted little or no attention, could substantially affect policy-making in all baskets of the EMP – hopefully progress in the political and security basket will then be easier to achieve. But once again Syria and Lebanon did not participate, for reasons connected to the situation in the Middle East, which leaves questions as to the viability of the Action Plan and the ultimate survival of the EMP itself.

WEU and the Mediterranean

WEU's Mediterranean Dialogue

The Maastricht Treaty closely associated the Western European Union (WEU) with the EU: WEU was appointed the operational military capacity of the CFSP. After the end of the Cold War WEU had reoriented itself from collective defence to the 'Petersberg Tasks',[17] i.e. crisis management, ranging from humanitarian and rescue operations and peacekeeping to peace enforcement. The association between both organizations was gradually reinforced; the development of the ESDP eventually led to the integration of WEU's Petersberg Tasks into the EU.

During the Cold War WEU had paid little or no attention to the Mediterranean; the main security issues at that time, i.e. the fear of Soviet intrusion into the area and the Middle East peace process, were left to NATO and the US respectively to deal with. Only after WEU's reactivation in the 1980s and urged on by its Southern European Member States did the Mediterranean begin to be considered an area of interest. In 1986 WEU created the Mediterranean Sub-Group of experts to consider Mediterranean security issues. In 1993 as the Mediterranean Group this became one of the working groups preparing the meetings of the WEU Council. The 1995 Common Concept, more or less the strategic concept of WEU, devoted considerable attention to the Mediterranean. It identified the main security issues in the Mediterranean: possible interruption of fuel supply, proliferation of WMD, the rise of political extremism, terrorism, the Cyprus issue and the Middle East peace process. 'The maintenance of political, economic and military stability in the region as well as a free flow of traffic through and into the Mediterranean' were named as priority objectives.[18]

In 1992 WEU started a 'Mediterranean Dialogue' of its own with eventually seven countries: Algeria, Egypt, Israel, Jordan, Mauritania, Morocco and Tunisia. This initiative, with focus on the Maghreb rather than on the Mediterranean as a whole, was inspired by the similar orientation of the Lisbon European Council that same month. It was felt in contrast to the Middle East, circumstances in this sub-region were quite favourable to the development of a close and effective dialogue. The Dialogue was guided by seven principles: dialogue, transparency, confidence, conflict prevention, sufficiency, peaceful settlement of conflicts and non-proliferation of armaments. These should address the main concerns of the participants: the distrust created in the South by the reorientation of WEU and NATO towards crisis management and rapid reaction forces and the Western concern over proliferation of WMD (Marquina, 2000a, pp.63–6; Ortega, 1999a). Because of its bilateral character, necessitating consecutive meetings on the same issues, the Dialogue proved to be very cumbersome.

In the end the achievements of the Mediterranean Dialogue remained very modest. Many of the WEU countries preferred to give priority to the Barcelona Process, while certain countries wanted to avoid duplication of NATO's Mediterranean Dialogue, resulting in limited interest in WEU's Dialogue. Meetings tended to concentrate on dissemination of information on the development of WEU itself, rather than on the possibilities for actual cooperation or even exchange of expertise, e.g. on crisis management. Proposals, some very detailed, for cooperation remained without response; e.g. a request by Egypt for assistance with de-mining operations was turned down. This resulted in disappointment in the Mediterranean partners, who felt 'dialogue for the sake of dialogue' to be both unsatisfactory and insufficient (Marquina, 2001, p.143). Although in itself the Dialogue constituted a – very general – CSBM, it lacked substance and far from realized its potential for security cooperation. Because of its bilateral character, it functioned as a North-South CSBM, but it did not address confidence and security between the Mediterranean countries themselves, although the risk of South-South disputes is by far the greatest.

In spite of the ever closer association between WEU and the EU, coordination between the two on Mediterranean issues was limited. WEU was not invited to attend the Barcelona Conference or any of the follow-up conferences, nor was it represented in the bodies of the EMP. When in 1998 WEU officials openly declared their willingness to contribute to the political and security chapter of the Partnership, their offer did not meet with any answer. The UK especially resisted WEU's involvement in the Barcelona Process: given that neither NATO nor the US were involved, London wanted to avoid WEU from acquiring a dominant position with regard to the security dimension of the EMP (Masala, 2000b, p.166). The Mediterranean Dialogue clearly involved all issues included in the political and security chapter of the EMP and so WEU could have contributed its – be it limited – acquis in this field, particularly as concerns the elaboration of the Charter for Peace and Stability. This would have been recommendable considering WEU's position as the Union's military arm, which might be called upon to implement CFSP decisions on the Mediterranean. A potential WEU contribution was dependent upon a formal demand from the EU however, which was never made. At the November 2000 Marseilles summit, in view of the near end of WEU as a separate entity and its integration into the EU – except for a small residual organization – it was decided to terminate the Mediterranean Dialogue.

Forces Answerable to WEU in the Mediterranean

In the context of WEU's reorientation to crisis management, a number of national and multinational military units were put at its disposal by the Member States: the Forces Answerable to WEU (FAWEU). These forces remain under national control, but at the request of WEU can temporarily be placed under WEU-command, (now in an EU framework, after the integration of WEU's crisis management tasks into the Union) for European operations. Three of the multinational units which were created have a Mediterranean character:

- The European Maritime Force (EUROMARFOR), created by France, Spain and Italy, has a small permanent multinational command, which is temporarily expanded for the duration of manoeuvres or operations. A High-level Interministerial Committee, consisting of the Chiefs of Staff and the Directors of Political Affairs of the participating countries, decides on the political and the general military guidelines of each operation and indicates the ships that will take part. As a maritime unit with an air force complement, EUROMARFOR is potentially a very flexible instrument. A ship can serve as a ready-made basis for land operations, which it can support with artillery or, in the case of an aircraft carrier, air force operations, and if a unit is equipped with landing craft or helicopters landing operations can be executed.
- The three countries also created a land unit along the same lines: the Rapid Deployment Euroforce (EUROFOR). A limited staff in Firenze is expanded for exercises or operations. No troops are assigned to EUROFOR permanently, an Interministerial Committee decides which units will participate in manoeuvres or operations; these would mainly be light units, enabling EUROFOR to be used as a rapid reaction force. EUROFOR can also operate jointly with EUROMARFOR for landing operations. On 15 May 1995 EUROFOR and EUROMARFOR were put at the disposal of WEU and the other Member States were invited to join them. Portugal already accepted this offer and joined both.
- In 1997 preparations started for the creation of an analogous Spanish-Italian Amphibious Force (SIAF), which is also available to WEU: a pre-structured, non-permanent force, with as its only permanent element two small nuclei of officers, each attached to the staff of the force of the other country.

It is clear that these units have a Mediterranean destination, though not exclusively. Because of an initial lack of information as to their purpose, the creation of EUROFOR and EUROMARFOR was greeted with mistrust by the Mediterranean states, who feared that these units, which were not included in a Euro-Mediterranean framework and would thus operate unilaterally, were intended for Western interventions on the Southern shore of the Mediterranean. Their creation was seen as being contradictory to the efforts within the EMP to promote dialogue and cooperation. A subsequent information campaign made clear that the units were not directed against the Mediterranean partners, but were rather meant to increase cooperation and interoperability between Western forces. On 14 May 1997 France, Spain, Italy and Portugal issued a declaration stating that they were 'prepared to implement actions of cooperation within the framework of EUROFOR and EUROMARFOR with Mediterranean countries, particularly those which maintain a dialogue with the Western European Union'. In the framework of the setting-up of CSBMs 'participation of those countries' forces, in conjunction with EUROFOR and EUROMARFOR, in some operations provided for in the Petersberg Declaration' was envisaged.[19] Joint operations involving troops from both sides of the Mediterranean would indeed be a very important CSBM and would considerably promote confidence between North and South and between the Southern countries. So far the offer, although successfully diluting the Southern countries' mistrust, has not resulted in actual cooperation however, apart from allowing observers to EUROFOR and EUROMARFOR manoeuvres (Echeverria, 1999b, pp.15–16; Pugh, 2000, pp.20–22).

The great weakness of EUROFOR and EUROMARFOR is the absence of a framework for them to operate in. Given its limited substance and its lack of cooperation on concrete issues, WEU's Mediterranean Dialogue did not constitute such a framework. Nor does the EMP as long as it does not provide for arrangements for Euro-Mediterranean military manoeuvres and operations. Without participation from the Mediterranean partners, the creation of EUROFOR and EUROMARFOR, although these units were and are very valuable in the context of the development of a European defence policy, could thus not serve as a CSBM for the Mediterranean.

Obstacles to a Security Partnership

Ongoing Disputes and Conflicts

Several factors explain why up to this day the achievements of the EMP in the field of security have remained so limited. The major obstacle to the implementation of the political and security basket of the Barcelona Declaration is the lack of progress in the Middle East peace process. The Arab-Israeli conflict, which in spite of negotiations and agreements goes from one crisis to the next, continues to strain relations between Israel and the Arab countries and between the latter and the EU, which is reproached with a too passive attitude. The impact of the conflict transcends it geographic limitations; it influences all initiatives for Euro-Mediterranean cooperation. For the Arabs, CSBMs can only be implemented if all partners accept the principles of international law, such as respect for sovereignty and territorial integrity, non-interference in domestic affairs and the right to self-determination, without which there is no basis upon which to establish confidence. Israeli occupation of Palestinian territory is seen as a violation of international law, so as long as the conflict has not been settled the Arab partners are not willing to discuss security. It is felt that first the existing conflicts and disputes, between Israelis and Palestinians, but also between Greeks and Turks, on Cyprus, in Algeria etc., should be solved before thinking of far-reaching arrangements for the prevention and resolution of future conflicts. In short, one cannot reasonably hope to establish security cooperation between countries which are involved in disputes or even, as in the case of the Israelis and Palestinians, in armed conflict.

By not addressing the ongoing conflicts and referring them to other fora, although in its Common Strategy the EU recognizes their resolution as preconditions for the achievement of the objectives of the EMP, the Partnership neglects the main security concerns of the Mediterranean partners. So it actually reduces its own chances of success, for until these conflicts are addressed, partners are not willing to discuss other security issues. The security dimension of the EMP thus remains limited to the lowest common denominator: measures which because of their limited scope give no cause for controversy. Although the EMP is valuable in itself as a forum for dialogue and as a CSBM, the fact that up til now the Partnership has been able to survive the subsequent crises of the Middle East peace process does not say anything about the achievements of the EMP as such. The failure of the Ministerial Conferences to adopt concrete measures and especially the non-attendance of Syria and Lebanon in Marseilles and Valencia are a severe warning: ultimately the EMP will not survive if no action is taken to settle the conflict in the Middle East. Only at the Brussels Conference did the partners for the first time 'violate' the formal separation between the Partnership and the peace process.

A factor which is related to the dominance of the Arab-Israeli conflict over all other Mediterranean issues is the impression among the Maghreb countries that since the creation of the Partnership the attention of the EU has been diverted to the Middle East. It is often felt in these countries that their interests would have been better served by the further development of their bilateral relations with the EU, which predate the EMP, than they are now by the multilateral Barcelona Process.

The situation in the Middle East is compounded by the possession – never officially recognized, but widely acknowledged – by Israel of nuclear weapons and its refusal to sign the NPT, which is a stumbling-block to the adoption of CSBMs, notably in the field of arms control and disarmament. In Israel's view accession to the NPT is possible only if peace treaties have been concluded with all Arab states, after which it will support the establishment of a WMD-free zone in the Middle East. Reasons given for not being willing to sign earlier are the country's lack of strategic depth, because of its narrowness, the constant hostility of certain neighbouring countries, the proliferation of other WMD and of ballistic missiles in the region and the fact that in conventional weapons the balance of power is much less favourable to Israel. Furthermore because of its strategy of 'deliberate ambiguity', Israel has always refused even 'softer' CSBMs in the field of nuclear weapons, such as public access to data or inspection of nuclear facilities. The Arab states refer to this Israeli stance to justify their refusal to agree to arms control and disarmament arrangements, especially in the field of WMD, which is why so far all initiatives towards this end have failed to produce significant results (Boniface, 2000, pp.174–5). In fact it is very difficult to agree on WMD-related CSBMs in a situation of permanent strategic imbalance: countries having a monopoly on certain WMD are not motivated to abandon them, because it would reduce their strategic advantage, while other countries seek to acquire such weapons or other WMD to compensate for their disadvantage. Thus in such a situation of uneven distribution of WMD, in casu nuclear weapons, they no longer serve as a regional security guarantee, as they will not result in a stable deterrence but instead stimulate proliferation, because of the linkages between the different categories of WMD (El-Sayed, 2000a, pp.136–48).

The impact of neighbouring regions on the countries of the EMP is a further impeding factor, notably in the field of arms control and disarmament. Israel refuses to consider arrangements to this end which do not include the WMD of e.g. Iran and Iraq, countries which it perceives as equally threatening to its security as Syria e.g., but which are not members of the Barcelona Process, making it very difficult to agree on measures in the context of the EMP. Security in the Middle East and the Gulf is indeed very much intertwined. Maybe in the long run the Partnership is therefore not the most suitable framework for far-reaching arms control and disarmament schemes. But because of the other obstacles to its political and security basket, partners were not even able to agree on the most modest arms-related CSBM, even though there is a wide range of not quite so far-reaching measures to be taken in this field which could very well be adopted in the framework of the Partnership.

It should be mentioned that the EU countries themselves still account for a considerable portion of the arms sales to the Mediterranean. Measures for arms control and disarmament would thus also require an earnest effort on the side of the EU, the arms exports policy of which ought to be consistent with the objectives of its Mediterranean security policy.

Perhaps the willingness of Turkey to discuss 'hard' security in the framework of the EMP should be doubted as well. Traditionally, Turkey, as a member of NATO, is a staunch ally of the US. Relations with the EU on the other hand have been clouded by frictions over Turkey's accession to the Union. These frictions were enhanced by the development of the ESDP and the possibility of EU military operations being conducted outside the NATO framework, which Turkey saw as a discrimination of the non-EU European Allies,[20] in spite of the fact that modalities for their extensive involvement were provided for. One can therefore question Turkey's willingness to accept a security role for the EU in the Mediterranean.

Distrust between North and South

An important factor of a more psychological nature is the climate of distrust which more often than not clouds relations between the two sides of the Mediterranean when it comes to security. The Arab countries notably feel that the West mainly sees them as potential enemies, which is why any security measures they propose are viewed with suspicion. So in the partner countries the concept of CSBMs is often resisted, particularly by the military establishment, because they are perceived as instruments by which the West hopes to gain an advantage. Export control regimes are seen as a way to limit the spread of modern science and technology, transparency measures can be a means of acquiring intelligence, arms control of limiting the armed forces of the South. CSBMs are thus feared to affect the countries' defence capability. For the Arab states the economic and cultural baskets of the EMP are the most important ones and they feel that the EU, because of its perceived preoccupation with security threats emanating from the Mediterranean, unduly emphasizes the politico-military dimension of the Partnership. Their impression is that Europe just wants to contain threats from the Mediterranean and is therefore waging a very traditional defensive policy. The 'securitization' of the migration issue and the visions of a 'Fortress Europe' which this evokes is another factor explaining this view. '11 September' carried with it the risk of a dramatic increase of the distrust between the West and the Arab world. There was a great danger that the events would be interpreted as an act of aggression by 'the' Arab world against 'the' West. Political leaders in Europe and the US therefore made it clear that their was no question of a 'war against islam'. The EU especially stressed that the perpetrators of the attacks, and they only, ought to be punished, provided their was hard evidence of their involvement, but that above all the underlying causes of extremism should be dealt with: the situation in the Middle East and poor socio-economic conditions, which make a good recruiting-ground for 'martyrs'.

The Arab states feel discriminated against because the West and especially the US seldom condemn Israel for its nuclear policy, while repeatedly and openly criticizing Arab proliferation of WMD. The notion of strategic imbalance should also been seen in a North-South context. Arab countries do not feel very much inclined to limit proliferation and possession of WMD knowing that the European members of the EMP are covered by the nuclear umbrella of NATO, with the UK and France possessing nuclear weapons of their own. They further reject the perceived inclination of the West to military intervention, as demonstrated during the Gulf War, the 1999–2000 Kosovo crisis and the 2003 Iraq crisis, and by the creation of EUROFOR and EUROMARFOR. These interventions are seen to contrast sharply with Western unwillingness to force Israel to implement Security Council resolutions. The Arab countries are indeed very suspicious of any risk of foreign intervention. It is feared that agreement to certain principles in the framework of the EMP can be used by the West as a pretext for intervention, e.g. for the sake of human rights or international law, especially by those countries which are regularly criticized for their human rights record. This is also seen as being in contradiction with the principle of non-intervention in internal affairs proclaimed in the Barcelona Declaration (Biad, 1999, pp.110–13; 2000a, pp.266–70). Of course, reactions to any given intervention will depend on the case at hand. During the Gulf War the large majority of the Arab regimes did support the military operations against Iraq. In the sense that each individual country perceives itself as a potential object of intervention however, one can say that a priori the Arab countries reject what they deem to be 'Western interventionism'. The gradual development of the ESDP and the creation of a European rapid reaction force are seen through this same lens and therefore once again arouse Arab suspicion. At an informal meeting in Zaragoza (22–23 March 2002) the EU Defence Ministers did state that efforts must be made to inform partners of the geographical scope and the cooperative nature of the ESDP in order to prevent its misinterpretation, but organizing a seminar (as was proposed) will not be sufficient to convince partners of the Union's 'honourable intentions'.

One should acknowledge that the Mediterranean states lack the experience of a process of CSBMs like the one in which the West was engaged with the Soviet Union. This is a factor to be taken into account when explaining their reluctant attitude towards CSBMs. But at the same time this lack of trust evidently is a strong plea in favour of CSBMs. The few countries which have joined a number of arms control arrangements, Cyprus, Malta and Turkey, are exactly the most Westernized partners. The suspicions of the partner countries vis-à-vis European security policy make it clear that, although the risk of disputes and conflict is bigger between or in Southern states, there is also a strong need for North-South CSBMs, in order to create the basis on which to establish Euro-Mediterranean security cooperation.

Terrorism is another issue which creates tensions between the EU and its Mediterranean partners. '11 September' led to a massive increase in the attention devoted to terrorism. The first reaction of the West was naturally to call for measures to defend itself against terrorist strikes. But effectively combating terrorism is only possible via close cooperation between all countries, not just the Western states. Only a wide platform of countries has any chance of success against internationally organized terrorist groups. And an operation against islamist terrorist groups would only be politically acceptable to the Arab and islamic states and to public opinion there if they too were involved. A coalition of Western countries only would again stimulate the image of a 'clash between civilizations', which ought to be avoided at all costs. A stepped-up effort in the framework of the EMP would in fact provide an answer to a long-standing request of its Mediterranean partners. But cooperation on terrorism demands a commitment on their side as well, not to harbour terrorist groupings. The main problem still remains the difficulty of finding an agreement on a definition of terrorism.

Another fact is that the EU is still not seen by its partners as an international actor with sufficient political weight to effectively influence the security issues discussed in the EMP. This has to do with the relative inefficacy of the CFSP; the achievements of the Second Pillar have indeed been limited because of its intergovernmental nature. It also has to do with the fact that the ESDP is still in a very early stage of development, which raises questions as to the capacity for action of the EU in the military field. There is of course also a connection with the impression of American dominance in the Mediterranean, specifically in the Middle East, which it is felt the EU is in no position to challenge. As a result partners are rather unwilling to discuss 'hard' security issues with the EU, which they perceive as too feeble an actor in this field, proof of which the Arab countries find in the Union's passive stance towards the Middle East peace process. Perhaps the relatively young age of the EU's security dimension and the limited experience and expertise of the Union in this field, can also partly explain why progress in the political and security partnership has been considerably slower than in the economic basket, which concerns the Union's core competencies. Indeed, Member States are often rather jealous of their national sovereignty in the fields of foreign and security policy and not all of them are that enthusiastic about the Union dealing with politico-military issues, so it is often difficult to find consensus between the Fifteen even before an item is tabled in the EMP.

An Unrealized Security Concept

The paralysis of the political and security partnership, as a consequence of the ongoing conflicts and the lack of trust between both shores, implies that the Union's comprehensive and cooperative approach to security on which the EMP is based has not, or at least not sufficiently, materialized on the ground. One must assume though that the Union is earnestly committed to its innovative approach, a fact which, although a formal security concept is yet to be adopted, can be deducted from the practice of the CFSP.

In Göteborg the European Council endorsed the EU Programme for the Prevention of Violent Conflicts, which makes conflict prevention into one of the main objectives of the Union's external relations, to be integrated in all of its aspects: the CFSP (and ESDP), development cooperation and external trade. The Programme lists EU instruments for both structural, long-term and direct, short term preventive actions, naming, *inter alia*, development aid, trade, arms control, human rights policies, environmental policies, political dialogue, diplomacy and capabilities for crisis management, military as well as civil. For next to the military capacity, the Union is also building a crisis management capacity in the field of police, justice, civil protection and civil administration. The same is advocated by the Commission, which pleads for a multi-dimensional 'proximity policy' based on close partnership.[21] This comprehensive approach, which makes use of the full range of available instruments, constitutes the specificity of the EU, as compared to NATO e.g., and also its potential strength.

The cooperative approach as well is a now well-established feature of the CFSP. As is evident from the partnership approach towards the Mediterranean and Central and Eastern Europe, the countries in the Union's periphery are seen as partners for security cooperation, rather than as mere objects of a unilateral EU security policy. On the basis of common interests and – the development of – shared values a joint security policy can be defined which is in the interest of all parties concerned. The comprehensive and cooperative approaches are indeed closely linked, for partnership and cooperation with the countries in Europe's periphery cannot be built on just the politico-military field, but require a broader base, to be established, *inter alia*, through close political dialogue and narrow economic relations.

Given the Mediterranean partners' distrust, the Union now has to perform a difficult balancing exercise. On the one hand the EU must avoid that in the wake of '11 September' relations with its partners are purely seen in terms of security or even antagonism. On the other hand the Union does have to proceed with the development of the ESDP, from which the Mediterranean cannot be excluded, and the political and security basket of the EMP.

An Inequitable Partnership

The dynamic of the EMP is for a great part dependent on the level of interest of each EU Presidency, as on the EU-side it is mainly the Presidency which has to provide the necessary impetus for new actions and which has to host and inspire the Ministerial Conferences. This is especially so in the area of security, because the Commission departments, which otherwise often function as the engine of further action, are much less involved in the preparation of policy in this field. On the other hand the regular meetings of senior officials at the different levels of the EMP assure that a certain dynamic will always be maintained. The repeated far-reaching proposals which they submit and the progressive elaboration of the Charter for Peace and Stability are proof of this. And although originally it were the Union's Mediterranean Member States who pushed for an enhanced Mediterranean policy, nowadays all Member States are committed to the EMP, because the interests of the EU as a whole are at stake. The administrative capacity of the consecutive Presidencies can differ greatly however, as smaller Member States have less means available for their very labour-intensive time as President-in-Office; this is a drawback of the CFSP in general.

Impetus, be it perhaps limited, is also provided by the policy-preparing bodies of the EU, such as the Political and Security Committee, the Council Working Groups, the High Representative for the CFSP and the Policy Planning and Early Warning Unit and, much more noticeably, by the relevant departments of the Commission and by the work done by the senior officials in the bodies of the EMP. The latter are very important as a driving force for the political and security partnership. The development of the ESDP and the enhancement of the administration of the CFSP by the inclusion of former WEU bodies and the creation of new structures will positively influence the role of the Second Pillar bodies as actors in the political and security partnership who can initiate proposals.

The EMP lacks an administration of its own however. There is no such thing as a EMP secretariat, even though the creation of such a permanent body has been proposed by a number of Mediterranean partners. The quarterly meetings of the Euro-Mediterranean Committee are insufficient for it to manage the daily running of the Barcelona Process. The necessary administrative and management tasks, including management of the MEDA Programme, are instead performed by the EU-bodies, in particular by the Commission departments. In combination with the fact that the EU Presidency chairs the Euro-Mediterranean Committee, thus giving it great power over agenda-setting within the EMP, this creates the impression that the Barcelona Process is rather more EU- than Mediterranean-oriented, which is a cause for friction between the EU and the Mediterranean partner countries. This was already the case at the very start of the Partnership: the Barcelona Declaration had been meticulously elaborated by the EU bodies, so at the Barcelona Conference the Mediterranean countries were more or less put in a 'take it or leave it' situation, without there being much room for amendments to the document (Jacobs, 2000, p.190). The impression of an inequitable Partnership is confirmed by the fact that most if not all meetings of the EMP are held either in the EU or on Malta, i.e. not in an Arab country, but it should be realized that this is not due to unwillingness on the European part, but to divisions among the partners (notably because of the Arab-Israeli conflict). Indeed, the dominance of the EU within the Partnership for a large part simply is the consequence of partners' inability to reach some kind of preliminary coordination among themselves, let alone to speak with a single voice as the Fifteen do. This is a consequence of the weakness of regional integration on the Southern shore of the Mediterranean. Implementing the organizational decisions of the Valencia Conference, particularly the concept of co-chairmanship, would do a great deal to restore the balance, but would not provide an answer to the lack of an EMP administration.

The EMP is an intergovernmental structure, meaning that decisions are taken unanimously by all participating states. This consensus-based approach makes for a slow and cumbersome decision-making process. In spite of the existence of shared security interests between both sides of the Mediterranean, it is very difficult to find consensus between 27 partners. There is in fact a double decision-making process, as first the Fifteen have to reach an agreement among themselves. The partners are a very diverse set of countries – the Mediterranean candidates for accession, Israel, and the Arab countries of the Mashrek and Maghreb – and they are further divided by a number of ongoing disputes and conflicts. But this diversity, although it renders decision-making difficult, at the same time constitutes the reason why a system of majority-voting in the EMP is unimaginable at least for as long as the ongoing conflicts in the region have not been resolved. Such a system would lead to the isolation of certain partner countries – Israel is of course the first that comes to mind – which might lead to their retreat from the Partnership. Supra-nationality demands a high degree of integration and trust between states, which at present do not exist in the Mediterranean. The EMP is therefore bound to continue as an intergovernmental structure.

One can discern a lack of 'cross-pillar' functioning within the EMP. The goals of democratization and politico-military cooperation, economic prosperity and understanding between cultures ought to be achieved in a consistent manner – this is the EU's comprehensive approach to security. But in practice each of the three baskets of the Partnership is run in a more or less autonomous way, without much coordination with the other pillars. In theory the Euro-Mediterranean Agreements ought to include provisions on political dialogue, human rights, rule of law etc., but in the agreements which have been concluded so far these provisions remain limited to very general stipulations. Political conditionality is thus in effect absent from the Euro-Mediterranean Agreements. The regulations on the MEDA programme link economic support to the promotion of human rights, fundamental freedoms and good-neighbourly relations, but here too in actual practice conditionality is very limited (Lannon, Inglis and Haenebalcke, 2001). Thus economic support is not used as an instrument to further the objectives of the political and security basket, while such a 'carrot' would be very useful in view of the non-binding character of the Barcelona Declaration and of the projected Charter for Peace and Stability.

Of course the EU should not impose too many conditions at once or it would risk alienating its Mediterranean partners, which might even pull back from the Partnership if they felt they were being confronted with conditions which they could not fulfil. One cannot hope to achieve all objectives at the same time; e.g. democratization or setting-up a framework of CSBMs is a gradual process. But the other extreme, granting economic support without any conditions at all, should be avoided as well. If not the EU ignores the fact that a number of regimes are themselves responsible for a number of causes of instability, internal (e.g. lack of democracy, socio-economic problems) as well as external (e.g. confrontational foreign policies). Without a minimum of conditionality, the EU might end up supporting regimes that commit grave human rights violations. By granting unconditional support to regimes with limited legitimacy, the EU will also turn public opinion in the countries concerned against the West. 'Cross-pillar' coordination is even more necessary after '11 September', which brought with it the risk that governments will abuse the 'terrorist' label to suppress all opposition.

There is one positive side to the relative autonomy of the three baskets of the Partnership: the slowing down of one pillar does not necessarily impact on the others. So while the political and security partnership still lacks substance and progress of its objectives is blocked by the conflict in the Middle East, the economic partnership, even though it too has far from fulfilled all expectations, has progressed much further. Ultimately however the Partnership cannot do without increased coordination. In this field too an 'EMP secretariat' could play a useful role.

Implementing the Charter for Peace and Stability

The Union's politico-military objectives are defined in the Common Strategy, which provides for the creation of politico-military instruments for the whole range of conflict issues, from conflict prevention over crisis management and resolution of conflicts to post-conflict peace-building, within the framework of a comprehensive partnership. If implemented, it will guarantee the interests of the EU: keeping Europe free from direct military threats and spill-over of conflicts, ensuring the security of European citizens abroad and safeguarding its economic interests. However, for the reasons stated above, the EU has so far not been able to reach agreement with its Mediterranean partners on the inclusion of all of these instruments into the security basket of the EMP. Up to date only a very limited number of CSBMs have been implemented in the framework of the EMP and these are all of rather limited scope:

- training seminars for diplomats;
- the EuroMeSCo network of foreign policy institutes;
- a register of bilateral agreements among the partner countries;
- exchange of information on partner countries' adherence to international conventions on human rights and arms control and disarmament;
- cooperation between civil protection services on natural and man-made disasters;

- regular dialogue itself in the Euro-Mediterranean Committee and through the meetings of senior officials.

These measures are limited firstly in that they only concern conflict prevention and do not include crisis management, resolution of existing or future conflicts and post-conflict peace-building. Secondly these are all 'soft' CSBMs; no measures in the military field, such as exchange of information on defence expenditure, arms control and disarmament – notably absent in spite of proliferation being one of the major security issues in the region – or joint manoeuvres and operations, have so far been provided for. Terrorism, which originally was also mentioned in the third basket of the Barcelona Declaration, gradually was dealt with exclusively in the framework of the political and security partnership, but without this leading to any concrete actions being taken.

The Charter for Peace and Stability has been conceived as an instrument to implement the political and security dimension of the EMP, through the institutionalization of a politico-military dialogue (being the creation of a policy-making entity), which should lead to the adoption of further CSBMs (including 'hard' CSBMs) and the creation of mechanisms for crisis management and post-conflict peace-building. The adoption of the Charter should gradually lead to the filling of the gaps in the political and security chapter of the EMP. From a 'long term possibility' mentioned in the Barcelona Declaration the Charter has thus gone to acquiring a pivotal role in the achievement of the politico-military objectives of the Partnership. But once again it must be very clear that no progress is possible without significant steps towards the resolution of the ongoing conflicts in the region and without a fundamental reinforcement of confidence between both shores of the Mediterranean.

Notes

1 PE 148.022/fin., 3 May1991, Report of the Committee on External Economic Relations on a revamped Mediterranean policy. Reporter: Mr. Eusebio Caro Pinto. A3-0121/91.
2 Commission Report to the European Council in Lisbon on the likely development of the Common Foreign and Security Policy (CFSP) with a view to identifying areas open to joint action *vis-à-vis* particular countries or groups of countries.
3 COM(94)427 final, 19 October 1994, Strengthening the Mediterranean policy of the European Union: establishing a Euro-Mediterranean Partnership.
4 The term 'partnership building measures' (PBMs) is also intended to put more emphasis on the non-military aspects of security. In order to avoid conceptual confusion, I will use the term CSBMs throughout for all measures dealing with 'hard' security, which is the main topic of this work, thus following Brauch's suggestion to limit the term PBMs to measures in the economic, ecologic and societal fields (Brauch, 2000a).
5 Although Claire Spencer, when interviewing the Political Director of the UK's Foreign and Commonwealth Office in 2000 noted a rather different motivation: 'When it was concluded that there should be four strategies, there was a deal between the Member States, frankly. The acceptance of Russia should be first; the Ukraine logically followed and then five Member States who are very obvious said: "What about us? What about

the South?". The deal was the next one would be the Mediterranean. I do not think it unfair to say that it did not have more attention than that at that stage and then someone said, "The Balkans are a big issue. Let us now take the Balkans as the fourth"' (Spencer, 2001b, p.40).

6 Several of the Mediterranean countries still have to cope with minefields constructed during World War Two.
7 COM(2000)0497 final, 6 September 2000, Communication from the Commission to the Council and the European Parliament to prepare the fourth meeting of Euro-Mediterranean Foreign Ministers: reinvigorating the Barcelona Process.
8 *Europe*, 13–14 and 16 November 2000.
9 Report from the Council to the European Council on the implementation of the Common Strategy of the European Union on the Mediterranean region, annexed to European Council. Göteborg, 15–16 June 2001. Presidency conclusions.
10 *Europe*, 22 September 2001.
11 *Europe*, 28 September 2001.
12 *Europe*, 29–30 October 2001.
13 *Europe*, 7 November 2001.
14 On 27 December 2001 the EU itself adopted a common position on combating terrorism (2001/930/CFSP), with the aim of reinforcing cooperation among the Member States in this field. A second common position of the same day (2001/931/CFSP), updated on 19 June 2002, defines 'terrorist acts' and includes a list of persons, groups and entities involved in terrorism.
15 *Europe*, 8 November 2001.
16 COM(2002)159 final, Communication from the Commission to the Council and the European Parliament to prepare the meeting of Euro-Mediterranean Foreign Ministers, Valencia, 22–23 April 2002.
17 Named after WEU's Petersberg Declaration (19 June 1992).
18 European security: a common concept of the 27 WEU countries. 14 November 1995.
19 *Europe*, 15 May 1997.
20 These are, besides Turkey: Hungary, Iceland, Norway, Poland and the Czech republic.
21 COM(2003)104 final, 11 March 2003, Wider Europe – neighbourhood: a new framework for relations with our Eastern and Southern neighbours.

Chapter 3

EU Policy and Conflict in the Mediterranean

Introduction

The objective of the EMP is to function as a region-wide framework for policy-making on Mediterranean security by the EU and the 12 partner countries combined. As was demonstrated in chapter 2, the achievement of this objective is to a very high degree dependent on the resolution of the ongoing disputes and conflicts in the region. This chapter examines EU policy towards these conflicts in the Middle East, North Africa and the Eastern Mediterranean and emphasizes the links between these policies and the success of the EMP. It concludes with a call for an active EU conflict resolution policy.

The Middle East Peace Process

Israeli Reticence, Arab Encouragement

In the early years of European integration the EC gradually moved away from the pro-Israeli position of the majority of the original Member States and adopted declarations which took much more account of the Palestinian view, which culminated in the demand that the PLO should participate in any peace negotiations and the recognition of the need for a homeland for and the right to self-determination of the Palestinian people, as expressed first in the London Declaration (29 June 1977) and then even more clearly in the Venice Declaration (13 June 1980). EC diplomacy was instrumental in the world-wide acceptance of the Palestinian claims as legitimate demands, and was appreciated as such by the Arab countries. Viewing the US' efforts as being insufficient and too exclusively tailored to Israel's needs to achieve an equitable and durable peace, the EC aspired to play a more active role itself. The absence of US support, the Israeli refusal to make concessions and intra-Arab divisions led to the failure of the European attempt, announced in the Venice Declaration, to launch a peace plan. The EC then reverted to a declaratory policy. Yet the successive crises in the Middle East forced the Member States to define a position and thus greatly stimulated European integration in the field of foreign policy (Gomez, 1998, pp.136–7; Gronbech-Jensen, 1999, pp.5–6). The EC also took the initiative in the economic field and created a major aid programme for the occupied territories, thus furthering its

Middle East policy objectives in an indirect way. These objectives can be summarized as:

- implementation of Resolutions 242 and 338, which enshrine the principle of land for peace;
- realizing the right to self-determination of the Palestinian people;
- security for all states in the region within recognized borders.

When after the Gulf War a peace conference for the Middle East was convened in Madrid (30 October 1991) Europe was intentionally sidelined by the US, which preferred Russia as co-sponsor. The EU was only granted a part in the financial and economic dimensions of the ensuing peace process.

Ever since, European aspirations to play a bigger political part in the peace process have always been rejected by Israel, and this pretty much regardless of the party in power, Likud or Labour. In the eyes of the Israelis the EU cannot act as an 'honest broker' because it is biased in favour of the Arabs. The EU's repeated allegedly 'pro-Arab' declarations are seen as proof. It is also felt that the EU does not fully appreciate the extent of Israel's security concerns and the necessities implied by its strategic situation, hence its failure to understand Israeli policies. The EU is furthermore perceived as being far too weak an actor in the politico-military field, without even the means to live up to the role which it claims for itself. With this judgement, Israel is very close to the views of its foremost ally, the US, which have always wanted to maintain their de facto leadership position in the politico-military dimension of the peace process. The view of Washington and Tel Aviv is that the regional parties should work out an agreement without interference from outside parties, which should limit themselves to facilitating the negotiations and should not try to further their own policy objectives or influence the terms of a settlement (Alpher, 1998, pp.82–4; Ben-Ami, 1998, pp.101–3).

This Israeli condemnation of EU policy ignores the fact that the Union has always tried to act even-handedly. The EU has indeed time and again condemned Israeli settlement policy, the disproportional repression of Palestinian protests and other acts which it judged to be obstacles to the progress of the peace process. But the EU has always condemned violence and extremism on both sides and has repeatedly urged the Palestinian Authority to deal with terrorists operating from within the Palestinian territories, even to the extent of setting up a special programme to assist the Palestinian Authority in taking counter-terrorist measures.[1] One of the primary objectives of the Union's Middle East policy has always been security for all states in the region. On the basis of this policy the EU should therefore be in a position to act as mediator in the peace process.

The frequent disagreements with Israel over the Middle East peace process have never interrupted the development of ever closer economic relations between the EU and Israel. The Union is Israel's major trading partner; trade with the EU represents over 30 per cent of Israeli exports and almost 50 per cent of its imports. Under the new Euro-Mediterranean Association Agreement, which came into force on 1 June 2000 and which confirmed the free trade regime for industrial products, cooperation was increased by the establishment of an institutional political dialogue, reflecting Europe's attachment to Israel as the only working democracy in the Middle East. Although at times the threat of slowing down negotiations on the conclusion of the Association Agreement was used to pressurize Israel, the EU never really made use of the instrument of economic sanctions against Israel to further its Middle East policy, in spite of its potential efficacy and of the Arab demand to do so (Stavridis and Hutchence, 2000, pp.56–9). The EU chose not to use economic sanctions, as this would completely antagonize Israel and preclude a possible role as mediator for the Union and thus the possibility to steer the peace process in a direction more favourable to its policy objectives. Or as Belgian Foreign Minister Louis Michel put it when asked in the European Parliament why suspending the Association Agreement as a way of putting pressure on Israel was not considered: 'I'm not sure this is the most subtle way of going about things'.[2] By adopting a lenient attitude towards Israel in the economic field the EU hoped in return to soften Israeli resistance to its involvement in the peace process.

But even Europe's economic policy is not always appreciated in Israel, which claims special treatment within the EMP because of its much higher state of development when compared to the other Mediterranean partners. The EMP, which economically is based on a North-South approach, is seen to undermine Israel's special economic status (Piening, 1997, pp.84–5; Tovias, 1998, pp.2–4). Europe's economic policy is of course consistent with its foreign policy, which is why, following differences over the subject with Israel, the Commission explicitly stated that the Association Agreement only covers Israeli territory as per the 1967 borders and not the Palestinian territories, to which the separate Interim Association Agreement of 1997 applies.[3]

The Arab countries on the other hand have welcomed the EU's Middle East policy, notably its critical attitude towards Israel and its position in favour of the realization of the Palestinian right to self-determination. For the Arabs the EU is a necessary counterweight to the influence of the US and its almost unconditional support for Israel. The Arabs have therefore at several instances called for greater European involvement in the peace process. At the same time they also realize of course that, because of its superpower status, the US can be a very effective broker. Furthermore several Arab regimes rely on US support to stay in power. For these reasons Arab countries have at crucial moments repeatedly chosen the side of the US instead of backing the European view on the peace process, in spite of their pro-European rhetoric (Gerges, 2000, pp.4–5). But the US do not always make use of their potential to further the peace process and often lapse into a passive attitude. Most recently e.g., instead of grasping the opportunity to end the cycle of violence of the 'Second Intifada' which the lull in the violence immediately after '11 September' provided, the US supported the harsh and un-reconciling policies which Israel adopted under the label of 'anti-terrorism'. With the US disappointing all hopes for a major peace initiative, the EU was left as the only international actor still trying to mediate, although it should be added that in the year following '11 September' the coherence of the EU position seemed to diminish rather than to increase, as a number of Member States, notably the UK, inclined towards the

American position. A larger European involvement would potentially provide a more constant impetus to the peace process and would make sure that diplomatic effort is maintained at all times. The EU also has close economic relations with the Arab countries of the Middle East, *inter alia*, through the Euro-Mediterranean Association Agreements. A role as co-sponsor would reflect Europe's position as the main donor to the peace process. It cannot be that the actor who contributes the most in the economic and financial field is not comparably represented in the political negotiations.

Because of its good relations with the Arab parties and the trust these have in the EU, the Union should act as a mediator alongside the US, to ensure that the views of both sides of the conflict are given equal attention, whereas now it seems that the Israeli position is over-represented. The US have indeed provided Israel with unparalleled amounts of economic and military aid, have been essential in ensuring its military superiority over its neighbours and, though often being critical of Israeli policies, have usually excused or defended its behaviour, especially in the Security Council. With the US and the EU both acting as mediators a balance would be reached between the parties. And while the US has the biggest potential influence on Israel, the EU has more leverage than the US when it comes to influencing the views of the Arab parties and convincing them to make certain concessions. Proof of this was provided by the Union's repeated successful intervention with the Palestinians to have the proclamation of an independent state postponed, and this in close coordination with the US. In 1999, when the interim period provided for in the 1993 Declaration of Principles ended, the EU succeeded in convincing the Palestinians to allow for an additional year for the conclusion of the final status negotiations and not to proclaim a state just yet, as it was feared this would provoke a severe crisis and might preclude a possible Labour victory in the upcoming Israeli elections. In return the Berlin European Council (24–25 March 1999) made a very explicit policy statement on the issue of a Palestinian state:

> [...] reaffirms the continuing and unqualified Palestinian right to self-determination including the option of a state and looks forward to the early fulfilment of this right [...] It appeals to the parties to strive in good faith for a negotiated solution on the basis of the existing agreements, without prejudice to this right, which is not subject to any veto [...] declares its readiness to consider the recognition of a Palestinian state in due course.

A year later the EU sadly had to make a similar intervention, for once again the parties failed to reach an agreement by the set deadline. These occasions do demonstrate that Washington and Brussels can work together successfully and on an equal footing to further the peace process and that a greater EU involvement would add value to the negotiations. The EU's leverage on the Palestinian side is indeed the single most important reason why the Union should act as mediator in the peace process alongside the US.

History has proved that on its own the US cannot settle the conflict. But in times of lesser American involvement in the peace process, the EU, without denying numerous significant achievements, has not been able to force a solution either, as became apparent after '11 September'. The European Council met on 21 September 2001 in extraordinary session to assess the international situation and called for a broad approach dealing with the underlying causes of terrorism, stating that

> the fight against terrorism requires of the Union that it play a greater part in the efforts of the international community to prevent and stabilize regional conflicts [and that] in particular, the European Union, in close collaboration with the United States, the Russian Federation and partners in the Arab and Muslim world, will make every endeavour to bring the parties to the Middle East conflict to a lasting understanding on the basis of the relevant United Nations resolutions.

Belgian Prime Minister Guy Verhofstadt announced a six-point plan whereby the EU would press for:

- the immediate reopening of direct dialogue, notably through a meeting, as soon as possible, between Arafat and Peres;
- the immediate resumption of security cooperation between the two parties;
- moderation on both sides; and
- the easing of restrictions on the circulation of goods and people; while the Union intended
- to maintain a long-term presence in the region and
- to strengthen concertation with the US, Russia and other partners.[4]

The troika and several European leaders started on a tour of the Middle East and a number of other islamic countries to express the European view on the events and to try and win partners for the resumption of the peace process. This way the Union hoped to be able to make use of the temporary pause in the violence, which probably presented the biggest opportunity to bring the parties around the table again since the beginning of the Al-Aqsa Intifada a year earlier. But the pause in the violence did not last for long: at the end of September 2001 Israelis and Palestinians clashed again. The window of opportunity went by unused, due to a great part to the intransigence of the Sharon government and the absence, still, of any American initiative to join the EU in its effort to revive the peace process. Thereafter EU involvement watered down as well, as divisions between the Member States arose. Violence continued unabated throughout 2002. When in 2003 the US made a change of regime in Iraq into their policy priority, a resolution of the Israeli-Palestinian conflict became even more remote. Since the EU Member States were themselves divided, no decisive action on the part of the EU could be expected either.

Only a combined and fully coordinated EU-US effort can succeed. Each of them should make full use of their leverage on the respective parties to put serious pressure on them to find a settlement. To put it more bluntly: although it could show its willingness to take into account its specific interests, the EU should not try to convince Israel of the justness of its policies, nor should the US do the same vis-à-vis the Arab side, because in the end they are not considered as 'honest brokers' by these respective parties. What they should do is use their power to actually force the parties on which they do have leverage to find a settlement. Besides, one should take into account that continued US passivity will end up undermining EU leverage on the Palestinians, for the longer the stalemate of the peace process persists, the more the Palestinian Authority looses popular support to the extremists in Palestinian society. Israel might just end up with the radicals taking power in Palestine and then all chances for dialogue would be effectively lost.

The US' economic presence in the region is smaller than that of the EU, in relative as well as in absolute figures, it imports about three times less petrol from North Africa and the Middle East than the Union and almost no gas, and its efforts as an international donor are much smaller. But in spite of these facts the US have always wanted to retain their position as the de facto sole sponsor of the peace process and are not willing to share responsibilities with the EU, at least not in the politico-military field.[5] They thus perpetuate Europe's frustration for being welcomed as a donor but not as a political actor. This frustration is exacerbated by Israel's wanton destruction of Palestinian infrastructure financed by the EU and its Member States, such as the Gaza port and airport. The main difference between Washington and Brussels in their approach to the peace process is that the former focuses on the process as such and the latter on the outcome. The US leave it to the regional parties themselves to decide on a suitable peace arrangement and offer only their good offices, without defending any specific option. This attitude is reflected in the Americans' unwillingness to pressurize Israel to change such or such a policy. The EU on the other hand clearly takes position on a number of outstanding issues and puts forward itself elements which it considers necessary for the achievement of a durable peace. So e.g. the EU spoke out in favour of a Palestinian presence in Jerusalem and of a Palestinian state. If parties take actions which go against EU views on a peace agreement, they are explicitly rebuked in the CFSP declarations. Furthermore the EU in its declarations attaches more importance to the respect for international law and the implementation of Security Council resolutions, while for the US it is more important that the parties reach consensus, even if this does not fully reflect international law. These are not fundamental differences however; broadly speaking, both the EU and the US strive after an equitable and lasting peace in the Middle East and they could thus very well work together. Besides, the fact in itself that, after several decades of negotiating, the conflict has still not been resolved, should lead to the awareness in Washington that the US by themselves will not end it (Charillon, 1998, p.216; Gordon, 1998, pp.23–32; Van Leeuwen, 1999).

The Peace Process and the EMP

Another reason why the EU should claim a larger involvement in the peace process is because of the huge impact of the situation in the Middle East on the development of the EMP. To start with, the EMP simply could never have gotten off the ground if it had not been for the positive atmosphere created by the conclusion of the 1993 Israeli-Palestinian agreement and the subsequent progress made in the Oslo framework. But most importantly, the EU was very soon forced to realize that the separation between the Partnership and the peace process, which was inscribed in the Barcelona Declaration and which worked well as long as the peace process stayed on track, was untenable. When the peace process broke down, the implementation of the political and security partnership of the EMP ground to a halt as well, as the Mediterranean partners refuse to discuss future security arrangements as long as the outstanding conflicts have not been resolved. The overwhelming influence of the peace process is evident in other areas as well, e.g. the negotiations on the Euro-Mediterranean Association Agreements, which to a large extent run parallel with the improvement of relations between the parties in the context of the peace process. The achievement of the objectives defined by the Barcelona Declaration is thus dependent on the progress of the peace process, which is why the EU should assume greater responsibility in it.

The correlation between the EMP and the peace process works both ways. At times when the peace process was in crisis, parties continued to meet and talk, be it sometimes at a reduced level, in the framework of the Barcelona Process, which thus in itself functioned as a CSBM complementary to the peace negotiations. This became particularly evident after the multilateral track of the peace process broke down and the EMP became the only forum where the regional parties meet in a multilateral framework. The Partnership thus more or less assumed the multilateral track's complementary function, i.e. reinforcing trust between the parties which should pave the way for success in the bilateral negotiations. Another example of the linkages between the EMP and the peace process is the treatment, within the Barcelona Process, of the Palestinian Authority on an equal footing with the sovereign states that have joined the Partnership – the political significance is clear (Moratinos, 1998a; Perthes, 1999a, pp.174–9).

This is one of the reasons why Israel is far from a staunch supporter of the Barcelona Process, another reason being, as already mentioned, that the EMP is felt not to take into account Israel's special economic position as compared to the other Mediterranean partner countries. On the other hand one could argue that the 1995 Association Agreement with Israel was only possible in the framework of the EMP, for on its own, as a purely bilateral initiative, it would have been unacceptable to the Arab countries (Ginsberg, 2001, p.124).

The overriding importance of the link between the peace process and the EMP was recognized by the EU in the June 2000 Common Strategy on the Mediterranean Region, where it is stated that

> the EU is convinced that the successful conclusion of the Middle East peace process, and the resolution of other conflicts in the region, are important prerequisites for peace and stability in the Mediterranean [but] while the EU will continue to play its full role in the Middle East peace process [...], this Common Strategy will cover the EU's contribution to the consolidation of peace in the Middle East once a comprehensive peace settlement has been achieved.

The objectives which the EU set itself in the Common Strategy are therefore only a confirmation of the above all complementary *de facto* role which it plays in the peace process and does not envisage a fundamental qualitative increase of the Union's involvement – this seemed to be a missed chance for an unequivocal claim for co-sponsorship. Instead:

- The EU will 'provide its expertise, submit ideas and make available its good offices [...] in order to facilitate the conclusion of peace agreements'.
- Once an agreement has been reached, the Union will 'promote conditions which will help the parties implement agreements concluded among themselves' and will 'contribute to the consolidation of peace in the region [...] notably through support to regional economic cooperation and integration and the expansion of trade flows'.
- The EU would also, 'in the context of a comprehensive settlement, and upon request by the core parties, give consideration to the participation of Member States in the implementation of security arrangements on the ground'.
- Finally and on a more general level, the Union will 'work towards strengthening stability in the Middle East [...] through its contributions to the implementation of the Euro-Mediterranean Charter for Peace and Stability once it is adopted and has entered into force'.

Only after '11 September' was the peace process addressed more explicitly, notably at the Brussels Euro-Mediterranean Conference, where the Middle East was the focus of attention. For the first time the EMP was used as a forum to adopt a very outspoken view on the steps to be taken to resume negotiations and on the objectives which these negotiations should achieve.[6] The Presidency Conclusions of the Conference repeated almost literally the words of the CFSP declaration released by the Council on 29 October 2001 on the occasion of the tenth anniversary of the Madrid Conference. In this the EU had reiterated

> its conviction that the 'peace process' framework so laboriously worked out in the course of negotiations and agreements between the various parties constitutes the only reasonable hope of putting and end to [the] conflict.

In view of the international situation, which demanded a breakthrough in the Middle East in order to rally the Arab countries behind the international coalition against terrorism and in order to signal that the West and the Arab world are partners yet, the Conference, at which Israel was represented by Shimon Peres, thus left the formal separation between the Partnership and the peace process, be it that this implied what was described as 'heated discussion'. Participants even went so far as to call for a Palestinian state:

> Ministers stressed that negotiations should lead: for the Palestinians, to the establishment of an independent, viable and democratic state and an end to the occupation of their territories; for the Israelis, to live in peace and safety within internationally recognized borders.

It was added that a comprehensive and lasting peace should also provide a solution to the refugee problem and should cover the Syrian and Lebanese tracks of the peace process as well. These explicit statements on behalf of the Partnership as a whole must be considered an important achievement of the Belgian Presidency and constituted an additional strong signal of the urgent need for a settlement in the wake of '11 September'. In the margin of the Conference the Belgian Presidency organized a meeting between Arafat and Peres who a few days before had had a fruitless meeting in Spain. According to the Presidency, some new ideas emerged from the meeting, notably to first realize the Palestinian state in Gaza. Although the meeting pushed to the background the actual Conference, relations were too tense to allow for any substantial achievements.[7] Hopes of significant progress at the occasion of the Euro-Mediterranean Conference were therefore disappointed. The same can be said of the Valencia Euro-Mediterranean Conference (22–23 April 2002), which confirmed the explicit statements made in Brussels.

EU Commitment on the Ground

A role as mediator or co-sponsor of the peace process would demand a bigger commitment on the part of the EU. In the first place there is the field of policy-making itself. Up until now EU policy objectives have never been formally summed up. They can of course be derived from the different CFSP acts on the Middle East, but there does not exist a common position to clearly outline, in one binding document, Union objectives (Lannon, 1999, pp.265–6). The joint actions on the Middle East concern policy instruments and do not refer to policy objectives. For such an important area of policy, *vis-à-vis* a region in which the EU is very active, not in the least as a financial donor and economic partner, a common position would be very useful as a policy framework, and would add continuity and a clear sense of direction. The formal definition of policy objectives for the Middle East would also further diminish the possibility of solo actions by Member States outside the CFSP framework, which affect the credibility of the Union and the effectiveness of its actions. The EU cannot allow internal divisions and has to speak with one voice in all international fora, which e.g. in the different bodies of the UN has not always been the case. Although there are differences in their approach, the Member States do agree on the fundamentals of Middle East policy however. Besides, the Member States should realize that none of them any longer has the ability to significantly influence events in the Middle East on its own.

More importantly, EU policy still is, to too great an extent, declaratory. At the beginning of the CFSP the Union fully committed itself to the Madrid process which had then just been initiated and which provided the first chance for a comprehensive peace settlement. A joint action was adopted expressing the Union's support for the peace process and outlining the instruments it would apply.[8] But the EU got to play only a secondary role. Its involvement in the bilateral track of the process, which is the main channel of negotiations, was minimal. In the complimentary multilateral track the Union had a bigger part to play, but even here it was sidelined in the most important working group in the politico-military field, the Arms Control and Regional Security Working Group

(ACRS). The EU therefore concentrated on the field in which its involvement was not contested and in which its institutions were most experienced: economic and financial support to the Palestinians. The Union emerged as the main donor to the region. Its support to the Palestinian territories culminated in the 1997 Interim Association Agreement. The EU also supported the establishment of the Palestinian Authority, notably by assisting with the creation of a police force and with the organization of the first Palestinian elections[9] and by providing financial support at very short term in times of need. Without European support, the Palestinian Authority cannot survive. All these actions contributed directly to the realisation of the Palestinian's right to self-determination and therefore were highly politically significant, but they could not hide the fact that the EU was absent from the main stage of the peace process, from the field of 'high politics', where the actual peace arrangements were discussed.

Only at the end of 1996, after several years of very limited political involvement and because of frustration over the slow pace of the Oslo process and the intransigent policies of Israel, did the EU take the initiative to try and increase its involvement and steer the peace process in the direction it desired. The appointment[10] of a special envoy, Spanish diplomat Miguel Angel Moratinos, and the temporary reticence of the US to assume the initiative resulted in a period of European activism and, after a period of hard work behind the scene, a number of important achievements:

- the agreement on Hebron, which provided for the redeployment of Israeli forces and the transfer of civil powers in the Palestinian part of that violence-stricken city (15 January 1997);
- the joint action establishing a counter-terrorism programme;
- the agreement on a code of conduct, meant to prevent tensions from rising, reassure the parties of each other's intentions and resume the deadlocked negotiations.

Although the latter ultimately was not implemented because of a renewed outbreak of violence, this was the first time the EU brokered a breakthrough in the peace process. But it seems that these successes of European diplomacy were not sufficiently pursued; neither the level of effort nor the momentum of the peace process itself could be maintained. The EU failed to obtain the status of co-sponsor of the peace process and let itself be sidelined again by the US, to be called upon only when Washington temporarily could not take the lead, because of a change of government for instance, or when its influence had to be brought to bear on the Palestinians, notably to have the proclamation of an independent state postponed. The Union has also shown little attention for the Syrian and Lebanese tracks of the peace process and has concentrated on the Israeli-Palestinian negotiations.

There thus seems to be a lack of continuity in the EU efforts concerning the Middle East peace process and especially a lack of action to try and implement its policies. The two main policy instruments used by the EU are still economic and financial support, mostly to the Palestinians, and the issuing of declarations. Four major joint actions were taken (not counting decisions amending or extending the original joint actions): on support for the peace process in general, on the organization of the Palestinians elections, on the counter-terrorism programme and on the appointment of a special envoy. In spite of the presence of the special envoy, EU action still is too dependent on the interest of any particular Presidency for the region or on its political will. Diplomatic activity can thus vary significantly from one Presidency to another. This has resulted in a lack of consistent effort to advance the peace process and the failure to follow up the successes that were achieved. Consequently, the Union's Middle East policy often does not surpass the stage of well-phrased declarations. The success of the Union's efforts of course partly depends on the US too. The Union has been able to achieve significant breakthroughs on its own on a few exceptional occasions, but a lasting achievement needs the backing of both Brussels and Washington. On the other hand, if this situation continues the Union's credibility with the Palestinians might be seriously undermined and its influence on the Palestinians affected. The CFSP needs results if the Union is to be recognized as an international actor of any significance. It also seems that in recent years Moratinos has been more or less overshadowed by Solana. Sending in the High Representative on every occasion which is considered that extra more important, while the special envoy tends to keep a very low profile, detracts from the latter's status as representative of the Union and the advantages of having a permanent envoy on the spot are lost or at least diminished.

Of course work behind the scene continues and the Union has made a significant contribution to the peace process, but it does appear that the EU could play a much bigger part. Europe, for the reasons cited above, should resolutely claim its role as mediator alongside the US and should together with the US initiate concrete peace proposals and work actively to implement them. In order to be able to really act jointly and use the available means in the most efficient and efficacious way, a permanent *ad hoc* structure should be set up to act as the driving-force of the peace process. All third party actors should be represented in this: in the first place the EU and the US, but the UN and Russia, which in Madrid was assigned a role as co-sponsor and aspires a renewed international status, have an important part to play too. The Union's representative can be the Special Envoy, who should re-assume the high-profile role of the early days of Moratinos' appointment, so as to become once again the influential and respected figure-head of European involvement in the peace process. This ad hoc structure should also tackle the Syrian and Lebanese tracks of the peace process. Brussels and Washington should make full use of their leverage and exert pressure on the respective parties, in order to bring peace to the Middle East as early as possible. If needs be, one can imagine the use of economic instruments to force the parties to the negotiation table: both Israel and the Palestinian Authority depend heavily on economic and financial relations with the US and Europe. The 'Quartet meetings' could fulfil this role if only all participants would muster the will to do so. This requires recommitting the US to the peace process, which in effect is the key to stability in the wide region, much more than just Iraq. In early 2003 a majority of

EU Member States did not support the military option to deal with Saddam Hussein, while the peace process was apparently forgotten.

The Union's claim to a role as co-mediator must be backed, as was done in recent CFSP declarations, by the willingness to contribute with observers or peacekeeping forces on the ground and to continue to provide the necessary means to finance accompanying measures and programmes, such as economic development of the Palestinian territories, institution-building and security measures. This may seem evident, but facts on the ground are that, quite contrary to the intentions which the Union expresses with regard to its role in the peace process, in 2002 the office of the special envoy suffered a reduction of 37 per cent of its budget. It took a letter from the Spanish Presidency to all Member States to find the money to buy Mr. Moratinos an armoured car – not exactly a luxury in his position. Here again the adoption of a common position on the Middle East, or even, considering the importance of the region, a common strategy, would prove fruitful, to force all Member States of the EU to fully commit themselves not only to the Union's policy objectives, but also to a continuous and upgraded EU role in all tracks of the peace process. In the first place, this demands political will, which in the past the EU has not had sufficiently.

In a speech back in 1998 Special Envoy Moratinos (1998b) neatly summarized the principles on which peace should be based:

> Right of all states and peoples in the region to live in peace within safe, recognized borders; respect for the legitimate aspiration of the Palestinian people to exercise self-determination, without excluding the option of a state; exchange of land for peace; non-acceptability of the annexation of land by force; rejection of terrorism of all kinds; good relations between neighbours; compliance with existing agreements and rejection of counterproductive unilateral initiatives.

Moratinos also outlined the necessary steps to be taken in order to arrive at this peace:

> No further settlement activity; no measures that pre-empt the final status negotiations; a further redeployment that is meaningful and makes a real contribution to building confidence; security measures that give confidence to all the citizens, Israelis and Palestinians; other confidence-building measures, such as developments with the Gaza airport and port, and the safe passage between Gaza and the West Bank.

Sadly enough his list remains as valid today as it was in 1998.

North Africa

Algeria

The EU has adopted a very passive attitude towards the ongoing crisis in Algeria. No common positions or joint actions have been adopted and only a very limited number of declarations have been issued. On just one occasion did the Union take political initiative, which even then was quite limited in scope: the troika visit to Algeria (19–20 January 1998). This was badly managed however, met with little cooperation from the Algerian government and hence did not produce any lasting results. Since then, as before, the Union has refrained from taking any initiative regarding the country, showing a regrettable lack of political will. Union policy on Algeria does not surpass rhetorical support for democracy and human rights. The troika again visited Algeria in June 2002 and returned with a very positive but quite unlikely message about the human rights situation that was heavily contested by human rights organizations.

At the same time the Union continues a policy of economic and financial support for the regime in order to enable it to introduce political and economic reforms, which in the view of the Union will lead to reconciliation. This support de facto has been more or less unconditional and has not been linked to the opening of sincere negotiations with the opposition movements and to respect for democracy and human rights. The EU did not make use of the economic instrument to pressurize the military regime, which instead has been able to count on the rather uncritical attitude of the Union and has acquired complete control over the state. The continuing purchase of Algerian oil and gas has been vital for the survival of the regime and have presented it worldwide as a respectable trading partner and a legitimate government (Aliboni, 1999a). The revenue from the oil and gas trade is the main factor keeping the regime in power and, probably, at the same time its main motivation for staying in power. Hydrocarbons represent 95 per cent of Algerian exports, 30 per cent of the GDP and 60 per cent of the national budget. Western petrol companies have invested billions in their operations in Algeria, which are heavily guarded and which, it seems, Western governments are not willing to put at risk. Union policy thus neglects the obvious fact that the persistence of the violence for by now more than a decade has clearly demonstrated that the military regime is unable or unwilling to find a lasting and equitable solution to the crisis and is even involved itself in the massacres.

The question should be asked whether under these circumstances the Union ought to have concluded a Euro-Mediterranean Association Agreement with Algeria, signed on the occasion of the Valencia Euro-Mediterranean Conference, a further token of support for the regime, especially so as the political content of these Association Agreements has tended to be limited, emphasis being put on economic cooperation, without real political preconditions being imposed. This is a clear example of a – deliberate – lack of coordination between the different baskets of the EMP. Economic support under the second basket of the Partnership continues in spite of the fact that Algeria obviously does not live up to the principles which it agreed to in the framework of the political and security partnership. Rather than 'admiring the courage of this Algerian administration to throw open their country's society and to conclude this Association Agreement with Europe', as chief EU negotiator Robert van der Meulen put it,[11] one should deplore the Union's lack of regard for actual conditions in the country. The launching of a technical assistance programme to police reform in Algeria (January 2002) is another project that raises doubts.

Several explanations can be found for the rigidity of Union policy and the EU's lack of initiative. When the crisis first erupted EU policies were to a very great extent influenced by those of France, which because of the colonial past was recognized by the other Member States as possessing greater expertise on Algeria and as having larger interests at stake. France adopted a very passive stance. Up to this day EU policy reflects the basic French view of economic support for the regime, without too many preconditions, so as to allow it to solve the crisis. France has always shielded Algeria from international criticism and has repeatedly blocked proposals for intervention, while the few occasions of international involvement, such as the troika mission, were limited in scope and produced at best limited results (Rich, 1998, pp.140–49). Remarkably, to a great extent the US too followed the French lead. Having limited interests in Algeria, except in the hydrocarbon sector, Washington as well adopted a rather passive attitude. The US did make discreet efforts to promote dialogue between the regime and the opposition, but ultimately their policy was more or less the same as that of France and the EU. Probably being the country which most dreads a second Iran and fearing the potential impact on the Middle East peace process and on stability in the whole of the Mediterranean, the US do not want to see the islamists gain power and therefore they too support the military regime. A clear example of this was the invitation extended to Algeria in March 2000 to join NATO's Mediterranean Dialogue, a very explicit expression of support for the regime, for when NATO's Mediterranean Dialogue was first launched in 1995 Algeria was not included because of its internal situation – ergo the Alliance in 2000 considered conditions in the country to be acceptable (Do Céu Pinto, 1998, pp.74–8; Garçon, 1995).

Another factor is of course the sheer complexity of the situation and the neigh impossibility of bringing around the table the military hard-liners on the one hand and the different rivalling armed islamist groups on the other hand. The fact that neither of them completely controls all of its forces complicates matters even further. In between the government and the armed opposition are the opposition parties which do not resort to violence, islamist and other. In this situation any mediation effort would meet with immense difficulties and would certainly involve protracted negotiations. EU involvement is further discouraged by the regime's rejection of any foreign intervention. Algiers opposes international investigations or mediation efforts, claiming that the perpetrators of the murders are well-known, that its own security forces and judiciary are able to deal with them, and that an investigation or dialogue with the islamists would only serve to legitimize them. Demands for foreign intervention are viewed as interference in Algerian internal affairs and even as contempt for the country's democratic institutions; the violence is done away with as acts of revenge by the islamists because of their loss in the elections. Algiers demands instead that the EU should take action against networks on the European continent supporting Algerian terrorist groups (Benyamina, 1998). At the same time any initiative not to the liking of the violent islamist groups might provoke terrorist strikes against Europe, a fear which at least in the years 1995–1996 was very real. Obviously, the fears engendered by the prospect of an islamist regime in Algeria still persist, even though objectively islamism does not pose a direct threat to the West nor does an islamist state necessarily have to be anti-Western.

The Member States of the Union are divided among themselves over the direction which a 'new Algerian policy' should take. The Northern Member States seem to be more willing to engage actively in some kind of conflict resolution, while most southern Member States fear the uncertainties implied by a replacement of the current regime. One of the dividing factors is the degree of credibility which the Fifteen attach to the official thesis of the regime that all massacres are committed by islamist groups, while the indications of the involvement of the regime itself in large-scale torture and killings rise daily in number. And of course the dilemma remains that the Union does not want to substitute one undemocratic regime for the other, wanting to make sure that it does not pave the way for undemocratic islamist currents. As the crisis has had little or no direct impact on Europe, apart from the terrorist wave hitting France, which can be said to have been provoked by France's support to the regime, there is little incentive for an active policy. In the climate reigning after '11 September' and the general spirit of a common fight against terrorism, and against islamist terrorism in particular, the Algerian regime's version of the story has the ear of the West even more than before. In such a situation an initiative aimed at bringing the parties around the table seems unimaginable.

The EU has also kept a low profile on the issue of islamism in the other North African countries, where the main security threat is spill-over of the Algerian conflict, and the policies of their governments on the subject. The Union probably has its own interests in mind and wants to avoid any cause for confrontation with the regimes concerned or with islamist and other opposition movements. One can therefore assume that the Union does not want to interfere as long as these countries are successful in preventing the rise of extremist islamism and as long as repression, against non-violent opposition movements especially, is not unduly excessive. The Union thus limits itself to economic and financial support and to – modest – support for democratization and respect for human rights. In the case of Egypt it should also be noted that this country is considered to be a very important partner in the Middle East peace process, as an Arab state which has concluded a peace agreement with Israel, which time and again lends strong support to all initiatives aimed to bring peace to that region and with which for those reasons close relations should be maintained.

Western Sahara

Next to the crisis in Algeria, another, often forgotten conflict, divides the Maghreb: the issue of Western Sahara. The EU has declined to become involved in the issue and has limited itself to verbally supporting the UN efforts to settle the matter, and even that rather reservedly. Just three CFSP declarations have been issued (29 December 1998, 21 June 1999 and 5 March 2003). Actual EU behaviour even tends to favour the Moroccan view of the issue, in spite of the Union's verbal support for the settlement plan and the right to self-determination of the Sahrawis. Officially none of the Member States accepts Morocco's annexation of the territory in 1975, especially not since the ICJ rejected Morocco's sovereignty claims. But the terms of the fishing treaty with Morocco, which is regularly renegotiated, remain ambiguous on the question of whether the Saharan waters are included, while European fishing practice effectively recognizes, and thus provides legitimacy to, Morocco's presence in Western Sahara. The Euro-Mediterranean Association Agreement with Morocco does not take the issue into account at all. Apparently, the EU has preferred to maintain close relations with Morocco, which is an important supporter of the EMP, rather than antagonizing it by pushing for a solution of the Western Sahara issue. If the principles of the Barcelona Declaration are to be fully applied, the Western Sahara issue should be settled according to the Resolutions of the Security Council and the EU should make use of its influence to put pressure on Morocco to implement them.

Libya

Libya is well known for being an 'Einzelgänger' in international politics and is very much closed to the outside world. It has been more and more internationally isolated ever since Muammar Gaddafi came to power in 1969. The Gaddafi regime adopted a nationalist and confrontational foreign policy, leading to grave tensions with several of the neighbouring countries and with the international community at large. The regime is also marked by its virulently anti-Western rhetoric, aimed especially against the US, but also against Westernized Arab elites.

The EU has extensive trade relations with Libya. The Union accounts for 90 per cent of Libya's oil exports and is the main market for other Libyan export products as well, while more than half of Libya's imports come from the EU. Because of the nature of the regime though, the country was not included in the network of cooperation agreements with the Mediterranean countries and the EU faithfully implemented all UN sanctions. Because of the sanctions regime Libya was not invited to participate in the 1995 Barcelona Conference. The absence of Libya from the EMP was a severe obstacle to the realization of its objectives. Clearly, region-wide confidence and security cannot be established without Libya taking part. For transparent and good-neighbourly North-South relations especially, Libya's participation is vital, given the distrust reigning relations between Tripoli and several if not most Western capitals, but there are tensions between the quixotic Libyan regime and its Southern neighbours as well. Recent developments concerning the sanctions regime and the international isolation of Libya are therefore potentially very beneficial for the future of the Partnership. Besides, regional integration among the Southern countries would also greatly benefit from a normalization of relations with Libya, especially through an amelioration of the functioning of the Arab Maghreb Union.

The transfer of the two individuals charged with the bombing of Pan Am flight 103 brought about the suspension of UN and EU Lockerbie-related sanctions. The EU stated (4 April 1999) that

> this will allow re-examining of the question of the Libyan Arab Jamahiriya's participation in the Barcelona Process, which the European Union deems desirable

[because] it is in the interest of stability in the Mediterranean basin that an important country, in a strategic position, such as the Libyan Arab Jamahiriya, should not be excluded from this dialogue.

It can indeed be argued that after the handing-over of the Lockerbie suspects and the trial, further isolation of Libya would be counterproductive. Confidence and security can only be established by interacting with the country and integrating it in the international community. In the EMP the Union possesses a prime instrument for doing so. Of course, this has to work both ways: if it wants the isolation and the sanctions to end, Libya should earnestly commit itself to the principles of international law and security, as they are e.g. included in the Barcelona Declaration (Aliboni, 2000a). This view reflects the traditional differences between Europe and the US over the relations with what the Americans used to call 'rogue states'. While Washington advocated complete economic isolation, the Europeans, partly to protect their economic interests of course, have always maintained that a 'critical dialogue' would be much more effective in inciting the Libyan regime to alter its policies. The EU was also very much opposed to the unilateral Iran-Libya Sanctions Act (Van Leeuwen, 1999).

The Union invited Libya to attend the third Euro-Mediterranean Ministerial Conference in Stuttgart (15–16 April 1999) as a 'special guest'. The Conference decided that the country would become a full member as soon as the UN sanctions were lifted and it had accepted the whole of the Partnership's acquis. The troika visited Tripoli on 18–20 September 1999 and was given assurances of Libya's adherence to the Barcelona acquis, which were confirmed in writing in a letter to the Presidency of 4 January 2000. This letter mentioned as condition however that Israeli and Palestinian membership of the EMP should be suspended until the conclusion of the Middle East peace process. Such a condition clearly goes against the idea of the Partnership as a global and inclusive framework and is unacceptable to the EU.[12] In a subsequent 'note verbale' of 26 January Tripoli then stated that the previous note was to be considered null and void and that the matter was still under debate; Tripoli therefore proposed further discussions. As a consequence of this volatile attitude the EU decided not to invite Gaddafi to visit the European institutions in Brussels just yet, a wish which he had expressed in early January 2000. Commission President Romano Prodi declared that 'an invitation would only be significant if we thus obtain a true breakthrough in our relations', a point which he thought had not been reached yet, adding that

> I have not spoken of an invitation to Gaddafi for starting up the fireworks – what I am interested in is peace in the Mediterranean.[13]

So far talks have not produced any concrete results. Obviously, the fickle nature of the regime makes a normalization of relations difficult. Libya ought to realize that it can only benefit from its full integration in the international community and that this also requires an effort on its own part.

The Eastern Mediterranean

Turkey and Europe

Europe's vital partner in the Eastern Mediterranean is Turkey. Ever since World War Two Turkey has been an important ally of the West and a key part of the Western security architecture. After the end of the Cold War and the demise of the Soviet Union, it became clear that Turkey's location at the crossroads of the Balkans, the Black Sea region, the Caucasus and the Middle East and its close relations with the newly independent Turkic states in Central Asia give it a unique position. This implies challenges and opportunities at the same time. As a Western-oriented and secular state with a muslim people Turkey has the potential to serve as a bridge between the West and the Arab Mediterranean partners – and countries in adjacent regions – and as an example and a bulwark of stability. It can also serve as a bridgehead for European operations in the region, with its large armed forces (over 600000 men) it can make a significant contribution to the ESDP and it insulates the EU from the Middle East. As such it is an obvious security partner for the EU. The political and strategic importance of the only muslim member of NATO became all the more apparent after '11 September', when Turkey became a key actor in the international coalition against terrorism, diluting the impression of a 'clash of civilizations'. But Turkey is confronted with many security risks emanating from the volatility of the security situation in its neighbouring regions and from the disputes in which it is involved itself, notably over Cyprus and the Aegean. Turkey also faces internal problems, such as the Kurdish issue and political instability. So the interest of the West in keeping Turkey as a stable ally and in maintaining its Western orientation and the close security cooperation with the country has increased rather than decreased since the end of the Cold War. From a flank member of the Atlantic Alliance Turkey has effectively become a front-line state (Akkaya, 1999, pp.122–3; Buzan and Diez, 1999, pp.47–8).

At the Luxembourg European Council of 12 December 1997, where the EU decided to launch the accession process for the Central and Eastern European applicants and Cyprus, Turkey was not yet considered to be in a position to join the EU, although eventual full membership was not excluded. This decision provoked fierce reactions from Turkey, where it was perceived as an outright rejection of its application. Political dialogue with the Union in the framework of the Association Agreement was suspended. Europe's policy of having Turkey not in, but also not out of the Union, thus resulted in a weakening of relations and created the danger of Turkey abandoning its European aspirations and moving its focus elsewhere, which would imply the loss of a vital partner for Europe's Mediterranean security policy. This would also mean that the EU would no longer be able to use the prospect of membership as an instrument to influence Turkish policies and that Turkey would be even less inclined to look for a compromise in its disputes with Greece and on the Cyprus issue. These risks clearly made the EU uneasy, so eventually the prospect of accession emerged again (Redmond, 1996, pp.191–2). At the European Council in Helsinki (10–11 December 1999) Turkey then formally obtained the status of candidate state. An Accession Partnership defines the priority areas where action is to be taken by the applicant through a National Programme, which in the case of Turkey includes important security issues.

The general principles of the Accession Partnership, which was defined by the Council on 8 March 2001, include peaceful settlement of disputes, resolving any outstanding disputes, and stability of institutions guaranteeing human rights and respect for and protection of minorities. One of the objectives to be completed or taken substantially forward by Turkey by the end of 2001 is the obligation to

> strongly support the UN Secretary General's efforts to bring a successful conclusion to the process of finding a comprehensive settlement of the Cyprus problem.

Among the medium-term objectives, which are expected to take longer to complete but work on which should begin in 2001, is the duty to 'make every effort to resolve any outstanding border disputes and other related issues' and to 'lift the remaining state of emergency in the South-East', the area where Turkish military forces are involved in operations against Kurdish guerrillas. The European Council will

> review the situation relating to any outstanding disputes, in particular concerning the repercussions on the accession process and in order to promote their settlement through the International Court of Justice, at the latest by the end of 2004.

It was stressed that compliance with the political criteria laid down at Copenhagen is a prerequisite for accession. In other words, Turkey's accession is dependent on its attitude in the Cyprus issue and on progress in its relations with Greece and it is up to the European Council to decide whether its conduct has been satisfactory. The prospect of accession, which the EU cannot deny Turkey because of its strategic importance, is thus at the same time used as an instrument to incite Ankara to actively contribute to the resolution of the outstanding disputes in which it is involved (Reuter, 2000, pp.8–11). So Turkey is now on the path to accession, but clearly the security objectives included in the political criteria will be among the most difficult to achieve and will still cause considerable friction.

As a candidate for accession and a member of NATO, Turkey is very closely involved in the elaboration of the ESDP, but the comprehensive arrangements for extensive consultation of all Allies and the possibility for them to participate in European operations have not satisfied the country. In view of its long-time membership of NATO Ankara feels it is now unjustly excluded from the Fifteen's security and defence policy. Taking into account its strategic position, which implies that most of the potential areas for EU operations are in its immediate neighbourhood, and the large numbers of troops which it could contribute to European operations, Turkey demands greater involvement in the ESDP. Ankara also doubts whether the Member States of the EU have the political will to really commit the necessary means to build up an effective military capacity. An aggravating factor in the eyes of Turkey is the advantageous position of Greece, which, having threatened not to ratify the Maastricht Treaty if it were not allowed to accede to WEU, in 1995 became a full member of this organization, where the foundations of the ESDP were laid.

Because of its dissatisfaction, Turkey has for a long time blocked the conclusion of an agreement on the modalities for the use of NATO assets for EU operations in the North Atlantic Council. One can assume that it was silently supported by the US or at least had its sympathy, as Washington above all wants to maintain the cohesion and indivisibility and the centrality of NATO. The US continue to put considerable pressure on Europe to induce it to include all Allies in the development of the ESDP to the fullest possible extent and, more specifically, have always strongly backed Turkey's candidacy for membership of the EU. The Americans attach particular importance to Turkey as a bridgehead for operations in the Middle East and the Gulf and as a partner in the Caucasus and Central Asia. So for the US Turkey's strategic position is paramount, while European policymakers attach more importance to the question of how Turkey will be integrated in the EU's political and security structures and what consequences Turkey's accession might have for the Union.

Perhaps Ankara hoped to be able use its veto power in NATO as a trump card in its relations with the EU. The question is of course whether Turkey's uncooperative attitude, rather than leading to changes in the ESDP, did not strengthen Europe in its resolve to create a military capacity of its own which can operate autonomously, even, if needs be, without having recourse to NATO assets and thus without being dependent on the consent of non-EU members. Clearly, the Union cannot detract from its autonomy of decision-making in favour of non-Member States. It is hard to imagine how the Union can involve Turkey even closer in the ESDP than it already is, without doing so. Eventually this issue will of course resolve itself when Turkey accedes to the Union, but until then it is a further factor increasing tensions between Brussels and Ankara and which makes the accession process even more difficult (Khalilzad, Lesser and Larrabee, 2000, pp.41–8). A compromise was reached just before the Laeken European Council (December 2001), but this was then rejected by Greece, which goes to show that Greece and Turkey can be equally obstinate when their interests are involved, even if their actions are detrimental to the policies of the EU. In the end the agreement between the EU and NATO was only signed in 2003.

EU membership would see Turkey on the other side of the table in the EMP, but in Turkish foreign policy the Partnership is not a priority issue. Above all, Turkey attaches much more importance to its candidacy for accession, for which the EMP is no alternative. In as far as it places Turkey on a equal footing with other Mediterranean countries for which membership is not an option, Turkey feels that the EMP diminishes its status. Ankara refuses to accept the EMP vision of Turkey as part of the European periphery rather than as a future Member State. Since the Helsinki Summit, Turkey has increased its involvement in the economic and social dimensions of the EMP, but it remains highly sceptical of the political and security partnership, which it perceives as further detracting from its status. As with the ESDP Turkey feels that, being a member of NATO, unlike the other Mediterranean partners, it is unjustly excluded from the decision-making side of the table. It therefore keeps its participation in the political and security dimension of the EMP to a minimum and emphasizes the importance of NATO as the preferred framework for Mediterranean security initiatives. Again as with the ESDP, Turkey's attitude would most probably change if it were a member of the EU and could fully participate in the definition of its Mediterranean policy (Tayfur, 2000).

The Aegean, Cyprus, the Kurds

The Union's central instrument for promoting peace and stability in the Eastern Mediterranean is the accession process. Given the strong desire of all three Mediterranean applicant states to join the EU, this is a potentially very powerful instrument indeed. Malta does not pose any problems in the field of security (Bin, 1995; Pace, 1999), but the disputes involving Greece, Cyprus and Turkey require an EU policy on 'hard' security *vis-à-vis* the area. It is clear that resort to violent solutions would immediately entail the loss or at least the long-term postponement of the prospect of membership. But in itself, if it is not accompanied by actual mediation efforts on the part of the EU, the possibility of accession does not suffice to incite the parties to the conflicts in the area to find a settlement for their disputes. An active EU policy is needed, aimed at bringing the parties together to work out their differences and making use of the accession process to pressurize all parties. The important interests of the Union in the area and notably the direct implication of a Member State and two applicants, one of which is a member of NATO, in the ongoing disputes, demand an EU initiative. Resolution of the ongoing disputes in the Eastern Mediterranean is also a precondition for the realization of the broader security objectives of the EMP, e.g. in the field of arms control and disarmament. Progress has been made, but one has to ask whether this is really due to EU involvement.

The Aegean There have been considerable EU efforts *vis-à-vis* the Greek-Turkish tensions, but the recent improvement in their relations seems to have much more to do with an increased willingness of the parties themselves than with any active EU policy. The earthquakes hitting first Turkey and then Greece in 1999 caused an unprecedented and mutual wave of popular support for the victims. The natural disasters made the process of reconciliation which had already begun acceptable to the public opinion in the two countries. The formal designation of Turkey as a candidate for accession at the Helsinki European Council, with Greek support, further improved relations between Athens and Ankara and with the EU and increased the willingness of the parties to earnestly engage in a process of creating mutual understanding. Both parties, it seems, have come to realize that allowing their relationship to be ruled by antagonism and nationalism, with the ever-present risk of escalation which this implies, works against their strategic interests, notably their desire to be fully integrated in the EU (Gundoglu, 2001; Lesser, 2000a, pp.187–8).

In the years immediately following the 1996 Imia crisis, the dispute over an uninhabited rocky islet which brought the two NATO Allies to the brink of war, the EU, alongside the US, played an active role as mediator between the two parties. Joint EU-US efforts after a lengthy and difficult process succeeded in bringing the two parties together and in compelling the Greek government to abandon its long-held policy of 'no talks with Turkey'. The willingness to talk was clearly motivated, at least in part, by the wish to maintain good relations with the EU, which for both parties was a political priority. The EU made use of this to play a mediating role and made sure to treat both parties to the dispute on an equal footing (Athanassopoulou, 1997). But the talks were interrupted by renewed tensions, caused notably by the decision of the Luxembourg European Council not to open accession negotiations with Turkey. The Union's hesitant and perhaps inconsistent policy on EU membership for Turkey thus resulted in alienating the country and in the breaking-off of its mediation efforts, which until then had been quite successful. Relations were further soured by the saga of PKK leader Abdullah Öcalan's unhindered escape from European custody, only to be arrested later by Turkish security. Thereafter the Union adopted a much more passive stance. Another problem straining the relations between Greece and Turkey and rendering conflict resolution in the area more difficult is the Greek attitude within the EU and Athens' use of its membership to obstruct certain Turkish claims, which is perhaps not countered enough by the other Member States.

The Kurds The Kurdish conflict has in fact been ended by military means, in spite of repeated EU calls for a political settlement. The EU especially condemned the repeated Turkish interventions in Northern Iraq, which by expanding the conflict into another country complicated the already tense security situation in the Middle East. The EU also repeatedly voiced its concerns at the tensions between Turkey and Syria, which also are related to the Kurdish issue. Syria provided support to the PKK and harboured its leader Öcalan. In October 1998, presumably with the silent backing of Israel and the US, militarily far superior Turkey threatened Syria with military action if it would not expel Öcalan and end support to the PKK. Mediation followed and on 20 October 1998 Turkey and Syria signed an agreement providing for an immediate end to all aid to the PKK. Öcalan and about 3000 fighters were forced to leave the country, Öcalan to start an odyssey which would eventually end with his arrest by Turkish agents. In this regard the EU has not been able to bring its influence to bear on Turkey. A military intervention in Iraq engenders a serious risk of re-opening the Kurdish conflict: Kurdish groups in Iraq aim to consolidate their power base in the North of that country, while Turkey seeks to occupy that part of Iraq in order to prevent a new uprising on its own territory as part of an attempt to create an independent Kurdistan.

In the field of human rights in general, more results have been achieved, although here too a lot remains to be done. The EU has taken firm viewpoints on the issue of respect for human rights. Because it is so directly linked to accession, it seems that the Union has been able to influence Turkish policy in this field. Apparently Ankara realizes that it is a *conditio sine qua non* for membership, especially because accession requires the assent of the European Parliament, which has adopted a very firm attitude in this regard.

Cyprus The Cyprus issue demonstrates that simple support for efforts by the UN and the US is insufficient. The Union's repeated declarations of support should have been backed by much more active involvement in the negotiations. Without this involvement the important decision of the Helsinki European Council to drop a settlement as a precondition for Cyprus' accession remained without effects on the ground.

In its June 1993 Opinion on Cyprus's application the Commission preferred the dispute over the island to be settled first, in order to avoid its internalization by the EU. But the EU took only limited initiatives to actively seek a solution to the conflict. Apparently it was estimated that the possibility of membership and the benefits this would entail for Cyprus as a whole and for Turkey would suffice to induce both Ankara and the Turkish Cypriots to find a compromise on the Cyprus issue. But the development of the accession process provoked very negative reactions instead. The fact that the EU earnestly considered to take the whole of Cyprus into the Union made the Turkish Cypriots stress their bid for sovereignty even more (Brewin, 2000, pp.16–30). Following the Luxembourg European Council Turkey and the Northern part of Cyprus announced a partial integration agreement. EU policy overlooked the fact that security and sovereignty issues rule the Cyprus conflict and not economic prosperity, which is why the economic benefits of membership by themselves proved to be far less of an incitement for the Turkish Cypriots to negotiate than had been expected.

There is some unease about the accession process among the Member States, because of the fear of the possible implications for the EU of the accession of a divided Cyprus, should negotiations fail to produce a settlement. The EU would then itself become a party to the dispute and would thus face an increased risk of involvement in unrest on the island or even in armed conflict. Another cause for unease lies in the fact that the Turkish Cypriot side is not represented in the accession negotiations, which raises questions as to the political legitimacy of the application and public support for it in the Northern part of the island. On the other hand the EU cannot shelve the application of a European country which meets all other accession criteria. Nor can the Union allow to let a non-Member State veto the accession of any applicant, especially not if this state acts in support of a regime which is not recognized by the EU (Nugent, 1998, p.134). Besides, public opinion in the North seems to have turned in favour of accession.

At the Helsinki European Council the Union's strategy concerning accession was changed. The European Council reiterated the view that 'a political settlement will facilitate the accession of Cyprus', which fulfils all political and economic criteria for membership. But in view of the absolute lack of progress in the negotiations, it was now explicitly added that

> if no settlement has been reached by the completion of the accession negotiations, the Council's decision on accession will be made without the above being a precondition.

Further and more importantly, Turkey was formally accepted as a candidate for accession, thus restoring the prospect of membership, but this was to be conditional on its attitude regarding its disputes with Greece and the Cyprus issue. The accession process was thus turned into a powerful incentive for Turkey and the Turkish Cypriots to accept a compromise on Cyprus.

Still it seems that the Union, by not taking any actual initiatives to further reconciliation and by limiting itself instead to supporting attempts by other actors, mainly the UN, failed to fully exploit this incentive, in spite of its great interest in the resolution of the Cyprus problem and its long-standing and oft-repeated commitment to the creation of a bi-communal and bi-zonal federation. It seems likely that because of the Union's leverage, active EU involvement would have considerably speeded up negotiations between the parties. The inactivity of the EU is reflected in the absence of common positions or joint actions on the Cyprus issue. One should also ask whether the EU has given sufficient incentives to the Greek Cypriots to negotiate; a settlement requires political will on both sides. On the other hand, in a reaction to the terms of the Accession Partnership, Turkey stated that it 'has never accepted any linkage between the efforts to find a solution to the Cyprus issue and its candidacy to the EU', claiming that the former is an issue just 'between the Turkish Republic of Northern Cyprus and the Greek Cypriot administration of Southern Cyprus'.[14] The prospect of accession very probably was a substantial factor contributing to the December 2001 agreement to resume direct negotiations. But once again this agreement in the first place was the result of active UN mediation. While Commissioner Verheugen was probably right in saying that 'the European Union has brought some movement through the planned accession. Otherwise nothing would have moved',[15] it does seem that progress could have been achieved much sooner had the decisions of the Helsinki European Council been followed by active EU mediation efforts.

Now that direct talks have been resumed the EU should work on the finding of a settlement jointly with the UN, which so far have acted as the driving force of the attempts to resolve the conflict, be it without success. The resumption of direct talks is the ideal occasion for the Union to join in. The fact that in early 2003 the talks floundered again, proves the necessity of strong EU involvement. An ad hoc structure could be created to take the lead in a renewed and joint effort at mediation. If they are willing to commit themselves the US could participate too. Using the carrot and stick approach, the EU should make full use of the possibilities offered by the accession process to broker an agreement. The Member States should be willing to commit the necessary forces to provide the security guarantees which both sides to the conflict would want, in the framework of either a remodelled UNFICYP, the UN force on the island, or a new EU operation. A settlement should of course be followed by economic and financial support for peace-building.

The status quo is not an option for Cyprus. The apparent stability is only superficial: on the ground the situation remains tense and the past eruptions of violence could easily repeat itself – the militarization of the island has increased the potential for violent conflict. As long as the conflict on Cyprus persists, it will continue to fuel Greek-Turkish tensions and thus make a settlement of Athens' and Ankara's bilateral disputes more difficult. And of course accession of a divided Cyprus remains problematic. Accession before a solution has been found is possible and the Northern part of the island could always join the EU at a later stage, like East Germany. But even though the possibility exists, internalizing a still potentially violent dispute is clearly not the most desirable option. Besides, accession of a divided Cyprus would create the remarkable situation, to say the least, that part of the territory of a Member State would be virtually occupied by the armed forces of a candidate for accession (Bertrand, 2000, p.121).

As a country with an undeniable European identity, but which is situated in the heart of the Middle East, and which maintains cordial relations with the whole of this region, Cyprus could serve as an example of democratic institutions and as a bridgehead of the Union. Furthermore Cyprus, because of its proximity to the unstable Middle East, is firmly committed to the EMP and the realization of the security objectives of the Partnership. Already it aligns its foreign policy with the CFSP and it is willing to participate in the development of the ESDP and abandon the non-aligned status which it maintained until now. The accession of a reunited Cyprus would therefore be of enormous value to the Union's Mediterranean policy (Couloumbis, 1996, p.211; Kramer, 1997, pp.25–6).

Active mediation The lack of an active policy on the side of the EU is witnessed by the absence of any joint actions or common positions on the Eastern Mediterranean. There is a large task ahead for the CFSP, which demands political will on the side of the EU. Now that a breakthrough seems possible, given the improved relations between Greece and Turkey, the restoration of relative stability in the Kurdish parts of Turkey and the resumption of UN-sponsored talks between the two Cypriot communities at the end of 2001, the EU should seize the occasion. A further passive attitude would not be reconcilable with the security objectives of the CFSP and the ESDP. In order to strengthen the parties' resolve to find a settlement and to give a clear signal of its willingness to contribute, the EU could announce the opening of accession negotiations with Turkey in the short term. Turkey's long-standing desire for membership would thus finally be translated into action, which would make a compromise on the outstanding disputes more acceptable to Turkey's government and public opinion. Making full use of the leverage provided by the accession process, a short term settlement should be possible.

A Conflict Resolution Policy

In order to establish a true Euro-Mediterranean security partnership, the EU should first and foremost commit itself to resolving all ongoing disputes and conflicts in the area. Only if this prime obstacle is overcome can ways of deepening the political and security basket of the EMP be considered, for quite simply as long as these conflicts persist the basic trust which is needed as a foundation for enhanced security cooperation is missing. Most if not all of the Mediterranean partners are in some way or another involved, or perceive the risk of becoming so, in one of the three major enduring conflicts which divide the region: the Cyprus issue, the civil war in Algeria and the Israeli-Palestinian conflict. The latter especially provokes high-running emotions and tensions which have region-wide implications and thus are mainly responsible for paralyzing the Partnership's security chapter. Under such circumstances, partners are focussed on maintaining a clear-cut profile in foreign policy, often under the pressure of public opinion, which does not leave room for the governments to discuss security cooperation. Peace and stability must be established in the short term before arrangements to guarantee the maintenance of peace and stability in the long run, by providing for conflict prevention and arrangements for crisis management, can be agreed upon.

Resolving the ongoing conflicts is also a matter of establishing the credibility of the EU as an international actor. Generally speaking EU involvement in conflict resolution in the Mediterranean has been rather limited. In the Cyprus issue and the Algerian crisis the Union certainly plays a very passive role. The Union's involvement in the Middle East peace process is much more substantial, be it that it has known its ups and downs, but even there the Union has achieved limited durable results. This generally passive stance has raised fundamental doubts about the Union's capacity and willingness to act in the politico-military field and explains partners' reluctance to engage in security cooperation with a partner which in their eyes has proved very little in this field. So the Union should actively work towards the settlement of ongoing conflicts in the region, not only because security cooperation is impossible while they persist, but also to demonstrate its resolve and its ability to wage an effective security policy and to commit the means necessary to that end.

It will indeed have to be the EU that will take the lead, for one should acknowledge that the EMP itself is not a suitable forum for resolving ongoing conflicts. On the contrary, these conflicts have prevented security cooperation in the Partnership from advancing far enough to include arrangements for conflict resolution and crisis management. The EMP was conceived as an instrument for prevention of future conflicts and not as a tool to resolve ongoing conflicts. This is the meaning of the Barcelona Declaration where it reads that the Partnership 'is not intended to replace the other activities or initiatives undertaken in the interest of peace' (Aliboni, 1998b, p.14). But practice has demonstrated that the separation between the Partnership and the Middle East peace process and, by extension, the other ongoing conflicts in the area, cannot be maintained: ignoring the partner countries' main security concerns has led to the paralysis of the EMP. This is a vicious circle: ongoing conflicts block the progress of the Partnership's security dimension, which thus lacks the means to deal with these conflicts. The only way to break this deadlock is if the EU itself assumes responsibility for the maintenance of peace and stability in its periphery and takes the lead in settling ongoing conflicts.

The EU should frame its actions in the overall objective of reinvigorating the EMP though, so as to give a clear signal to its Mediterranean partners of its will to make an earnest effort and to commit all the required means to achieve peace and stability for all states in the region. The Union could thus correct the prevailing impression in the partner countries that it is only interested in the security basket of the Partnership for the sake of its own security rather than earnestly aspiring to establish a Mediterranean area of peace and stability.

Although the EMP itself cannot resolve the ongoing conflicts, it can contribute to their resolution, through regular dialogue and by improving relations and increasing understanding between partners. The Union should take care to keep its Mediterranean partners fully informed of its actions, through the political dialogue of the EMP. One possibility would be to provide for 'Euro-Mediterranean Middle East information gatherings': regular and official but informal gatherings in which all partners are invited to participate on a voluntary basis, with the purpose of keeping all partners informed of events and policies that strongly influence the Partnership but are dealt with by partner countries outside the EMP framework. The Middle East peace process would be a priority subject of such gatherings, but other conflict areas could also be covered. Thus a privileged Euro-Mediterranean forum for dissemination of information would be created, next to the existing EMP meetings, which would serve to enhance the status of the Partnership (Aliboni, 2000b, pp.11–12). Besides informing all partners of its actions, the EU should also effectively involve in its actions those regional parties which are themselves concerned by any specific conflict, in a way best suitable for the case at hand. Unilateral EU action might increase distrust in the partner countries about the Union's intentions and diminish the acceptability and thus the chances of succes of any initiative, whereas action in close cooperation with the partner countries directly concerned would benefit from increased legitimacy and would in itself function as a North-South CSBM.

The very limited number of common positions and joint actions on the Mediterranean is a witness to the general passivity of the EU. There are no common positions or joint actions on Greek-Turkish tensions and the Cyprus issue, the civil war in Algeria or the dispute over the Western Sahara. Common positions on the Maghreb are limited to those on the sanctions regime against Libya. On the Middle East originally four joint actions were taken, followed by a number of later decisions to amend or extend these. For the remainder the EU has limited itself to issuing declarations. This is not to say that declarations cannot have an important impact; the CFSP declarations in support of the creation of a Palestinian state e.g. are proof of the contrary. The absence of common positions and joint actions also does not necessarily imply total inactivity. Efforts at mediation and negotiation take place without being made explicit in a formal CFSP framework. With regard to some conflicts however, notably the issues of Algeria and the Western Sahara, EU passivity really is almost complete. And even where action is taken, in the Middle East and, to a far lesser extent, in the Eastern Mediterranean, the lack of common positions and joint actions has important drawbacks. While in some cases the policy objectives of the Union can be derived quite clearly from the consecutive CFSP declarations or European Council conclusions, in other cases EU policy remains very vague. A clear-cut common position or joint action would increase the visibility of the CFSP and would bind all the Member States to a clearly defined policy, which would leave less room for solo actions by individual Member States, which still happen all too often. A clearly defined policy should not only include a hierarchy of objectives, but should also cover the range of diplomatic, economic and military instruments to be applied to attain these and should be followed by actual implementation on the ground. Policy objectives should be framed in the general objectives of the EMP.

Next to involving its Mediterranean partners, the EU should also seek cooperation with other potential partners. The UN are a first obvious partner for conflict resolution. The Union's attitude in the Iraqi crisis, notably the rejection by a majority of the Member States of military action without explicit authorization by the Security Council, indicates its strong commitment to the UN system and multilateralism. In all of the ongoing conflicts in the region the EU supports the implementation of Security Council Resolutions and UN actions in the field, sometimes very actively, like in the Middle East, sometimes though with much less vigour or even only verbally, like on Cyprus and on the issue of Western Sahara. Regarding the conflict in Algeria the UN sadly have adopted the same passive attitude as the EU. So an active EU conflict resolution policy can be, and where the EU is active today already is, based on Security Council Resolutions, which provides EU actions with increased legitimacy. But cooperation between both international organizations can go much further than that. At the June 2001 Göteborg European Council the Swedish Presidency, in the framework of the elaboration of the ESDP, proposed the building of an effective partnership with the UN in the fields of conflict prevention and crisis management. Cooperation on conflict prevention would focus on collection and exchange of data, analysis of situations and diplomatic action. In the field of crisis management the idea is to ensure that the developing European military and civilian capacities, which will enlarge the international pool of means available for crisis management, provide real added value to the UN, by guaranteeing the compatibility of training, exchanging information on the planning and implementation of operations and coordinating operations on the ground. Next to the Balkans and Africa, the Middle East will be given highest priority in this reinforced cooperation.[16]

In this philosophy the EU should not only step up its efforts at conflict resolution, but should also act jointly with the UN, so as to ensure that both organizations' initiatives are fully consistent and that the available means are used in the most efficient and efficacious way. This is especially the case with regard to Cyprus and the Western Sahara, where the UN are the leading actor in the ongoing attempts at conflict resolution. In these two cases one can imagine that the Union and the UN, instead of operating separately, create an ad hoc structure and launch a single renewed initiative to find a final settlement. Regarding Algeria it is up to the EU, as part of an active conflict resolution policy, to propose options for increased UN involvement to the Security Council.

The second partner for conflict resolution is of course the US. They are still seen by the Mediterranean countries as the strongest international actor, which can bring the most pressure to bear. Experience has shown that often actions can only succeed if they have the explicit backing of the US. Over the years it has also become clear however that the US alone is not in a position to resolve the ongoing conflicts in the Mediterranean. Successful cases of EU-US cooperation, on Greek-Turkish tensions, but especially in the Middle East, demonstrate that joint efforts have the biggest chance of success. The elaboration of the CFSP and the ESDP should not be seen as directed against the US. Although Washington has a different approach to Mediterranean security issues from that of Brussels, the EU and the US where they are both involved share the same basic objectives. Therefore, like with the UN, the EU should act jointly with the US through *ad hoc* structures where both Europeans and Americans are involved in conflict resolution efforts, notably in the Middle East, on Cyprus and regarding Greek-Turkish tensions. This does however require agreement on the instruments to be applied, which was completely absent in the case of Iraq.

The need to settle the ongoing conflicts before any further progress towards a security partnership can be achieved, was openly recognized by the EU in the aftermath of '11 September', at least with regard to the conflict in the Middle East. The Middle East attracted the most attention because the settlement of the conflict between Arabs and Israelis would greatly contribute to avoiding the perception of a 'clash of civilizations' going on and would enable the US to rally Israel and the Arab countries alike in their global coalition against terrorism. Only Commission President Romano Prodi drew a more general picture at the extraordinary European Council meeting of 21 September 2001, emphasizing the need to

> extend the EU's active participation in settling international crises and preventing conflicts, which will require a multiplication of efforts with regard to countries around the Mediterranean.[17]

A programme for action indeed.

Notes

1. Joint action adopted by the Council on the basis of Article J.3 of the Treaty on European Union on the establishment of a European Union assistance programme to support the Palestinian Authority in its efforts to counter terrorist activities emanating from the territories under its control (97/289/CFSP) (29 April 1997).
2. *Europe*, 29 August 2001.
3. Euro-Mediterranean Interim Association Agreement on trade and cooperation between the European Community, of the one part, and the Palestine Liberation Organization (PLO) for the benefit of the Palestinian Authority of the West Bank and the Gaza Strip, of the other part (signed on 24 February 1997).
4. *Europe*, 22 September 2001.
5. The US' aspiration to monopolize the peace process has not been limited to Europe; the UN too time and again have been sidelined by Washington.
6. Euro-Mediterranean Conference of Ministers for Foreign Affairs. Brussels, 5–6 November 2001). Presidency Conclusions.
7. *Europe*, 8 November 2001.
8. Joint action adopted by the Council on the basis of Article J.3 of the Treaty on European Union, in support of the Middle East peace process (94/276/CFSP) (19 April 1994).
9. Council decision supplementing joint action 94/276/CFSP adopted by the Council on the basis of Article J.3 of the Treaty on European Union, in support of the Middle East peace process, concerning the observation of elections to the Palestinian Council and the coordination of the international operations for observing the elections (95/403/CFSP) (25 September 1995).

10 Joint action adopted by the Council on the basis of Article J.3 of the Treaty on European Union in relation of the nomination of an EU special envoy for the Middle East peace process (96/676/CFSP) (25 November 1996).
11 *Euromed Special Feature*, 15 January 2002.
12 *Europe*, 10–11 January 2000.
13 *Europe*, 6 and 7 January and 1 February 2000.
14 *Europe*, 16 November 2000.
15 *Europe*, 19 January 2002.
16 European Union Programme for the Prevention of Violent Conflicts. Göteborg, 15–16 June 2001.
17 *Europe*, 22 September 2001.

Chapter 4

Building a Euro-Mediterranean Security Partnership

Introduction

An active conflict resolution policy is a prerequisite for an enhanced Euro-Mediterranean security partnership. This chapter deals with its indispensable complement: opening up the ESDP can create trust between both shores and can open the way to the institutionalization of the EMP and to deepened politico-military cooperation. The chapter further deals with arms control, disarmament and non-proliferation, which are governed by particular circumstances, and with the organization of the EMP, to conclude with an appeal to the Union to muster the political will to take the lead in the sensitive issue of Euro-Mediterranean security.

From CSBMs to Crisis Management on the basis of the ESDP

Opening Up the ESDP

Once the EU initiates an active conflict resolution policy in order to address the immediate obstacles to Euro-Mediterranean security cooperation, the deepening of the political and security basket of the EMP can be considered. The EU can however also give an immediate and very strong signal of its wish to engage in a true and equitable security partnership with its Mediterranean partners by opening up the ESDP to participation by all EMP countries. A deepening of the political and security partnership is called for in the guidelines for a Euro-Mediterranean Charter, which should set up 'an enhanced political dialogue, in the appropriate institutional framework and on adequate levels', and in the Valencia Action Plan, which states that 'cooperation on conflict prevention with a special emphasis on crisis management' is required. Following preparatory work under the Spanish and Greek Presidencies in 2002, the Political and Security Committee in early 2003 put forward proposals for strengthening dialogue in the field of the ESDP, which were endorsed by the Council on 19 March 2003, with a view to strengthening mutual understanding and exploring more concrete ideas for co-operation.

The ESDP already provides for far-reaching cooperation with the European members of NATO which are not part of the EU and with all applicant states to the EU. So Turkey, which fits into both categories, and Cyprus and Malta are already involved. These countries will be kept regularly informed of the development of the ESDP through meetings at political, military and expert levels, a dialogue which will be intensified in times of crisis, they will be allowed to detach liaison officers to the European Military Staff and they will have the possibility to participate in EU operations. The units which they earmark for possible participation will be included in the EU catalogue of available headquarters, forces and equipment, so an element of joint force planning is implied. Close cooperation is also being developed with Canada, Russia, Ukraine and with NATO as an organization.

The EU could very well open up the ESDP to all Mediterranean partners in the same way. The advantages would be very substantial. In the first place, joint participation in military structures is a very powerful CSBM. The opening-up of the ESDP would entail a wide scope of cooperation activities. It would allow for a large-scale exchange of information, it would offer the Mediterranean partners the possibility of being involved in the ongoing planning process and, in times of crisis, in decision-making, and this at an early stage; it would also make possible participation in military manoeuvres and in actual humanitarian, peacekeeping and peace enforcement operations performed by the EU in the Mediterranean and in other areas. Thus, it would function as a North-South CSBM, diluting partners' suspicions regarding the development of a European military capacity by directly involving them. So an 'open door policy' could be the way to reconcile the two EU policy imperatives that emerged very clearly in the wake of '11 September', i.e. avoiding that relations with its partners are clouded by an atmosphere of suspicion and antagonism and proceeding with the development of the ESDP – a complicated balancing act indeed. The advantages of joint participation in the ESDP also work horizontally, so at the same time the opening-up of the ESDP constitutes an important South-South CSBM.

Another major advantage is that from a practical point of view this proposal is easy to implement. The decision-making structures of the ESDP and the mechanisms for involving non-EU Member States are already in place and the military capacity is taking shape. Involving the Mediterranean partners in these existing structures is thus only a matter of political will on the side of the EU. The proposal as such does not imply any financial effort on the part of Europe. It would be recommendable though to subsidize the Mediterranean partners' participation, for experience has shown that the cost of cooperation activities and of delegating diplomatic and military personnel often works as an impediment to full participation. Opening up the ESDP would really amount to the continuation of the now defunct Mediterranean Dialogue of WEU in the EU framework, at a very much enhanced level. In fact, when WEU's role as an operational organization was ended, the Mediterranean Dialogue should have been transferred to the EU along with WEU's other operational elements, instead of just terminating it. Now the limited but nonetheless existing acquis of the WEU Dialogue has been lost and a gap has been created in relations between the EU and its Mediterranean partners as regards security and defence, just at the time when the Union is fully involved in developing its own capacities in these fields.

Even setting aside the advantages, opening up the ESDP is a necessity, precisely because of the South's distrust towards the North, which such a move would certainly help to diminish. Unilateral or 'all-European' crisis management operations would be unacceptable to the Mediterranean partners, in view of the current fear of 'interventionism'. Unilateral action would probably even be counterproductive and could lead to an antagonization of relations between both shores. So the 'expeditionary logic' of an EU doted with specific military capacities suitable for interventions on the opposite shore, which should be able to quench every potential security threat, does not apply. The structural imbalance between both shores and, at the same time, their interdependence render any idea of a 'Fortress Europe' guarding itself unilaterally against security threats issuing from the South completely unrealistic (Ravenel, 2000, p.89). Only joint Euro-Mediterranean operations, or at least operations which have been the subject of extensive consultations in a Euro-Mediterranean framework, would be politically acceptable to the governments and certainly to the public opinion in the partner countries. The EU could thus not hope to play its newly acquired crisis management role in the Mediterranean without fully involving its partners in the EMP. In other words, the cooperative approach to security which characterizes the Partnership should be introduced into the ESDP in order to make it possible for the Union to fulfil its crisis management role in the Mediterranean.

In order to fully dispel all distrust *vis-à-vis* the ESDP, the Union should formally frame the ESDP in a comprehensive security concept. With regard to the Union's Mediterranean periphery, as with regard to other regions and the global level, a security concept should define EU objectives and instruments for the whole spectrum of external policies, in order to make clear that in the comprehensive approach security policy (the politico-military dimension) is just one of a range of policies that together aim for long-term stabilisation. With regard to the Union's crisis management task in the Mediterranean, i.e. short-term security policy, a security concept should clearly confirm the 'Euro-Mediterranean option' of jointly implementing crisis management in an 'EU+12' framework. The legitimacy that is needed for crisis management, can be gained by EU action in the long-term. That way partners would no longer have any reason to doubt the purpose of the ESDP. Besides, a security concept for the ESDP also is a necessity for technical reasons of policy-making: it should serve as a framework for the planning tasks of the EU Military Staff, the composition of the rapid reaction force depends on the types of operations to be implemented and on the geographical scope of the ESDP etc. Political considerations come into the game as well. Military operations demand uncontested legitimacy and thus have to be founded on documents that clearly define when military action is possible. Furthermore the adoption of a comprehensive security concept could diminish the reluctance to engage in the ESDP of the Union's 'neutral' Member States, which fear the silent militarization of the CFSP. Since in the comprehensive approach all external policies are put on the same height, each operating according to its own rationale, 'securitization' can be avoided.

Opening up the ESDP would be a relatively easy step, because it 'simply' means involving the Mediterranean partners in an existing structure, and a far-reaching one at the same time, because it directly goes to the core of 'hard' security cooperation: joint manoeuvres and operations. The latter part could be difficult to sell to public opinion in the partner countries. In the same philosophy as the cooperation arrangements provided for in the projected Euro-Mediterranean Charter, participation in the ESDP could be offered to the partner countries on a voluntary basis and would evolve gradually, also because the ESDP is still in its early stages of development. Ultimately, the results of the opening-up of the ESDP depend on the successful further elaboration of the European security and defence dimension. The partners could start with the appointment of liaison officers and regular dialogue, with manoeuvres and operations following in a later stage. One can imagine that first significant progress should be made in the field of conflict resolution before these latter stages materialize. On the other hand, opening up the ESDP and an active EU conflict resolution policy can go hand in hand – they are in fact mutually reinforcing. If conflict resolution should imply European military operations or an EU contribution to UN or other operations, an observer or peacekeeping force in the Middle East e.g., the legitimacy and acceptability of such operations would be far greater if the Mediterranean partners were already involved in the ESDP. If the EU should open up the ESDP, this would of course demand political will on the other side as well. All partners should participate for this CSBM to be most effective. And should they refuse an invitation to participate, partners can no longer complain about a lack of transparency or vagueness of intentions regarding the ESDP. In short, opening up the ESDP would force both sides of the Partnership to really bring their long-stated commitment to Euro-Mediterranean security cooperation into practice.

One should not forget the civilian side of crisis management. The EU is also developing a civilian crisis management capacity. Objectives include the creation of a pool of 5000 police officers available for operations abroad; 200 prosecutors, judges and correctional officers to ensure a functioning criminal justice process; experts to take on assignments within the civilian administration; and civil protection intervention teams consisting of up to 2000 personnel. In this field as well close involvement of the non-EU European members of NATO and the applicant states is provided for, so the civilian crisis management capacity could be opened for participation by the Mediterranean partners along the same lines too. In fact cooperation in this non-military field would perhaps be more acceptable to the partner countries and could thus be a means of involving them in crisis management operations in a gradual way, starting with the civilian dimension.

Institutionalizing the Security Partnership

Initiating an active conflict resolution policy and opening up the ESDP are the measures which the EU should take to make possible a deepening of the Euro-Mediterranean security partnership, including conflict prevention, crisis management and post-conflict peace-building. This would amount to the implementation of the Charter for Peace and Stability. Joint participation of all partners in the ESDP would be a firm basis on which to found these further steps.

As provided for in the Guidelines for the Charter, further measures for security cooperation should be framed in an enhanced political dialogue; this institutionalized dialogue would then serve as the policy-making entity within the political and security basket of the EMP. In the framework of the ESDP a regular dialogue with all participating countries is already provided for, at the political, military and expert level, crowned by meetings at the level of Ministers for Foreign Affairs and Defence. Meetings at these levels will be held at least twice during each EU Presidency with the candidates for accession and the non-EU European members of NATO ('EU+15' format) and with the latter separately ('EU+6' format). If the ESDP were opened up to the Mediterranean partners, a third forum could easily be added, grouping the Fifteen and the Mediterranean partners ('EU+12'). Overlaps between these groupings do not pose a problem, for next to the dissemination of information on the development of the ESDP, different subjects and regions would be covered by each forum. Besides, there already is a complete overlap between the 'EU+15' and 'EU+6' formats.

The meetings at 'EU+12', next to their function of informing the Mediterranean partners about the development of the ESDP, could then at the same time serve as the enhanced political dialogue of the political and security partnership of the EMP. A single institutional framework would thus emerge, with meetings ranging from expert level, through the military and senior official/diplomatic level, to the level of Foreign and Defence Ministers. Contrary to the other baskets of the Partnership, there are now no meetings of sectoral Ministers within the political and security chapter. Within the EMP security issues are only discussed at a ministerial level at the general Euro-Mediterranean Ministerial Conferences. Meetings of Foreign and Defence Ministers at 'EU+12', once each Presidency e.g., dealing only with the first basket of the EMP, could provide additional impetus to the security dimension of the Partnership and would certainly give it a higher profile. At these ministerial meetings the general programme of action for each Presidency could be discussed. The voluntary and consensual or intergovernmental character of politico-military cooperation as agreed in the Guidelines can be maintained. At a time when even within the EU majority decision-making with regard to the CFSP, and the ESDP in particular, is still a far-off dream, one should not look for supra-nationality in the EMP, where the partner states especially are very careful of their national sovereignty. At all these different levels, from experts to ministers, with meetings at regular intervals and as required, the full scope of Euro-Mediterranean security issues could then be discussed, including the ESDP, and decisions could be taken by the 27 partners, at the appropriate level, on the adoption of further CSBMs and arrangements for crisis management.

The advantage of combining the politico-military dimension of the EMP with participation in the ESDP is that partners would be much more involved in policy-preparation and decision-making within the EU, at an early stage, so that eventually a truly joint Euro-Mediterranean security policy can emerge, rather than a policy which first is defined by the Union in the appropriate EU bodies and which is then presented to its partners in the framework of the EMP. Another advantage is that by directly linking participation in the ESDP to further Euro-Mediterranean CSBMs, even though they have a North-South and South-South effect at the same time, as these involve all 27 partners, still the sense of reciprocity would be greater for the partners. The adoption of further measures for security cooperation would be more acceptable to partners' governments and public opinion alike, as this would be matched by their involvement in the ESDP.

In order to really give body to the political dialogue, one could go even one step further than introducing regular meetings at all levels, as in the 'EU+6' and 'EU+15' formats, and create an additional body: a sort of permanent council at 'EU+12', preferably at ambassadorial level, which, like the other levels, would at the same time function as a forum for participation in the ESDP and for an enhanced Euro-Mediterranean security dialogue. Within the political and security basket of the Partnership, this permanent council would be the highest organ, except for the less regular meetings of sectoral, i.e. Foreign and Defence Ministers, each Presidency; and except of course for the general Euro-Mediterranean Ministerial Conferences and the Euro-Mediterranean Committee, which cover all three baskets of the EMP. At ambassadorial level, a permanent council would increase the profile of the political dialogue and it would have the necessary authority to take decisions on politico-military issues. As a permanent body it would be able to follow-up events much more closely and to have more extensive consultations. The meetings of the permanent council could be prepared and its decisions implemented by meetings on the other levels: senior officials, military and experts. A permanent council is not provided for in the 'EU+15' and 'EU+6' formats, but in these groupings there is no need for such a body. A forum for permanent dialogue with the non-EU European members of NATO is already at hand, in the North Atlantic Council, while the 'EU+15' format will eventually disappear as all applicant states successively join the EU. For most of the Mediterranean partners membership of the EU (or NATO for that matter) is not being envisaged though, so in this context a permanent body is in order so as to ensure the continuity of the dialogue with these countries.

The permanent council would then on the one hand be the main forum for dialogue with the Mediterranean partners with regard to the development of the ESDP and the cooperation activities developed in that framework. On the other hand in the framework of the EMP it would constitute a body which can deal with regular exchanges of information on agreed subjects and notification of unusual or unscheduled matters on a daily basis; appropriate mechanisms and procedures ought to be elaborated. It would thus assume a conflict prevention and early warning function. Next to this the permanent council would also follow up the daily running of the political and security basket and the implementation of all agreed CSBMs. So the permanent council would replace the quarterly meetings of senior officials as the managing body of the Partnership's first basket.

Both NATO and the OSCE have developed Mediterranean dialogues of their own, each with its own particular approach and with little coordination between them. The main achievement of NATO's Mediterranean Dialogue is the development of concrete military cooperation activities, crowned by the participation of a number of Dialogue countries in NATO peace support operations on the Balkans. The merit of the OSCE's Mediterranean dimension lies in the dissemination of its expertise in the fields of conflict prevention and peaceful settlement of disputes. Because neither of these Mediterranean initiatives possesses the same wide membership as the EMP, nor its comprehensive and multilateral character, the EMP is the best suitable framework to achieve the objective of a Mediterranean area of peace and stability. Aligning the programmes of activity of NATO and the OSCE so that they complement the agenda of the EMP would therefore seem to be the most efficient and effective way of putting the available means to good use (Biscop, 2002a).

In order to be able to perform its functions, the permanent council would have to be backed by the necessary organizational support. Several structures can be set up (Aliboni, 2000b, pp.16–28; Biad, 1999, pp.109–22).

- A communications network between the Ministries of Foreign Affairs, at the diplomatic level, can allow for secure and rapid communication between the 27 partners. This measure implies the elaboration of procedures, the designation of contact persons and the installation of the necessary soft- and hardware.
- A situation centre can collect and analyze data on a series of agreed items, which are provided by the partner countries on a regular basis, and can monitor the implementation of agreed CSBMs. For the purpose of crisis management it could monitor any situation which is under the consideration of the permanent council. One can imagine the establishment of a cell of analysts which through a series of agreements is granted access to intelligence made available by the individual partner countries and by similar bodies, notably the Policy Planning and Early Warning Capacity established within the CFSP, the Satellite Centre in Torrejón (Spain), which was transferred from the WEU to become an agency under the CFSP, and any other arrangements for pooling intelligence that might be established in the framework of the CFSP.
- A conflict prevention centre (CPC) can develop and then manage permanent mechanisms for the notification of unusual or unscheduled events and, as the Guidelines for the Charter provide, 'procedures of clarification, mediation and conciliation for settling disputes between parties by peaceful means of their own choice'. In these fields the experience and expertise of the OSCE would prove very useful; here the Mediterranean dimension of the OSCE and the EMP would be truly complementary. The Mediterranean activities of the OSCE could easily be focussed on issues relevant to a CPC for the Partnership. The OSCE's Mediterranean Partners for Cooperation have in fact proposed the creation of a CPC for the Mediterranean analogous to the existing OSCE centre. Although this proposal has not been acted upon by the OSCE, it does show that there is room for such mechanisms in the Mediterranean.

A similar construction was actually agreed upon in the framework of the Arms Control and Regional Security Working Group, before these talks were suspended as the multilateral track of the Middle East peace process ground to a halt, which indicates that under more favourable circumstances it ought to be quite feasible. The most important characteristic of this structure is that it provides for truly Euro-Mediterranean bodies, i.e. at 27, at all levels, from Ministers to experts, for preparation of policy, for decision-making as well as for the implementation of decisions. All CSBMs aim for full reciprocity, between North and South in the first place, so as to dispel any distrust, but since they are taken at 27, they have a South-South effect at the same time. The result should be an equitable security partnership and a Euro-Mediterranean security policy, based on joint assessment of security issues and joint definition of the ways to respond to them.

The Charter for Peace and Stability should be the document establishing the basic structures and objectives of an enhanced Euro-Mediterranean security partnership. In order to signal its significance and ensure maximal compliance, the adoption of the Charter, preferably by a meeting of the Heads of State and Government of the Partnership, should be a solemn occasion (Daguzan, 1999). The ultimate aim should be a legally binding treaty, but this is a very long-term perspective. Even though the Charter, as has already been decided, would be politically binding only, which under the current circumstances is the only feasible way of adopting it, the institutionalization of the security partnership as described above would on its own ensure that dynamic is maintained, because of the permanent dialogue it would imply and because of the drive of each institution to prove its right of existence.

Adopting Additional CSBMs

Once this basic framework is set up and building on the activities implied by the participation in the ESDP, other CSBMs can be implemented.

- A code of good conduct can be adopted, identifying the principles directing the relations between the partners. Examples of principles are: the indivisibility of security, meaning that all states have a right to security and that no state can increase its security to the detriment of another; the comprehensive nature of security, i.e. recognition of the fact that security is the sum of not only military, but of political, economic, demographic, ecological and other factors as well and that therefore an integrated approach is in order; the concept of sufficiency, implying that security policy is strictly defence-oriented and that states refrain from developing a military capacity going beyond their legitimate defence requirements; transparency, which is indeed the general principle underlying all CSBMs; and the principle of good faith in implementing all agreements (Biad, 2001, pp.100–104). Such a code of good conduct would also reconfirm and detail a number of the principles already included in the Barcelona Declaration: respect for the sovereign equality and territorial integrity of states, for the inviolability of frontiers, for the fundamental rights and freedoms and for the right to self-determination of peoples; avoidance of the threat or the use of force; peaceful settlement of disputes; non-intervention in internal affairs; and the general principle of cooperation. The code could become an integral part of the Charter for Peace and Stability. Perhaps the elaboration of such a code could be the first task of a conflict prevention centre, so as to create the general framework first before

moving on to the establishment of concrete mechanisms for early warning and dispute settlement.
- The expertise present in the EuroMeSCo network of foreign policy institutes can be put to its full use by viewing the network as an extension of the capacities established in the EMP. Mechanisms should be defined allowing the Partnership to avail itself of EuroMeSCo when analysis of situations is needed or for the elaboration of proposed CSBMs (Aliboni, 2000b, p.24).
- Observers can be exchanged, liaison officers detached and joint manoeuvres organized, not only in a South to North direction, but in the opposite direction and between the Southern partners as well. Other possible measures for military cooperation are exchanges between military academies and other military bodies, cooperation between defence institutes, seminars on strategic doctrines, mutual visits, including to 'sensitive areas', etc.
- In order to reinforce the Euro-Mediterranean perspective in strategic thinking, the establishment of a Euro-Mediterranean institute for strategic or security studies might be considered, which should lead to the development of a common strategic language. This exercise would contribute to avoiding conceptual and terminological misunderstandings and to dispelling prejudices; it would therefore be an important CSBM in its own right (Echeverria, 1997b, p.2). As such an institute would gradually build up expertise, it could make an important contribution to policy-making in the EMP.
- Cooperation between border personnel, from joint training to joint patrolling, would contribute to avoiding border incidents and could achieve significant results in the fight against arms and drug trafficking, one of the 'soft' security issues with which all EMP countries are confronted (Brauch, Marquina and Biad, 2000b, pp.331–2). Cooperation in this field would of course be very desirable to the EU Member States, which seek to stem illegal immigration from the Mediterranean area.
- Acting on partners' proposals, cooperation in the fight against terrorism can be developed. Possible measures are the exchange of information between police services, setting-up a database on terrorist movements, compiling a catalogue of relevant national legislation in the partner countries, developing a joint approach to the financing of terrorist groups etc. The obstacle which still has to be overcome however is to find consensus on the definition of terrorism. This demands political will on both sides of the Mediterranean. The Arab countries should recognize that in the struggle against Israeli occupation not everything is permitted; EU Member States should limit political asylum to true political dissidents only and exclude terrorists.
- Land- and sea-mines constitute an important problem in the Mediterranean, notably on Cyprus, along the Greek-Turkish borders and in the Middle East, where Egypt especially faces an immense problem caused by left-over minefields from the Second World War and its own wars with Israel. Partners have at several instances launched proposals for Euro-Mediterranean cooperation in this field, but these have not been acted upon, in spite of Europe's high profile role in the fight against anti-personnel landmines. A unit

within the EMP could act as facilitator, bringing together Mediterranean states seeking assistance with de-mining and EU Member States and other countries and international organizations offering help. Such a unit could also function as coordinator of ongoing de-mining operations in the area and it could set up a database of the situation regarding mines in the partner countries (Sánchez Mateos, 2000).
- A similar task of coordination could be assumed in the field of disaster relief, on the basis of partners' participation in civilian crisis management. The existing Steering Committee of the Euro-Med System for the Prevention, Mitigation and Management of Natural and Man-made Disasters could be enhanced and organizational support could be supplied by a unit within the EMP. Its purpose would be to coordinate partner states' contributions to civilian crisis management and the different cooperation activities taking place in this field. Coordination would notably be necessary with participation in the civil emergency planning activities in the framework of NATO's Mediterranean Dialogue. By focussing the Alliance's Mediterranean programme in this field on the EMP objectives, NATO and the Partnership would operate in a complementary way. In this field the link between the first and second pillars of the Partnership is evident. Disaster relief ranges from humanitarian aid to refugees in the case of armed conflict, to aid in the case of natural disasters or incidents causing pollution. In these fields monitoring by a situation centre would be useful too.
- The nature of the area calls for the implementation of naval CSBMs (Pugh, 1997; Roy, 2001). The measures proposed above also apply to naval forces, e.g. exchange of information, prior warning of force movements, joint manoeuvres etc. More specific CSBMs could be added, e.g. cooperation in the fields of the prevention of naval incidents and search and rescue operations. One possibility in order to promote cooperation in these fields is the creation of a Euro-Mediterranean maritime agency (Calleya, 1999a, pp.4–5). This could develop mechanisms for joint action, coordinate available means and set up an exercise programme. In the long run this could evolve into the creation of a Euro-Mediterranean coastguard, dealing not only with maritime safety, but also with maritime pollution and illegal trafficking.
- An important task not to be forgotten is the communication of the objectives of the security partnership to the general public, through the media. The averse public opinion is an important factor explaining the reluctance of number of partner countries to join in security cooperation with the West. The public, on both sides of the Mediterranean, should therefore be convinced of the mutual benefits of a security partnership.

Most of these CSBMs could also be implemented without the establishment of an institutionalized dialogue as provided for by the Charter for Peace and Stability. A number of the 'soft' CSBMs especially might be implemented at an earlier stage, perhaps even before progress in the resolution of ongoing conflicts can be achieved. This would represent the gradual approach to the creation of a Euro-

Mediterranean security partnership: starting with relatively 'easy' CSBMs and gradually moving on to the core of politico-military issues. It seems however that in the Mediterranean this would imply a very long-term process indeed. The option of opening up the ESDP and building a security partnership on that basis therefore seems preferable; it might function as a sort of 'shock therapy'.

Euro-Mediterranean Crisis Management

The final touch to this network of CSBMs should be arrangements for crisis management: Euro-Mediterranean humanitarian, peacekeeping and peace enforcement operations. Conflict prevention can indeed fail or can demand the presence of forces on the ground as the only means of avoiding the eruption of violence. Far-reaching and long-term though it may seem, opening up the ESDP could significantly speed up the establishment of crisis management arrangements, as it goes right to the heart of security cooperation, and because of the positive effect of the experience of jointly participating in EU manoeuvres and operations. In fact, once the ESDP is firmly established the most efficient way of organizing Euro-Mediterranean crisis management would most probably be to consider the opened-up ESDP as the military arm of both the EU and the Partnership at the same time. If events within the territory of the Partnership might demand an intervention of any kind, the case should first be considered within the EMP, by the Ministers of Foreign Affairs and Defence, acting upon a recommendation of the permanent council, who could decide to launch a Euro-Mediterranean operation. An operation initiated in such a Euro-Mediterranean framework would be viewed in a totally different perspective by the partners than unilateral European action and would greatly benefit from this increased legitimacy.

The existing capacities and procedures of the ESDP could then be used to implement the decision to launch an operation. Current arrangements for participation in the ESDP by non-Member States provide that these will take fully part in the daily management of the operation through a Contributors' Committee, but that the EU, notably the Council and the Political and Security Committee, retains political control and strategic direction of the operation. If however an operation were initiated by the Ministers of the 27 partner countries in the framework of the EMP, they and the permanent council should exercise political control and strategic direction, in order to guarantee a balance between the EU and the Mediterranean partners. This balance should also be ensured in the operational planning of the operation at hand, e.g. by temporarily expanding the responsible planning capacity with staff from the partner countries, and in the composition of the force headquarters on the ground. This planning capacity could be one of the national and multinational headquarters made available by the states participating in the ESDP, or the Union could avail itself of NATO capacities. Through their participation in the ESDP the partners would also have an input in the permanent process of generic planning, i.e. the elaboration of a typology of operations, of the requirements in terms of headquarters, forces and equipment for the different types of interventions, and of rules of engagement. As in the EU and faithful to the voluntary character of the EMP, the rule should be that states who are not prepared to participate in a proposed operation should not prevent the states that are willing from taking an initiative – a kind of 'constructive abstention' arrangement. Next to Euro-Mediterranean crisis management, partner countries could of course still be invited to participate in EU operations in other areas, according to the regular ESDP arrangements.

Such an arrangement would be in line with the division of labour between the EU and NATO/the US that seems to be emerging. One can safely assume that the US would welcome a larger European contribution to maintaining peace and security in the periphery of the Union, so that American means could be redirected elsewhere. American criticism regarding Europe's meagre performance during the Kosovo air campaign and Washington's subsequent demand for a greater European effort are recent indications leading to this supposition. The same goes for the current concentration of American means for the 'war on terrorism'. But already several years before, American unwillingness to always assume responsibility for crisis management in the European periphery became apparent. When in 1997 Albania sank into anarchy, Washington had it known that it would not intervene in what it considered to be a European problem in which no American interests were directly at stake. Nor therefore would NATO which, as was stated quite literally – and quite contrary to one of the main criticisms of the Alliance's opponents – had no intention of being the world's policeman. One should also not forget that the US only intervened in the successive crises on the territory of former Yugoslavia after all EU attempts to settle the conflict had failed. It therefore seems probable that, once the ESDP is fully operational, through the day-to-day practice of policy-making and of consultations between the EU, NATO and the US a division of labour will gradually develop in which the Alliance/the US will only intervene for crisis management on the European continent if EU means prove to be insufficient or if main American interests are directly concerned (Biscop, 2002b, p.482).

In the context of Euro-Mediterranean arrangements for crisis management, the two multinational European units with a Mediterranean character, EUROFOR and EUROMARFOR, should be opened for participation by the partners too. The best way of dispelling any remaining distrust as to their purpose is to have the partners join these forces, on a permanent basis, so that they truly become Euro-Mediterranean units. As such they could be the ideal instrument for crisis management operations in the Euro-Mediterranean area. Both units have a flexible structure which would easily allow for the participation of additional countries.

In due course, as the spirit of cooperation increases, additional multinational Euro-Mediterranean units might be created. A force could be set up composed of contingents from the Maghreb countries e.g., which share French as a common military language. The important thing is that all forces should be open to participation by partners from both sides of the Mediterranean, in order to avoid any ambiguity as to their purpose. Several partner countries, notably Egypt and Jordan, have a wide experience with participating in peace support operations in a UN framework. Partners have even participated in IFOR and SFOR, in a NATO context. This proves that joint Euro-Mediterranean crisis management operations must be possible, both inside the territory covered by the Partnership and outside it, e.g. in Sub-Saharan Africa. Euro-Mediterranean multinational forces could indeed very well contribute to UN operations; such joint actions would constitute a very strong CSBM.

Specific training modules could be set up with regard to the whole range of crisis management operations, in the framework of the ESDP. Joint exercises strengthen ties and help to unify concepts and procedures. A Euro-Mediterranean institute for security or strategic studies could contribute to this, through its function of developing a common security vocabulary and by organizing staff courses for officers of the partner countries. A number of partners are already involved in bi- or multilateral military manoeuvres. Egypt e.g. plays a leading role in the Bright Star programme, large-scale manoeuvres involving air, land and sea forces from over a dozen countries, including the US, a number of EU Member States and several Arab countries, both members of the EMP and others. This example shows that the will to participate in a multilateral exercise programme is present.

The voluntary character of the security partnership should be respected. Security cooperation is only possible on a voluntary basis – pressurizing states to participate will not result in increased confidence. It should therefore be possible that initially CSBMs are implemented with the participation of just a limited number of partners. The success of the first CSBMs to be introduced is the only argument that can convince other partners to join. Creating a Euro-Mediterranean security partnership is a gradual process – one cannot hope to establish the desired structures and CSBMs all at once. But opening-up the ESDP might be the booster that is necessary for security cooperation in the Mediterranean to take off.

Arms Control, Disarmament and Non-Proliferation

With regard to arms control, disarmament and non-proliferation, obstacles to surmount before any measures can be adopted are considerably higher than in other fields, because of the particular circumstances in the Mediterranean and, specifically, in the Middle East.

A first major obstacle is the situation of strategic imbalance in the Middle East. Israel is not willing to relinquish its regional monopoly on the possession of nuclear weapons, which is used by its Arab neighbours as an argument against limits on their acquisition of biological and chemical weapons and on the conventional arms build-up, which they seek in order to counterbalance Israel's strategic advantage. In the Arab philosophy introducing arms-related CSBMs in such a situation would perpetuate the condition of strategic imbalance. A consequence of this situation is that if it comes to disarmament, all categories of armaments, from WMD to conventional types, will have to be dealt with at the same time, in a global programme, because all categories combined define the balance of forces which the regional parties want to achieve. No Arab country will be willing to consider limiting its forces if Israel's nuclear capacity remains outside the negotiations (Biad, 1997, p.5; El-Sayed, 2000a, p.151). Evidently, a breakthrough would only be possible once peace in the Middle East has been firmly established and relations between the current antagonists are ruled by mutual confidence and security – actual disarmament is thus a very long-term perspective.

The second obstacle is even more difficult to overcome, as it surpasses the EMP. Partners' security is not only a matter of relations with fellow partners, but is also influenced by countries which do not belong to the Partnership. Again, this is especially the case in the Middle East, where countries like Iraq and Iran have a substantial impact on the security situation – the 2003 Iraq crisis is the obvious proof. Partners in this area are not willing to consider actual disarmament, if countries such as these are not also involved in any proposed arrangement. When it comes to nuclear weapons, one must even take into account states which are yet further off: India and Pakistan. One must therefore conclude that the EMP is too limited a forum for the adoption of substantial disarmament measures, especially with regard to WMD, but the same goes for conventional weapons as well. A way needs to be found of involving neighbouring states which have a significant influence on the security perception of partner countries, if disarmament in the region is to have any chance of success (Lemke, 2000, p.97).

Still, a number of important arms-related CSBMs can and should be implemented within the Partnership, starting with CSBMs aimed at increasing transparency and moving on to non-proliferation measures, so as to freeze the existing amount of WMD and other armaments, to be followed in the long run by a disarmament programme.

In the first place transparency measures can be taken. As a first, 'soft' CSBM partner countries should fully cooperate with the existing UN Register of Conventional Arms, registering imports and exports of a number of conventional weapons. Arab partners currently refuse cooperation because they insist on the inclusion of WMD in the register. The creation of an enhanced register in a Euro-Mediterranean framework, including other categories of armaments and providing more detailed information, could therefore be the next step. The management of such a register could be entrusted to the situation centre proposed above. This measure should not pose a problem for the Arab countries, on the condition that Israel too would fully comply or, in other words, that it should end the ambiguity regarding its nuclear installations. This can best be done in the context of the NPT.

All partners should indeed become party to the major arms control agreements. Most of them already are, but a number of significant players still have to join the NPT, BTWC, CWC and CTBT. Adherence to these agreements is one of the undertakings which is explicitly mentioned in the Barcelona Declaration. The Palestinian Authority is not party to any of them, nor to the 1925 Geneva Protocol, which has been ratified by all other partners. Strictly legally speaking Palestine is not yet a state, though it certainly is an international actor sui generis, given e.g. its treatment in the EMP on an equal footing with the other partners. Pending formal statehood, the Palestinian Authority could already make a unilateral statement in which it commits itself to comply with the provisions of the said agreements. Such a move would be an important signal and it would deny other partners the possibility of using Palestine's non-commitment as an argument for not joining the agreements themselves. For the countries concerned, attention should also be given to the implementation of the Pelindaba Treaty, which aims at the establishment of a nuclear weapons-free zone in Africa.

Membership of these agreements by all partners would be a significant step. First of all, all partners would then be in the same position, which should make it easier to discuss arms-related issues between them. Secondly, proliferation of the WMD covered by the agreements would at least be frozen at the current level. Even when taking into account the influence of non-partner countries on partners' security, this ought to be a feasible step. Thirdly, transparency would be increased through the verification and inspection regimes included in a number of agreements, notably the CWC and the NPT. Following up partners' compliance could also be a task for the EMP situation centre proposed above. Arrangements for joint Euro-Mediterranean verification could be elaborated, with the participation of partners from North and South, as an important CSBM. Again, success depends on the willingness of Israel to disclose its nuclear installations to international inspection; given that all European countries and the US are subject to it as well, Israel has no rightful argument against joining the NPT. On the other hand, the Arab countries could make the first move, as a token of good-will. At the same time all partners that possess nuclear weapons could make a unilateral statement in which they guarantee that they will not use these weapons, or the threat of them, against any other partner state.

At the same time as generalizing membership of these agreements, other non-proliferation measures could be taken as well. The partners should define criteria to govern the transfer of defence equipment within the EMP. Arrangements can be modelled on existing EU export policy and on the guidelines of bodies as the Nuclear Suppliers Group, the Zangger Committee, the Australian Group, the MCTR and the Wassenaar Arrangement. Membership of these bodies should be promoted as well. Any arrangements should not only cover WMD technology and dual-use goods, but also conventional weapons, including small arms and light weapons. Arrangements should have a Euro-Mediterranean character; i.e. they should not only cover North-South arms transfers, but South-South transfers too. These measures demand political will on the side of the EU as well; the Union should adhere to strict criteria regarding arms sales to countries in the area and should refrain from all transfers to countries involved in conflict or even disputes which potentially might evolve into conflict.

In the longer term actual disarmament measures can be considered. A disarmament programme should refer to the notion of sufficiency, i.e. the commitment to refrain from developing a military capacity beyond legitimate defence requirements and to adopt a non-offensive defence posture, which was already included in the Barcelona Declaration and which, in the framework of the Charter for Peace and Stability, is to be confirmed in a code of conduct. Through the permanent dialogue in the security partnership, the concept of sufficiency could be more clearly defined; criteria could be elaborated in order to make its implementation on the ground possible. A system similar to the Treaty on Conventional Armed Forces in Europe (CFE) can be imagined. As the concept of sufficiency is taken into account, partners should arrive at a situation of 'equal security' for all, in which no single state has a dominant position over any other partner country. The ultimate result should be a gradual programme for reduction of forces and armaments, conventional and non-conventional. The advantage of making sufficiency the central notion in a programme of disarmament is that the influence of non-EMP states on the security needs of partner countries can be taken into account. A certain degree of disarmament should thus be possible within the Partnership. In a later stage and when suitable fora have been found, further disarmament measures can then be elaborated with the participation of states neighbouring the EMP, notably in the Middle East. The project of creating a Middle East and, by extension, a Mediterranean zone free of WMD should be fitted in this context too. This commitment too is included in the Barcelona Declaration.

Settlement of the ongoing conflicts, certainly in the Middle East, is a precondition for the adoption of any CSBMs in this field. As long as the causes of proliferation have not been dealt with, the demand for armaments will not decrease. Another important requirement is full reciprocity between the North and South of the Mediterranean. When setting up a Euro-Mediterranean arms register e.g. the EU Member States should disclose complete information as well and they should comply with all non-proliferation arrangements too. Partners want to discuss not only 'horizontal non-proliferation', i.e. preventing additional, notably Arab, countries from acquiring WMD, but also 'vertical non-proliferation', i.e. the reduction and ultimately the elimination of the existing stocks of WMD, notably on the Northern shore of the Mediterranean. Care should therefore be taken not to create the impression that arms-related measures are solely aimed at the Southern shore of the Mediterranean.

Organizing the EMP

A Secretariat for the Partnership

The EMP lacks an administration of its own. This fact contributes to a large extent to partners' perception of the Partnership as being inequitable, for the absence of any Euro-Mediterranean body leaves the daily running of Partnership activities almost exclusively in the hands of the European side of the EMP, which is contrary to the basic idea of cooperation underlying the Partnership. In this sense the Partnership is not Euro-Mediterranean at all.

An EMP secretariat should therefore be set up. This can be created by detaching officials and experts from the Commission and from partners' national administrations, to jointly administer the Partnership. The views of all partners could then be taken more into account in every stage of policy-making, from the preparation of policy by meetings of diplomats, officials, experts and the military and by the secretariat to be created, over decision-making in the political bodies, to implementation of policy by the secretariat and the individual countries. A secretary-general can be appointed, to assume the function of head of staff and to follow-up and coordinate the implementation of Partnership activities. In order to really create a sense of shared ownership, the secretary-general should be a national of one of the partner countries. For the same reason, the secretariat should be located on the Southern shore of the Mediterranean. The bodies to be created in the framework of an institutionalized political and security partnership, notably a situation centre and a conflict prevention centre and any other organs, could be integrated into the secretariat. An EMP secretariat would have the extra benefit of giving additional impetus to the Partnership, for each administration seeks to prove its own usefulness. The creation of a secretariat, in combination with the implementation of the organizational decisions of the Valencia Conference, would therefore certainly strengthen the internal dynamic of the Partnership.

Coordinating the Three Pillars of the Partnership

The achievement of a Euro-Mediterranean area of peace and stability does not solely depend on the politico-military dimension of the EMP. Politico-military cooperation can make a significant contribution to confidence and security-building and conflict prevention, and arrangements for crisis management are a necessary instrument of a Euro-Mediterranean security policy. But the events of '11 September' have demonstrated that even possession of the greatest military might on earth, including the most advanced technology, by itself cannot guarantee security. The comprehensive approach means that durable peace and effective long-term conflict prevention can only be achieved if cooperation in the field of security policy (the politico-military dimension) is accompanied by democratization, economic development and understanding between cultures. Lack of democratic institutions and the impossibility of expressing needs through regular political channels, the huge economic gap between both shores of the Mediterranean and, within the South, between governing elites and poor masses, the general lack of understanding between the Arab and Western worlds: these are the factors that create instability and must therefore be tackled along with military threats to security. Such is the nature of the comprehensive approach to security on which the Partnership is based. One can hope that, very gradually, a harmonization of values will occur among the 27 partners. In the – very – long run partnership could lead to the emergence of a Euro-Mediterranean 'security community': a group of states that, through extensive interaction and communication, have come to develop shared norms and values and a mutual expectation not to use coercion as a way of resolving disputes (Adler and Barnett, 1998).

A number of more specific reasons plead in favour of the comprehensive approach too. For example, the growing number of intra-state conflicts cannot be prevented by CSBMs, because there is only one state-actor involved. Internal balances must be restored to prevent such conflicts. The particular nature of civil-military relations in the Mediterranean constitutes another reason. In several of the partner countries the military play a significant role in politics. In such cases engaging in security cooperation unconditionally, without taking into account the nature of civil-military relations, could be contrary to the Partnership's objectives in the field of democratization and respect for human rights and fundamental freedoms.

Recognizing the comprehensive nature of security does not suffice: it must also be implemented through the policies of the Partnership. Firstly, on a general level, all external policies should aim to preserve and enhance those 'global public goods' which have to be sufficiently present in order to achieve stability: security, the rule of law, welfare, sustainable development, the environment. Secondly and more specifically, policies under all three baskets towards any given country or group of countries in the Mediterranean should be effectively aligned and integrated. In other words, economic policy *vis-à-vis* a partner state should be consistent with that country's respect for human rights and its willingness to engage in security cooperation; if necessary economic policy must be used as an instrument to promote the achievement of the objectives of the other baskets of the Partnership. Several measures are possible: economic pressure and the offering of benefits can be used as measures of crisis management; through different mechanisms economic support can be partly linked to increasing the budget for e.g. social policy and diminishing military expenditure, or to improving the human rights situation etc. (Aguirre, 1998, pp.30–31).

The economic instrument must be used carefully, in order to avoid alienating countries from the Partnership by putting exaggerated demands – chances of influencing countries' policies are much higher within the Partnership than outside it. But it must be clear that unconditional economic and financial support is out of the question; a minimal degree of conditionality must be introduced. The EU should also provide the proverbial carrot however. The Union can only hope to count on the goodwill of its partners regarding the security chapter of the Partnership, if Europe itself earnestly works for the achievement of a true free trade area as provided for in the economic basket (Tovias, 2001). As things are today, the economic partnership seems to benefit almost exclusively the EU side of the EMP, while the Southern partners are struggling with the difficulties implied by necessary, but painful economic reforms – this situation too cannot be allowed to continue. For EU action to earn legitimacy, the Union should devote effort to all 'global public goods' mentioned above.

Regional vs. Sub-Regional Approach

It has been suggested that adopting a sub-regional approach would be a way of advancing the security basket of the Partnership (Aliboni, 1998b, p.14). The idea is that in some specific sub-regions of the Mediterranean, the Maghreb or the Eastern Mediterranean e.g., circumstances are more favourable than in others or than in the Mediterranean as a whole, to advancing politico-military cooperation. A sub-regional approach would circumvent the stalemate in the peace process and would make it possible to take into account the specific needs and characteristics of each sub-region. However, such an approach denies the indivisibility of security in the Mediterranean. In the politico-military field, the most prominent issues, e.g. proliferation and violent islamism, are not confined to certain sub-regions, but concern the whole of the Mediterranean and therefore demand a global approach. By focussing on the conflict in the Middle East as the cause of the lack of progress of the Partnership's security dimension, the advocates of the sub-regional approach further ignore that in fact the obstacles also concern the whole of the Mediterranean. Closer security cooperation is blocked because of ongoing conflicts in the whole of the region, including in those sub-regions where conditions are supposed to be more favourable, and because of the distrust between both shores of the Mediterranean. For these reasons, continuation of the global Mediterranean approach is in order.

The global approach does not exclude the possibility of 'constructive abstention' or some sort of 'enhanced cooperation' however, which is indeed evident because of the voluntary character of the security partnership. It is quite likely that at first not all partner states will be willing to adopt a proposed CSBM. Another possibility is that a limited number of partner states, because they are members of another international framework, or because they are involved in a dispute, propose certain specific CSBMs. Turkey and Greece e.g. could agree on certain naval CSBMs in the context of their dispute over the Aegean, or Spain and Morocco could propose joint measures, or the members of the AMU. In such cases the partner states that are 'able and willing' should be allowed to advance and set an example, but the others should always have the possibility to join any arrangements at a later date, because the ultimate aim is a Euro-Mediterranean security partnership at 27. This is the view taken by the Commission, which recommended that

> partnership building measures should be implemented in a flexible way so that these questions could be addressed by a smaller number of partners wishing to advance more quickly, without prejudice to the principle that all Barcelona partners have the right to participate if they so wish.[1]

The EU should also support regional integration on the Southern shore, such as in the AMU and the Arab League, for integration is a CSBM in itself. Specific measures aimed at supporting the existing structures should be part of the Partnership's programme. This was recognized in the Valencia Action Plan, which expressed strong support for South-South integration, e.g. in the 'Agadir Process', comprising Morocco, Tunisia, Egypt and Jordan. The AMU, and other structures, can continue to attend the Euro-Mediterranean ministerial conferences with observer status. In these structures partners can consult each other and perhaps define common views on certain issues prior to Partnership meetings. This would at least partly redress the current situation, in which the EU can speak with a single voice while partners each act separately. The regional structures can however never be the Union's official interlocutor in the Partnership, unless they unite all partner states. If not and the Arab League were to represent its members in the EMP, this would leave Israel isolated, all the more so as Cyprus, Malta and Turkey will eventually become members of the Union. One option therefore is that Israel (and Turkey for that matter) should be allowed to join the Arab League, which should then change its name, so as to become a Middle Eastern regional organization (Said, 2000, pp.52–3).

The Partnership and the CFSP

The importance of the Mediterranean to the EU and the CFSP is evidenced by the adoption of the common strategy regarding the region. The CFSP, and the ESDP in particular, are still developing, and so is, for that reason, the Union's identity as an international actor. Yet its Mediterranean policy and the EMP which resulted from it can already be considered examples of what one hopes will constitute the specificity of this European identity in international politics. The comprehensive and multilateral approach to security and the whole concept of partnership as an instrument of foreign policy are indicators of a foreign policy which, far more than that of other actors, takes into account equity and cooperation between international actors, human rights and fundamental freedoms, economic development and understanding between cultures. The aim is long-term stability by working to promote the essential 'global public goods' – this amounts to a permanent effort at conflict prevention. Rather than being threat-based, this is a positive, objective-based approach. The use of coercion is not excluded, but only as an instrument of last resort, if all other means have failed. In the face of crises, the EU still more often than not fails to find consensus on the approach to adopt and thus fails to act decisively, but with regard to its long-term policies, the comprehensive approach does seem to be emerging as 'the' European way. This EU approach is comprehensive:

- by setting wide objectives that surpass the politico-military field;
- by combining instruments from the whole range of EU external policies;
- by addressing the security of regions and states as well as individuals (through promoting their access to 'global public goods');
- by including other actors in policy-making through cooperation and partnership;
- by its worldwide scope (which does not exclude a specific regional responsibility).

Because of the Union's interests in the Mediterranean, the EMP should be one of the priorities of the CFSP. The success of the Partnership and of EU policy on the Mediterranean in all fields is not only vital to assuring the Union's interests in its Southern periphery, it is also vital to the credibility of the CFSP as such. The Union cannot allow the EMP to fail, for that would at the same time be the failure of the CFSP. A stepped-up effort on the part of the EU with regard to conflict resolution and advancing politico-military cooperation through the ESDP is therefore in order.

Union policies in the Mediterranean once again reveal the well-known weaknesses of the CFSP. Foremost is the still prevailing declaratory character of Europe's foreign policy. Ambitious objectives and strong commitments often stay without implementation on the ground. The Union's verbal support to the UN efforts regarding Cyprus and the Western Sahara and its inactivity concerning Algeria are all cases in point. The second major point is the intergovernmental nature of the CFSP and the several weaknesses which this implies, notably a difficult decision-making process, because of the need for unanimity, and the tendency of the larger Member States to go solo. The latter is often the case when Member States have a special relationship with certain countries, mostly because of a former colonial link; the UK and Cyprus, France and Lebanon and Algeria are just two examples. Sometimes action by an individual Member State can have a positive outcome, but essentially solo action without consulting the fellow Member States undermines the CFSP. The same occurs when the larger Member States by keeping certain important decisions to a closed group create a 'directoire'. This happened e.g. prior to the informal European summit in Ghent on 19 October 2001, when the UK, France and Germany met separately to discuss the military implications of '11 September' and operations in Afghanistan, in spite of the obvious importance of these matters to all Member States and the links to the Union's Mediterranean policy. Organizational support for the CFSP at the level of the EU is still limited, which means that the successive Presidencies have to largely bear the burden. Substantial differences in capacity between the Presidencies thus have an influence on policy and long-term consistency is often lacking, as Presidencies concentrate the available means on policy areas in which they have a specific interest. Finally, the Union still lacks a security concept as strategic framework for its external policies. These and other deficiencies have to be overcome in order to increase the efficiency and efficacy of the CFSP as a whole.

Another matter to be addressed by the CFSP is the link between security in the Euro-Mediterranean area and other regions. This link is very apparent in the field of arms control and disarmament, where partners in the Middle East want to involve non-EMP countries because of their influence on their security situation. The link is also evident when it comes to hydrocarbons: the Mediterranean is a passageway for oil and gas from the Gulf and, ever more, from the Caucasus and Central Asia. The security situation of partners bordering these regions is obviously also determined by developments there. The Union should therefore also develop a security policy *vis-à-vis* these regions.

As the most powerful international actor within the EMP, the Union should assume the responsibility for advancing the establishment of a true and equitable Euro-Mediterranean security partnership. The Union should find the political will to take to the initiative. An active conflict resolution policy and the opening-up of the ESDP are the steps which the Union can set to effectively launch the security basket of the Partnership. On that basis a deepened security partnership can be established in the most efficient and efficacious way. Then of course the Mediterranean partners too should live up to the commitments which they took upon themselves in the Barcelona Declaration.

If the security dimension of the Partnership were enhanced on the basis of partners' participation in the ESDP, the EMP could function as a comprehensive system for conflict prevention and conflict resolution. The CSBMs implemented in the framework of the Partnership's security dimension, together with support for democratization and respect for human rights, and with, in the other baskets, economic and financial support and the project of a free trade area, and the dialogue between cultures and civil societies, would all serve to prevent conflicts.

Arrangements for the peaceful settlement of disputes and for crisis management would cover the field of conflict resolution. Programmes for post-conflict rehabilitation would be the end-piece. This ambitious programme demands firm political will on the side of both the EU and the Mediterranean partners. Opening up the ESDP would constitute a very clear signal though; partners' participation in the ESDP, going straight to the core of security cooperation, would be an excellent basis on which to found a comprehensive and equitable Euro-Mediterranean security partnership. The EU should therefore make the first step and open the doors of the ESDP.

Note

1   COM(2000)0497 final, 6 September 2000, Communication from the Commission to the Council and the European Parliament to prepare the fourth meeting of Euro-Mediterranean Foreign Ministers: reinvigorating the Barcelona Process.

Chapter 5

From Common Interests to Joint Actions

Introduction

This final chapter summarizes the main findings and recommendations of the book, in order to present a clear picture of the importance, the urgency and, above all, the feasibility of EU action in the field of Euro-Mediterranean security.

The Euro-Mediterranean Security Environment

If one looks at the Mediterranean through the lens of security, and of the politico-military dimension of security specifically, the obvious starting point of the analysis is the definition of the interests of the Union in the region. Which EU interests, in the economic, political and other fields, have to be safeguarded by a European security policy? One can then assess, on the basis of an analysis of the security situation in the Mediterranean, which are the potential threats to these European interests. The next question then is which should be the objectives of a security policy for the Mediterranean and which instruments should be applied to attain them. At the same time one needs to establish to which degree the Union's interests are shared by its Mediterranean partners, in order to determine whether these shared interests provide enough common ground to found a joint Euro-Mediterranean security policy upon, which is the assumption on which the EMP is based.

At a broader level, a similar approach should in fact be adopted in order to arrive at the definition of a security concept for the whole range of EU external policies. A security concept is a necessary policy framework for the daily running of the Union's external action, a framework which currently is lacking. Since the creation of the ESDP and the possibility of EU military operations which this implies especially, the need for a clearly defined security concept has become all the more urgent – the EU cannot go on building a military capacity without determining what to use it for.

When analyzing the security situation in the Mediterranean, it immediately becomes clear that it still is a rather unstable region. Unlike its stable Northern counterpart, the Southern shore is characterized by the existence of important disputes and even violent conflicts, the most important of which, the Israeli-Palestinian issue, has been clouding the region for decades. Another important characteristic of the Mediterranean, as compared to other regions in the world, is its very high degree of militarization, in the conventional field, but also in the field of proliferation of WMD. Regional integration on the other hand is very limited, certainly in the politico-military field, in which regard the existing international organizations in the area are particularly weak. Hence the absence of adequate mechanisms for conflict prevention and crisis management.

Yet contrary to the claims of certain alarmist observers, a closer look reveals that no direct security threat to the EU arises from the Mediterranean. This has actually been evident for a long time, but after '11 September' reconfirmation of this fact seems to be in order. The Southern states would not have the military and technological means to pose a serious threat to the Union and of course they would have to take into account the prospect of massive retaliation by superior military means. But above all, it would simply not be in the interest of any of them to commit an act of aggression against the Union, in view of the strong economic interdependence between both shores. For most if not all of the Mediterranean states the Union is the most important trading partner by far; conversely, the Union is highly dependent on the Mediterranean as a transport route for energy and on gas produced in the Mediterranean itself. Given the disputes dividing the countries of the region and the pre-eminence of contested authoritarian regimes, the risk of conflict is indeed foremost to be situated between and within the Mediterranean countries, not between the Union and the South. Such South-South conflicts can endanger the security of EU citizens abroad though, can jeopardize the Union's economic interests and do imply a certain risk of spill-over effects on Member States of the Union.

The threat of extremist islamism and terrorism to the EU should not be exaggerated either, even though after '11 September' it is tempting to consider this the main security threat. First of all, one should absolutely avoid to equate islamism and terrorism. Islamist movements seeking to obtain their goals through political action must be regarded as regular political actors, whether one agrees with their political programme or not. Secondly, islamist movements in the first place have a domestic agenda, directed against the ruling regimes in the South; this also holds true for extremist islamist factions which revert to violence as a way of achieving their objectives. So the Union is not their target, all the more so because of its even-handed policies with regard to the Middle East and the Arab and Muslim world in general, which are very much appreciated in the South. Again, it are the Southern countries themselves that run by far the greatest risk, which is exactly why they have demanded the inclusion of anti-terrorist measures in the EMP from the beginning.

Of course '11 September' presents an exception in that a Western country was attacked directly. In the Arab and Muslim world the US are regarded as the cornerstone of Israel's position in the Middle East; through their uninterrupted and almost unconditional support for the latter country the US block the settlement of the Israeli-Palestinian conflict. This American policy has at least created a breeding ground for extremism, making it possible to recruit suicide attackers. The US' almost exclusively military reaction to the events and their hardened attitude regarding the conflict in the Middle East, where they allowed the Sharon government a free hand, have reinforced anti-American feelings. Needless to say, the US military intervention in Iraq, justified by an unproved link with international terrorism and possession of WMD, has alienated large parts of worldwide public opinion. The EU adopted a very different attitude however. Wanting to avoid the impression of a 'clash of civilizations' at all costs, the Union called for a broad approach to the now omnipresent 'war on terrorism', an approach stressing the underlying causes of terrorism: bleak poverty and harsh repression. The EU as such also did not support military action as a way of disarming Iraq. Once again the Union does not come into the picture as a potential target of islamist terrorism.

Next to the ongoing disputes and conflicts, the basic causes of instability in the Mediterranean are extreme poverty and a lack of democratic institutions, which undermine the legitimacy of existing regimes, often of a very authoritarian nature, and which create a breeding ground for extremism of all kinds. A gap exists, between governing elites and poor masses within the partner countries, and between the rich Northern and the underdeveloped Southern shores of the Mediterranean. Such gaps between 'haves' and 'have-nots' in terms of access to essential 'global public goods' are detrimental to the stability of the international system.

A Comprehensive Approach to Security

This security environment demands a comprehensive approach: a permanent and structural effort at long-term stabilisation by preserving and strengthening those 'global public goods' that are vital to international stability: security, the rule of law, welfare, sustainable development, the environment. This can only be achieved through multilateral cooperation and partnership. Promotion of these 'global public goods' is the overall objective for the whole range of EU external policies, but each according to its own rationale and dynamic, so that 'securitization' of policy fields other than the politico-military is avoided. Working towards 'global public goods' is a positive agenda that will earn the Union the legitimacy that is needed when more forceful external action is required; this focus on positive objectives rather than threats allows the security dilemma to be avoided. The comprehensive approach has a global scope: in a globalised world, the security of the Union is inseparably linked to the stability of the international system as such, so global objectives should be set. But at the same time the Union does have a specific responsibility with regard to its periphery, both because factors of insecurity originating here will have a more direct impact on the Union and because as the nearby actor with the means at hand the Union has a duty.

But: the need for a comprehensive approach should not lead to the politico-military dimension being forgotten. In a region that is troubled by disputes and even armed conflicts and that faces militarization and proliferation, a politico-military contribution to the comprehensive approach is vital:

- in order to ensure that the Union remains free from direct security threats;

- in order to resolve the ongoing conflicts and disputes in the region, which greatly hinder if not paralyze Euro-Mediterranean cooperation in all fields;
- in order to prevent conflicts between or within Mediterranean states, which can jeopardize the Union's economic interests and the security of European citizens abroad and which could imply spill-over effects to Member States.

These objectives demand an active security policy on the part of the EU. On the one hand politico-military measures of conflict prevention are needed, a process of confidence and security-building, which in view of the militarization of the region should give special attention to arms control, disarmament and non-proliferation. On the other hand mechanisms are required for the resolution of ongoing and possible future conflicts, including arrangements for crisis management and peaceful settlement of disputes. Arrangements for post-conflict rehabilitation should complete the picture.

The foundation for a joint Euro-Mediterranean policy in these fields exists: the common economic interests of both shores. In the economic field both shores are very much mutually dependent and therefore have a strong common interest in maintaining peace and stability. The common economic interests outweigh by far the military issues that could potentially arise between North and South. A security policy safeguarding the Union's interests, which is of course the essential objective of any policy, could thus at the same time serve the interests of the Mediterranean partners. A joint policy does indeed seem to be the only one with any chance of success. A unilateral European security policy, based on the notions of power projection and intervention, would be politically unacceptable to partners and would certainly lead to an antagonization of North-South relations.

Standstill of the EMP

Having established the need for a politico-military dimension to the Union's Mediterranean policy and the objectives which it should achieve, one can then look at actual EU policy. Policies towards the region as a whole, through the political and security basket of the EMP, should be considered, as well as policies towards specific conflicts and disputes. One can then assess the efficacy of EU policy in safeguarding the Union's interests and one can establish whether the Union has effectively built on the existence of common interests to initiate truly joint Euro-Mediterranean policies.

It was indeed the need for a Mediterranean security policy that in 1995 resulted in the creation of the EMP. The Union's Southern Member States, which were most concerned by the new-found prominence of Mediterranean security issues after the end of the Cold War, were the driving forces behind this initiative. Their motivations were very pragmatic: fearing to be marginalized in a Union expanding eastward, they demanded an enhanced Mediterranean initiative in order to balance off the Union's extensive involvement in Central and Eastern Europe. But their lobbying did lead to the launching of a comprehensive partnership with the

Mediterranean, replacing the bilateral and almost exclusively economic policies which had governed European relations with the region up until then. The Barcelona Declaration includes far-reaching principles and ambitious objectives in the politico-military field, mainly with regard to conflict prevention; it provides *inter alia*, for an extensive system of CSBMs and substantial measures with regard to arms control, disarmament and non-proliferation. The projected Euro-Mediterranean Charter for Peace and Stability would add to this an institutionalized political dialogue and arrangements for crisis management and post-conflict peace-building. These objectives are reconfirmed in the Union's Common Strategy for the Mediterranean, which outlines EU goals regarding the region and the basic strategy to achieve them, through the EMP. The overall objective is the creation of a Mediterranean area of peace and stability. The important common economic interests of the Union and the Mediterranean countries were translated into an ambitious economic and financial partnership with the ultimate aim of establishing a Mediterranean free trade area by 2010. The Partnership is completed by a social, cultural and human affairs basket.

With the take-off of the EMP, the Union abandoned the exclusive economic focus of its Mediterranean policy; for the first time the politico-military field was included as an issue to be covered by Euro-Mediterranean cooperation. Given the neglect for Mediterranean security issues which had prevailed during the Cold War and in view of the early stage of development of the CFSP at that time, this was a very ambitious and significant step indeed. The EMP embodies the innovative comprehensive approach to security that is outlined above. The Mediterranean states are considered to be partners for the Union's security policy, rather than its objects.

However, this innovative approach has not yet materialized on the ground, because the political and security partnership was paralyzed and until today has seen very little implementation of partners' commitments. Only a very small number of CSBMs with a rather limited scope have been adopted, which do not come even close to realizing the ambitious undertakings in the Barcelona Declaration. The elaboration of the Charter was a significant step, which is most noteworthy for complementing the Barcelona Declaration by providing for an enhanced political dialogue and by adding the establishment of arrangements for crisis management and post-conflict rehabilitation to the Partnership's objectives. But time and again the approval of the Charter has been postponed, so that it still is only an informal working document, to be formally adopted when political circumstances are more favourable. Implementation of the Partnership's other baskets is far from optimal as well, although the economic and financial partnership has progressed more than the others. The three pillars are, to some degree at least, up and running, so in this sense the Union is somehow bringing its comprehensive approach to security into practice: the politico-military issues on the Euro-Mediterranean agenda are integrated into a much broader network of multilateral and bilateral relations. Economic and financial cooperation are the main focus of the Partnership; indeed, given the deplorable lack of implementation of the security basket, it could hardly be otherwise. For in spite of the Union's intentions, it is as yet unable to give body to the security partnership. Political dialogue remained at a very low level and no joint Euro-Mediterranean security policy could be defined, let alone implemented. The few CSBMs which were adopted are the only concrete achievements so far; a general security policy for the area still has to follow. The high expectations of the Mediterranean partners were thus disappointed.

Two main causes can be discerned for the failure of a fully-fledged Euro-Mediterranean security partnership to materialize. The first reason is to be found in the Union's inefficacious policy or often even the lack of policy regarding the different disputes and ongoing conflicts in the region. First and foremost, Euro-Mediterranean cooperation is blocked by the enduring conflict in the Middle East. As long as no durable and equitable settlement has been found for the persisting Arab-Israeli conflict, there is no basis for confidence between partners and hence no willingness to engage in a process of CSBMs, let alone to discuss further security cooperation, such as joint mechanisms for crisis management or arms control, disarmament and non-proliferation schemes.

The launching of the Partnership was possible precisely because of the positive spirit generated by the Oslo process – when this died, the spirit of cooperation in the EMP more or less died as well. In order to avoid the conflict in the Middle East from blocking the functioning of the Partnership, the two were in fact formally separated from the beginning, but practice has proved that this unrealistic separation cannot be maintained. One cannot hope to exclude one of the participants' most important security concerns from the discussions if one wants to create a genuine security partnership. Every single one of the Euro-Mediterranean Ministerial Conferences which followed Barcelona was clouded by the successive crises in the Middle East, making progress in the politico-military field all but impossible. All partners did continue their participation in the EMP, which makes it into the only multilateral forum where Israel and the Arab countries are still interacting and which demonstrates partners' belief in the inherent value of the Partnership, but this situation cannot go on indefinitely. That the Partnership lived through all of the crises in the Middle East is a positive fact, but it can hardly be called a real achievement. In the end, the Partnership will not survive if the peace process is not brought to a good end and effective measures for security cooperation can be adopted – dialogue just for the sake of dialogue is not enough to continue the EMP.

What the Union lacks is an active conflict resolution policy. Since the Partnership itself is not equipped to deal with current conflicts, as precisely because of them no such far-reaching security mechanisms were feasible, the Union itself should take the lead in finding a settlement for the ongoing conflicts in the Mediterranean. Arab countries expect the Union to translate its even-handed policy with regard to the Middle East conflict, which is apparent from the Union's successive CFSP statements, into actions on the ground and reproach the Union with an all too passive attitude, resulting in under-representation of its views and thus of the Palestinian interests in the peace process. This is of course also due to the American unwillingness to allow the EU to act as mediator on an equal basis and also to plain passivity on the part of the US, especially after '11 September', when the Union ended up as the only international actor still actively trying to revive the peace process. Without a joint European-American effort no progress is possible. The conflict in the Middle East is of course the most prominent, and the one in which the EU plays the most active role, but the same goes for the other ongoing conflicts and disputes in the Mediterranean: Western Sahara, Algeria, Cyprus, the Aegean. With regard to these equally urgent issues the Union has adopted a much more passive attitude, in spite of the potentially very efficacious instruments – economic relations and the enlargement process offer ample 'sticks and carrots' – which it has at its disposal. A settlement of these issues must be achieved or significant progress must at least be made, before the Euro-Mediterranean security partnership can be substantially advanced: up to the Union to take the initiative.

The second major reason for the stagnation of the EMP is that all too often relations between partners, especially in the field of security, are overshadowed by a lack of trust, both between the Northern and Southern shores and, because of the ongoing disputes and conflicts, between the Southern states themselves. In the perception of the partners, the EU in the first place still sees them as a source of security threats rather than as partners for security cooperation. They therefore feel that the Union puts far too much emphasis on the politico-military dimension of the EMP, while they themselves attach far more importance to the full implementation of the economic and financial partnership, which they feel the Union is reluctant to do. Having in mind the Gulf War and the intervention in Kosovo, the partners fear to become the object of what they deem to be 'Western interventionism'. In the mid-1990s the formation of two multinational military units by the Union's Southern Member States, EUROFOR and EUROMARFOR, was already viewed with much suspicion. As they were not involved, partners considered these units to be mainly directed against them. The development of the ESDP and the creation of a rapid reaction force for the EU are now viewed in the same light. The 2003 Iraq crisis only added to partners' suspicions.

In combination with the fact that, due to the paralysis caused mainly by the Middle East conflict, the security basket of the Partnership has not really come off the ground, which implies that the partnership approach to security which was envisaged by the Barcelona Declaration has not materialized, it is understandable that partners are tempted all too easily to view the development of the ESDP as a return on the part of the Union to the earlier 'interventionist' logic and the abandonment of the cooperative security concept. In the wake of '11 September' the danger is of course that mutual distrust rises even more and that relations will be dominated by a perception of antagonism. One should also take into account that contrary to the Member States of the EU, partners have limited experience with CSBMs, which means that they are more reluctant to engage in a process of security cooperation than on reasonable grounds one might perhaps expect. The dominance of the European side within the different bodies of the Partnership is another factor explaining unease with the EMP. The Partnership lacks a sense of shared ownership; partners feel they have insufficient influence on the agenda of the Partnership and have to undergo the desiderata of the Union. Particularly with regard to the political and security basket, this situation creates a lack of confidence, which is a necessary prerequisite for enhanced security cooperation.

The Way Ahead

In order to overcome these obstacles to Euro-Mediterranean security cooperation, the EU should in the first place wage an active conflict resolution policy towards all ongoing conflicts and disputes in the area.

With regard to the Middle East peace process, the EU should resolutely claim its role as co-sponsor alongside the US. A greater involvement of the Union would provide substantial added value to the peace process. With the US, which almost unconditionally support Israel, as only mediator, the Israeli side is over-represented; Washington's in fact often passive attitude leaves Israel a free hand. The label of anti-terrorism, so popular with governments worldwide since '11 September', should not be abused as an excuse not to engage in dialogue with the Palestinians. Only negotiations can lead to a settlement; the alternative is that extremists gain the upper hand on both sides – in so far as that is not yet already the case. With the EU as additional mediator the interests of both sides would be equally represented. The most important – very practical – reason why the Union is needed as mediator is that, whereas the US have leverage on Israel, the Union has far more leverage on the Palestinian side. Both Israel and the Palestinian Authority depend on the vital support of Washington and Brussels respectively. Therefore a joint EU-US effort, making effective use of their leverage on the respective parties to pressurize them into returning to the negotiating table, is the only way that can lead to a settlement.

In the Eastern Mediterranean as well the EU should assume responsibility and should actively work towards a settlement of the disputes between Greece, Turkey and the two Cypriot communities. The central instrument which the Union can apply to that end is the accession process. Given the strong wish of applicant states Turkey and Cyprus to join the Union, this would indeed be a very efficacious instrument. But on itself the prospect of membership and the conditions for accession imposed by the Union are insufficient to incite the parties to achieve a settlement of the outstanding disputes. The resuming of negotiations on Cyprus was indeed attributed to the pressure generated by the accession process, but is certainly not due to active EU involvement. It really seems that this breakthrough could have been achieved much earlier if the Union had made more effective use of the desire for membership of the parties. By any means, the Union should play a much more active part now that negotiations are once again underway, instead of limiting itself to verbal support for the efforts of the UN. The direct involvement of one Member State and two applicant states in interrelated disputes over Cyprus and the Aegean which have led to violent incidents in the past and which on one occasion at least threatened to escalate into a full-scale war, demand an urgent and substantial EU contribution to the efforts to find a settlement.

EU security policy towards North Africa too has so far been very passive. It seems rather that the Union is not considering adopting a clear position regarding the ongoing violence in Algeria as long as the steady supply of gas is assured and their is no spill-over of the violence to neighbouring countries. By waging this overly pragmatic policy of containment the Union *de facto* supports the military regime and provides it with international legitimacy, in spite of now undeniable evidence of its implication in the killings. The conclusion of a Euro-Mediterranean Association Agreement with Algeria is the ultimate proof of the Union's complete lack of regard for conditionality of its support to the country. Union policy regarding the Western Sahara is characterized by the same – again all too – pragmatic approach: the Union limits itself to verbally supporting UN actions to find a settlement, but essentially does not trouble the Moroccan government in any way concerning the matter. In its actual behaviour towards Morocco the Union even goes so far as to de facto recognize its claims on Western Sahara. The other North African countries are not really troubled by any questions regarding their respect for the principles which they committed to in the Barcelona Declaration either. Only with regard to Libya does the Union – rightfully – adopt a stronger attitude, in order to pressurize the regime into conforming to internationally accepted principles, as a first step on the way to its integration into the EMP. The Union should at least have a critical dialogue with the regimes in question and should carefully make use of the economic instrument to influence their policies. Union policy towards North Africa demonstrates the lack of coordination between the three pillars of the Partnership: economic and financial support are provided under the EMP's second basket without taking into account compliance with the political and security commitments of the first pillar. The Union thus undermines the comprehensive approach to security, by ignoring respect for human rights and democratization as factors of security and stability.

A significant effort at conflict resolution on the side of the EU must be the first step, in order to pave the way for enhanced security cooperation. At the same time, the Union could open up the ESDP for participation by all Mediterranean partners, along the same lines as it is now open to the candidates for accession, to the non-EU European members of NATO and even to Russia and Ukraine. Joint participation in the Union's military structures would be a very powerful CSBM, both between the Northern and Southern shores and, because of the multilateral character of the ESDP, among the Southern states themselves. Involving the Mediterranean partners would dissipate their distrust towards the development of the ESDP. It would thus provide an answer to the second major cause for the Partnership's stagnation: the continuing distrust between North and South. At the same time, on the basis of partners' participation in the ESDP, a very close, institutionalized Euro-Mediterranean security dialogue could be constructed, from expert to ministerial level, covering all stages of policy-making, from preparation of policy to its implementation. Thus a truly joint Euro-Mediterranean security policy could be achieved. Indeed, such an effectively cooperative policy would be the only one with a chance of success, for unilateral European actions would not be acceptable to the partners, which would quickly reject any initiative bearing only the semblance of 'interventionism'. Opening up the ESDP is a readily available instrument, which demands only political will on the side of the EU, but which would certainly constitute a very strong signal of trust and of the Union's desire for cooperation rather than confrontation with its Mediterranean partners.

The enhanced security dialogue which can be built on the foundation of the ESDP could be optimized by the establishment of a permanent council at ambassadorial level within the first basket of the Partnership, to function as a permanent body for security dialogue with sufficient authority to make policy in the field of Euro-Mediterranean security. Such a permanent council ought to be supported by a communications network and bodies such as a situation centre and a conflict prevention centre, which are to provide the necessary capacity to monitor events, to give early warning and to manage the implementation of all CSBMs and cooperation activities. These bodies can be part of an EMP secretariat, the creation of which is necessary in order to make possible truly joint management of the activities of the Partnership by all 27 partners; it would also promote coordination and integration of policies under all three baskets of the EMP, which currently is very limited. The appointment of a secretary general from one of the Mediterranean partners would crown this construction, which should be sufficient to create a sense of shared ownership. Thus the framework would be created in which further CSBMs could be adopted, starting with transparency measures and with the ultimate aim of establishing Euro-Mediterranean arrangements for crisis management. The same gradual approach could be adopted in the field of arms control, disarmament and non-proliferation.

A European security policy towards the Mediterranean demands a difficult balancing act of the Union. On the one hand the Union must absolutely avoid that relations with the Mediterranean countries are dominated by 'hard' security issues and distrust. The ample attention devoted in EU external policies to human rights, democratization, economic development, dialogue between cultures etc. is exactly one of the merits of the Union and certainly of the EMP. On the other hand the Union's interests in the Mediterranean do demand a policy on 'hard' security in the area, which cannot be excluded from the further development of the CFSP and the ESDP. The existence of common interests however, shared by all partners, provides the basis on which a common Euro-Mediterranean security policy can be founded. By opening up the ESDP to its Mediterranean partners and building enhanced security cooperation on that basis, the Union can achieve the creation of an equitable Euro-Mediterranean security partnership. In order to make this possible, a substantial effort in the field of conflict resolution is needed. The comprehensive approach to security which can then be implemented seems to be the only way to realize the objective of a Mediterranean area of peace and stability.

Bibliography

Adler, E. (2000), *A Mediterranean Canon and an Israeli Prelude to Long Term Peace*, Jean Monnet Working Paper in Comparative and International Politics No. 34.

Adler, E. and Barnett, M. (1998), *Security Communities*, Cambridge, Cambridge University Press.

Agapiou–Josephides, K. (1996), 'La Perspective de l'Adhésion de Chypre à l'Union Européenne', *Law and European Affairs – Revue des Affaires Européennes*, Vol. 6(4), pp. 353–7.

Agata, P.S. (1994), 'Le rôle de la Ligue arabe', in Centre d'Études et de Recherches Internationales et Communautaires (ed.), *La Méditerranée: Espace de Coordination?*, Economica, Paris, pp. 95–106.

Agha, H.J. (1994), 'The Middle East and Europe: the post-Cold War Climate', in H. Miall (ed.), *Redefining Europe. New patterns of Conflict and Cooperation*, Pinter, London, pp. 241–52.

Agha, H.J. (1995), 'Islamic Fundamentalism and its Image in the Western Media', Al-Ahram Center for Political and Strategic Studies Strategic Papers, Vol. 4(25), pp. 1–12.

Aguirre, M. (1998), 'The Limits of Conflict Prevention and the Mediterranean Case', *Mediterranean Politics*, Vol. 3(3), pp. 21–37.

Akagül, D. (1998), 'Le Cinquième Élargissement de l'Union Européenne et la Question de la Candidature Turque. La Fin d'un Cycle, mais Quelles Perspectives?', *Revue du Marché Commun et de l'Union Européenne*, Vol. 41(419), pp. 359–69.

Akarcali, B. (1996), 'L'Union Douanière et la Turquie', *Law and European Affairs - Revue des Affaires Européennes*, Vol. 6(4), pp. 350–352.

Akgönenç, O. (1997), 'Mutual Security Expectations in the Eastern Mediterranean Region', Foreign Policy, Vol. 21(1–2), pp. 1–6.

Akkaya, Ç. (1999), 'Die EU-Türkei-Beziehungen sowie die Rolle der Türkei als besonderer Faktor für die Außenbeziehungen der EU zu Zentralasien und zum Nahen Osten', in W. Zippel (ed.), *Die Mittelmeerpolitik der EU*, Nomos, Baden-Baden, pp. 115–32.

Algieri, F. (1996), 'In Need of a Comprehensive Approach: the European Union and Possible External Security Challenges', in F. Algieri, J. Janning and D. Rumberg (eds.), *Managing Security in Europe. The European Union and the Challenge of Enlargement*, Bertelsmann, Gütersloh, pp. 189–207.

Ali, M.A.J. (1994), 'Arms Control and Confidence Building Measures in the Middle East', in F. Tanner (ed.), *Arms Control, Confidence Building and Security Cooperation in the Mediterranean, North Africa and the Middle East*, Mediterranean Academy of Diplomatic Studies, Malta, pp. 1–9.

Aliboni, R. (1991), *European Security across the Mediterranean*, Chaillot Paper No. 2, WEU Institute for Security Studies, Paris.

Aliboni, R. (1993), 'Instability South of the Mediterranean: Recommendations for the West', The International Spectator, Vol. 28(3) pp. 87–96.

Aliboni, R. (1994), 'Factors Affecting Mediterranean Security', in F. Tanner (ed.), *Arms Control, Confidence Building and Security Cooperation in the Mediterranean, North Africa and the Middle East*, Mediterranean Academy of Diplomatic Studies, Malta, pp. 10–12.

Aliboni, R. (1995), 'Southern Europe and the United States: the community approach', in J.W. Holmes (ed.), *Maelstrom. The United States, Southern Europe and the Challenges of the Mediterranean*, The World Peace Foundation, Cambridge (MA), pp. 169–85.

Aliboni, R. (1996), 'Collective Political Cooperation in the Mediterranean', in R. Aliboni, G. Joffé and T. Niblock (eds.), *Security Challenges in the Mediterranean Region*, Frank Cass, London, pp. 51–64.

Aliboni, R. (1998a), 'Confidence-Building, Conflict Prevention and Arms Control in the Euro-Mediterranean Partnership', *Perceptions*, Vol. 2(4), pp. 1–6.

Aliboni, R. (1998b), 'Re-Setting the Euro-Mediterranean Security Agenda', *The International Spectator*, Vol. 33(4), pp. 11–15.

Aliboni, R. (1999a), *Un Caso di Conflitto Mediterraneo, l'Algeria e il Ruolo Politico dell'Islam*, lecture in the Residenza Universitaria A. Lamaro – E. Pozzani, Rome 30 June.

Aliboni, R. (1999b), *NATO and the Mediterranean: Energy Risks*, paper presented at the conference on 'Transatlantic Approaches to the Mediterranean. Impact of the new NATO on North and South perspectives', Washington DC, 24–25 May.

Aliboni, R. (1999c), 'European Union Security Perceptions and Policies towards the Mediterranean', in S.J. Blank (ed.), *Mediterranean Security into the Coming Millennium*, US Army War College, Carlisle (PA), pp. 125–41.

Aliboni, R. (1999d), *The Mediterranean and the New NATO. The European Vision: Political and Security Issues*, paper presented at the conference on 'Transatlantic Approaches to the Mediterranean. Impact of the new NATO on North and South perspectives', Washington DC, 24–25 May.

Aliboni, R. (1999e), 'Italy and the Mediterranean in the 1990s', in S. Stavridis, T. Couloumbis, T. Veremis and N. Waites (eds.), *The Foreign Policies of the European Union's Mediterranean States and Applicant Countries in the 1990s*, Macmillan, London, pp. 73–97.

Aliboni, R. (2000a), *Including Lybia? EU, Arab World and the US*, paper presented at the conference on 'Lybia: Current Relations and Future Prospects', Washington DC, 25 February.

Aliboni, R. (2000b), *Building Blocks for the Euro-Mediterranean Charter on Peace and Stability*, Euromesco Paper.

Aliboni, R. (2001), *The Role of International Organizations in the Mediterranean*, Hellenic Foundation for European and Foreign Policy Occasional Papers No. 2.

Aliboni, R. (2002), *Working Group I – First Year Report: Security and Common Ground in the Euro-Med Partnership*, EuroMeSCo report.

Allen, D. and Smith, M. (1984), 'Europe, the United States and the Arab-Israeli Conflict', in D. Allen and A. Pijpers (eds.), *European Foreign Policy-Making and the Arab-Israeli Conflict*, Martinus Nijhoff, Den Haag, pp. 187–210.

Alpher, J. (1998), 'The Political Role of the European Union in the Arab-Israeli Peace Process: an Israeli Perspective', *The International Spectator*, Vol. 33(4), pp. 77–86.

Alpher, J. (2000), 'The Political Role of the EU in the Middle East: Israeli Aspirations', in S. Behrendt and C.-P. Hanelt (eds.), *Bound to Cooperate – Europe and the Middle East*, Bertelsmann, Gütersloh, pp.193–208.

Aly, A.M.S. (1996), 'The Shattered Consensus – Arab Perceptions of Security', *The International Spectator*, Vol. 31 (4), pp. 23–52.

Anciaux, R. (1997), *Vers un Nouvel Ordre Régional au Moyen-Orient?*, L'Harmattan, Paris.

Anderson, E. and Fenech, D. (1994), 'New Dimensions in Mediterranean Security', in R. Gillespie (ed.), *Mediterranean Politics*, Pinter, London, pp. 9–21.

Antoniou, A. (1999), 'A Political Economist's View of the Recent Developments in Cyprus', in S. Baier-Allen (ed.), *Looking into the Future of Cyprus-EU Relations*, Nomos, Baden-Baden, pp. 105–13.

Apostolides, K. (1998), *Cyprus and the enlargement of the European Union*, Jean Monnet Working Paper in Comparative and International Politics No. 15.
Aronson, G. (1996), *Arms Control and Proliferation in the Middle East*, Foundation for Middle East Peace Special Report.
Asmus, R.D., Larrabee, S.F., Lesser, I.O. (1996), 'Mediterranean Security: New Challenges, New Tasks', *NATO Review*, Vol. 44(3), pp. 25–31.
Athanassopoulou, E. (1997), 'Blessing in Disguise? The Imia Crisis and Turkish-Greek Relations', *Mediterranean Politics*, Vol. 2(3), pp. 76–101.
Attina, F. (2001a), 'Partnership and Security: some Theoretical and Empirical reasons for Positive Developments in the Euro-Mediterranean Area', in F. Attina, S. Stavridis (eds.), *The Barcelona Process and Euro-Mediterranean Issues from Stuttgart to Marseille*, Giuffrè, Milan, pp. 17–50.
Attina, F. (2001b), 'Partnership-Building', in F. Attina, S. Stavridis (eds.), *The Barcelona Process and Euro-Mediterranean Issues from Stuttgart to Marseille*, Giuffrè, Milan, pp. 269–87.
Avran, I. (2000), 'Europe: vers un Rôle Politique Effectif au Proche-Orient?', in J.-P. Chagnollaud, R. Dhoquois-Cohen and B. Ravenel (eds.), *Palestiniens et Israéliens: le Moment de Vérité*, L'Harmattan, Paris, pp. 189–205.
Axt, H.-J. (1997), 'Cyprus on the Treshold to the European Union: Preconditions, Implications and Scenarios', in H.-J. Axt and H. Brey (eds.), *Cyprus and the European Union. New Chances for Solving an Old Conflict?*, Südosteuropa-Gesellschaft, München, pp. 170–96.
Axt, H.-J. (1999), 'Cyprus and the EU: Avoiding Wishful Thinking and Designing German Foreign Policy', in S. Baier-Allen (ed.), *Looking into the Future of Cyprus-EU Relations*, Nomos, Baden-Baden, pp. 213–29.
Aybet, G. (1999), 'Turkey and European Institutions', *The International Spectator*, Vol. 34(1), pp. 103–10.
Aykan, M.B. (1999), 'The Turkish-Syrian Crisis of October 1998: a Turkish View', *Middle East Policy*, Vol. 6(4) pp. 174–91.
Badini, A. (1995), 'Efforts at Mediterranean Cooperation', in J. W. Holmes (ed.), *Maelstrom. The United States, Southern Europe and the Challenges of the Mediterranean*, The World Peace Foundation, Cambridge (MA), pp. 103–24.
Bagci, H. (1997), 'Cyprus: Accession to the European Union – a Turkish View', in H.-J. Axt and H. Brey (eds.), *Cyprus and the European Union. New Chances for Solving an Old Conflict?*, Südosteuropa-Gesellschaft, München, pp. 159–69.
Bagci, H. (1999), 'Turkish Reactions to the EU Approach', in S. Baier-Allen (ed.), *Looking into the Future of Cyprus-EU Relations*, Nomos, Baden-Baden, pp. 39–50.
Baier-Allen, S. (1999a), 'Assessing the Impact of the EU Accession Process on the Cyprus Conflict: Incentive for Conflict Resolution?', in S. Baier-Allen (ed.), *Looking into the Future of Cyprus-EU Relations*, Nomos, Baden-Baden, pp. 171–86.
Baier-Allen, S. (1999b), 'Conflict Prevention through Development Cooperation: the EU Approach in the Maghreb', in P. Cross and G. Rasamoelina (eds.), *Conflict Prevention Policy of the European Union. Recent Engagements, Future Instruments*, Nomos, Baden-Baden, pp. 32–47.
Balta, P. (1997), 'La Méditerranée en tant que Zone de Conflits', *Revista CIDOB d'Afers Internacionals*, Vol. 16(37), pp. 1–9.
Baquer, M.A. (1997), '¿Existe una Coherencia Estratégica entre los Países del Sur?', *Revista CIDOB d'Afers Internacionals*, Vol. 16(38–39), pp. 1–7.
Barbé, E. (1995), 'En Busca de la Cooperación y la Seguridad en el Mediterráneo o el "Espíritu de Barcelona"', *Anuario Internacional CIDOB*, Vol. 7, pp. 1–9.
Barbé, E. (1996), 'The Barcelona Conference: Launching Pad of a Process', *Mediterranean Politics*, Vol. 1(1), pp. 25–42.

Barbé, E. (1998), Turbulencia en el Mediterráneo: Desafíos Globales, Conflictos Locales y Espacios Regionales, Centre for Euro-Mediterranean Studies Research Paper No. 1, University of Reading.

Barbé, E. and Izquierdo, F. (1997), 'Present and Future of Joint Actions for the Mediterranean Region', in M. Holland (ed.), *Common Foreign and Security Policy. The Record and Reforms*, Pinter, London, pp. 120–135.

Bar-On, H. (1999), 'Israel and its Troubled Mediterranean Neighbours', in N.A. Stavrou (ed.), *Mediterranean Security at the Crossroads: a Reader*, Duke University Press, Durham (N. Ca.), pp. 244–60.

Barre, R. (1993), 'La Coopération Euro-Maghrébine, une Grande Chance pour l'Europe', *Confluences Méditerranée*, Vol. 3(7), pp. 1–5.

Basbous, A. (1999), 'La Crise Algérienne et l'Union Européenne', in P. Cross and G. Rasamoelina (eds.), *Conflict Prevention Policy of the European Union. Recent Engagements, Future Instruments*, Nomos, Baden-Baden, pp. 25–31.

Baudin, P. (1990), 'La Méditerranée, Partenaire ou Enjeu?', *Revue du Marché Commun*, Vol. 33(335), pp. 187–96.

Ben Ali, D. (1996), 'La Sécurité dans le Bassin Méditerranéen: Évolution en Afrique du Nord et Impact sur la Région', in Defence Studies Centre (ed.), *Proceedings. La Coopération Euro-Méditerranéenne: Hypothèses de Base et Résultats*, Royal Defence College, Brussels, pp. 47–54.

Ben-Ami, S. (1995), 'Regionales Gleichgewicht. Der Friedensprozeß aus Israelischer Sicht', *Internationale Politik*, Vol. 50(7), pp. 9–15.

Ben-Ami, S. (1998), 'Europa y el Conflicto de Oriente Próximo', *Política Exterior*, Vol. 66(12), pp. 97–111.

Ben Haha, Y. (2001), 'Euro-Mediterranean Partnership: Implementation and Prospects', in I. Bourloyannis-Tsangaridis (ed.), *Development of Euro-Mediterranean Relations. Perspectives and Problems*, Hellenic Foundation for European and Foreign Policy Occasional Paper No. 1, pp. 28–35.

Bentsur, E. (1994), 'Israel's Vision on the Goals and Principles of the Regional Security and Arms Control Process', in F. Tanner (ed.), *Arms Control, Confidence Building and Security Cooperation in the Mediterranean, North Africa and the Middle East*, Mediterranean Academy of Diplomatic Studies, Malta, pp. 1–4.

Benyamina, A. (1998), 'Foreign Interference in the Situation in Algeria: the Algerian Government's Position', *Cambridge Review of International Affairs*, Vol. 11(2), pp. 184–95.

Bertrand, G. (2000), 'L'Adhésion de Cypre à l'Union Européenne: un Déblocage du Conflit par le Bas?', in S. Saurugger (ed.), *L'Élargissement de l'Union européenne ou la Construction d'un Objet Politique Problématisé*, l'Harmattan, Paris, pp. 118–35.

Biad, A. (1996), 'Security and Cooperation in the Mediterranean: a Southern Viewpoint', in R. Aliboni, G. Joffé and T. Niblock (eds.), *Security Challenges in the Mediterranean Region*, Frank Cass, London, pp. 41–9.

Biad, A. (1997), 'Les Possibilités du Désarmement en Méditerranée', in A. Marquina (ed.), *Les Élites et le Processus de Changement dans la Méditerranée*, Stradémed, Toulon, pp. 1–16.

Biad, A. (1998), 'L'Algérie et la Méditerranée: Perception de Vulnerabilité et Besoin de Coopération', in A. Marquina (ed.), *Perceptions Mutuelles dans la Méditerranée. Unité et Diversité*, Publisud, Paris, pp. 255–73.

Biad, A. (1999), 'Conflict Prevention in the Euro-Med Partnership: Challenges and Prospects', *The International Spectator*, Vol. 34 (2), pp. 109–22.

Biad, A. (2000a), 'Code of Conduct for Good-Neighbourly Relations in the Euro-Mediterranean Partnership', in H.G. Brauch, A. Marquina and A. Biad (eds.), *Euro-Mediterranean Partnership for the 21st Century*, Macmillan, London, pp. 259–80.

Biad, A. (2000b), 'The Debate on CBMs in the Southern Mediterranean', in H.G. Brauch, A. Marquina and A. Biad (eds.), *Euro-Mediterranean Partnership for the 21st Century*, Macmillan, London, pp. 115-27.
Biad, A. (2001), 'La Charte Euro-Méditerranéenne: Cadre pour le Partenariat de Sécurité', in FMES (ed.), *Euro-Méditerranée 1995-1999. Premier Bilan du Partenariat. Actes du colloque*, Publisud, Paris, pp. 99-110.
Bin, A. (1995), 'Security Implications of Malta's Membership of the European Union', *The International Spectator*, Vol. 30(3), pp. 5-26.
Bin, A. (1997), *Mediterranean Diplomacy. Evolution and Prospects*, Jean Monnet Working Paper in Comparative and International Politics No. 5.
Bin, A. (1998), 'Strenghtening Cooperation in the Mediterranean: NATO's Contribution', *NATO Review*, Vol. 46(4), pp. 24-7.
Bin, A. (2000), 'The Security Dialogue towards the Mediterranean', *Revista CIDOB d'Afers Internacionals*, Vol. 19(49), pp. 1-5.
Bin, A. (2001), 'Mediterranean Dialogue', *NATO Review*, Vol. 49(Autumn), p. 9.
Biscop, S. (2000), *De Integratie van de WEU in de Europese Unie. Europa op Weg naar een Europose Defensie-Organisatie*, Acco, Leuven.
Biscop, S. (2001a), 'Un Défi Considérable: la Dimension Sécurité du Partenariat Euro-Méditerranéen', *Revue du Marché Commun et de l'Union Européenne*, Vol. 44(445), pp. 93-5.
Biscop, S. (2001b), 'Het Euro-Mediterraan Partnerschap en Veiligheid. Een Moeizaam Proces', *Vrede en Veiligheid*, Vol. 30(1), pp. 39-52.
Biscop, S. (2001c), 'Het Middellandse Zeegebied in het Europees Veiligheids- en Defensiebeleid', *Internationale Spectator*, Vol. 55(11), pp. 536-40.
Biscop, S. (2001d), *The European Union and the Eastern Mediterranean. The Need for Conflict Resolution*, Veiligheid en Strategie No. 67.
Biscop, S. (2002a), 'Network or Labyrinth? The Challenge of Coordinating Western Security Dialogues with the Mediterranean', *Mediterranean Politics*, Vol. 7(1), pp.92-112.
Biscop, S. (2002b), 'In Search of a Strategic Concept for the ESDP', *European Foreign Affairs Review*, Vol. 7(4), pp. 473-90.
Biscop, S. (2003a), 'Ouvrir l'Europe au Sud, la PESD et la Sécurité Euro-Méditerranéenne', *Revue du Marché Commun et de l'Union Européenne*, Vol. 46(465), pp. 101-5.
Biscop, S. (2003b), 'Opening up the ESDP to the South: A Comprehensive and Cooperative Approach to Euro-Mediterranean Security', *Security Dialogue*, Vol. 34(2), pp. 179-193.
Bistolfi, R. (2000), 'L'Europe et la Méditerranée: une Entreprise Virtuelle?', *Confluences Méditerranée*, Vol. 10(35), pp. 1-9.
Blanc, P. (2000), *La Déchirure Chypriote. Géopolitique d'une Île Divisée*, L'Harmattan, Paris.
Blank, S. (2000), 'The Mediterranean and its Security Agenda', *Mediterranean Quarterly*, Vol. 11(1), pp. 24-48.
Blunden, M. (1994), 'Insecurity on Europe's Southern Flank', *Survival*, Vol. 36(2), pp. 134-48.
Bojji, A. (1999), 'La Charte Euro-Méditerranéenne pour la Paix et la Stabilité', in Ggroupement d'Études et de Recherche sur la Méditerranée (ed.), *L'Annuaire de la Méditerranée 1999*, Publisud, Paris, pp. 223-8.
Boniface, P. (2000), 'Arms Control in the Mediterranean Area: a European Perspective', *Mediterranean Politics*, Vol. 5(1), pp. 167-88.
Bonvicini, G. (1995), 'The Role of Human Rights in European Political Cooperation and Applications in the Middle East', in E. Ahiram and A. Tovias(eds.), *Whither EU-Israeli Relations? Common and Divergent Interests*, Peter Lang, Frankfurt AM, pp. 269-77.
Brauch, H.G. (1996), 'Energy Interdependence in the Western Mediterranean', *Mediterranean Politics*, Vol. 1(3), pp. 295-319.

Brauch, H.G. (2000a), 'From Confidence to Partnership Building Measures in Europe and the Mediterranean: Conceptual and Political Efforts Revisited', in H.G. Brauch, A. Marquina and A. Biad (eds.), *Euro-Mediterranean Partnership for the 21st Century*, Macmillan, London, pp. 27–58.

Brauch, H.G. (2000b), 'Partnership Building Measures for Long-Term Non-Military Challenges Affecting North-South Relations', in H.G. Brauch, A. Marquina and A. Biad (eds.), *Euro-Mediterranean Partnership for the 21st Century*, Macmillan, London, pp. 281–318.

Brauch, H.G., A. Marquina and A. Biad (2000a), 'Introduction: Euro-Mediterranean Partnership for the 21st Century', in H.G. Brauch, A. Marquina and A. Biad (eds.), *Euro-Mediterranean Partnership for the 21st Century*, Macmillan, London, pp. 3–25.

Brauch, H.G., A. Marquina and A. Biad (2000b), 'Beyond Stuttgart: Prospects for Confidence and Partnership Building Measures in Euro-Mediterranean Relations for the 21st Century', in H.G. Brauch, A. Marquina and A. Biad (eds.), *Euro-Mediterranean Partnership for the 21st Century*, Macmillan, London, pp. 319–50.

Braverman, A. (1995), 'Wasser: Element des Friedens und des Konflikts', *Internationale Politik*, Vol. 50(7), pp. 51–4.

Bremmer, I., Clément, S., Cottey, A. and Dokos, T. (1999), 'Emerging Subregional Cooperation Processes: South-Eastern Europe, the Newly Independent States and the Mediterranean', in A. Cottey (ed.), *Subregional Cooperation in the New Europe. Building Security, Prosperity and Solidarity from the Barents to the Black Sea*, Macmillan, London, pp. 213–40.

Bretherton, C. and Vogler J. (1999), *The European Union as a Global Actor*, Routledge, London.

Brewin, C. (1999), *European Union Perspectives on Cyprus Accession*, Centre for Euro-Mediterranean Studies Research Paper No. 2, University of Reading.

Brewin, C. (2000), *The European Union and Cyprus*, Eothen, Huntingdon.

Brey, H. (1997), 'Economic Performance and Competitiveness: the Republic of Cyprus', in H.-J. Axt and H. Brey (eds.), *Cyprus and the European Union. New Chances for Solving an Old Conflict?*, Südosteuropa-Gesellschaft, München, pp. 55–62.

Brey, H. (1999), 'Regional Economic Context: Cyprus, Europe and the Middle East', S. Baier-Allen (ed.), *Looking into the Future of Cyprus-EU Relations*, Nomos, Baden-Baden, pp. 93–104.

Brey, H. (1999), 'Turkey and the Cyprus Question', *The International Spectator*, Vol. 34(1), pp. 111–21.

Brisepierre, P. (1999), 'Le Maroc, Élément Fondamental de Sécurité et de Stabilité en Afrique du Nord', *Défense nationale*, Vol. 55(10), pp. 18–27.

Bruyere, P. (1996), 'Les Problèmes de Sécurité', in Defence Studies Centre (ed.), *La Coopération Euro-Méditerranéenne: Hypothèses de Base et Résultats*, Royal Defence College, Brussels, pp. 87–145.

Burgat, F. (1996), 'L'Islamisme en Face', in Defence Studies Centre (ed.), *Proceedings. La Coopération Euro-Méditerranéenne: Hypothèses de Base et Résultats*, Royal Defence College, Brussels, pp. 35–46.

Buzan, B. and Diez, T. (1999), 'The European Union and Turkey', *Survival*, Vol. 41(1), pp. 41–57.

Calabrese, J. (1997), 'Beyond Barcelona: the Politics of the Euro-Mediterranean Partnership', *European Security*, Vol. 6(4), pp. 86–110.

Calleya, S.C. (1997), 'The Euro-Mediterranean Process after Malta: what Prospects?', *Mediterranean Politics*, Vol. 2(2), pp. 1–22.

Calleya, S.C. (1998), *Security Considerations in the Euro-Mediterranean Area*, Hellenic Foundation for European and Foreign Policy Occasional Paper No. 7.

Calleya, S.C. (1999a), *The Establishment of a Euro-Med Conflict Prevention Centre*, Euromesco paper.
Calleya, S.C. (1999b), 'Regional Security Challenges in the Mediterranean', in S.J. Blank (ed.), *Mediterranean Security into the Coming Millennium*, US Army War College, Carlisle (PA), pp. 93–110.
Calleya, S.C. (2000), *Is the Barcelona Process Working? EU Policy in the Mediterranean*, Zentrum für Europäische Integrationsforschung Discussion Paper No. 75.
Calleya, S.C. (2001), 'Between Partnership, Association and Enlargement: the Case of Malta', in F. Attina and S. Stavridis (eds.), *The Barcelona Process and Euro-Mediterranean Issues from Stuttgart to Marseille*, Giuffrè, Milan, pp. 249–68.
Cameron, F. (1999), 'Cyprus and the EU: the Next Steps', in S. Baier-Allen (ed.), *Looking into the Future of Cyprus-EU Relations*, Nomos, Baden-Baden, pp. 11–22.
Carpenter, T.G. (1999), 'The Mediterranean Cauldron', in N.A. Stavrou (ed.), *Mediterranean Security at the Crossroads: a Reader*, Duke University Press, Durham (N. Ca.), pp. 69–88.
Cavanagh Hodge, C. (1999), 'Turkey and the Pale Light of European Democracy', *Mediterranean Politics*, Vol. 4(3), pp.56–68.
Chagnollaud, J.-P. and Ravenel, B. (1993), 'Pour une Politique Méditerranéenne de l'Europe', *Confluences Méditerranée*, Vol. 3(7), pp. 1–4.
Charillon, F. (1998), 'La Stratégie Européenne dans le Processus de Paix au Moyen-Orient. Politique Étrangère de Proximité et Diplomatie du Créneau', in M.-F. Durand and A. De Vasconcelos (eds.), *La PESC. Ouvrir l'Europe au Monde*, Presses de Sciences Po, Paris, pp. 195–225.
Charollais, F. (1997), 'Bilan des Forces en Méditerranée: une Nouvelle Aproche après Barcelone', in A. Marquina (ed.), *Les Élites et le Processus de Changement dans la Méditerranée*, Stradermed, Toulon, pp. 1–11.
Charriot, M. (1995), 'La Turquie: un Difficile Partenaire pour l'Union européenne', *Revue du Marché Commun et de l'Union Européenne*, Vol. 38(390), pp.430–2.
Chatelus, M. (2000), 'La Méditerranée Orientale et la Mer Noire dans la Géopolitique des Hydrocarbures', in M. Bazin, S. Kançal, J. Thobie and Y. Tekelioğlu (eds.), *Méditerranée et Mer Noire entre Mondialisation et Régionalisation*, L'Harmattan, Paris, pp. 125–51.
Chater, K. (1996), 'Mediterranean Security: the Tunisian Viewpoint', in R. Aliboni, G. Joffé and T. Niblock (eds.), *Security Challenges in the Mediterranean Region*, Frank Cass, London, pp. 65–80.
Chenal, A. (1995), 'La France Rattrapée par le Drame Algérien', *Politique étrangère*, Vol. 60(2), pp. 415–25.
Chesneau, J. (2000), 'À Propos d'une Politique Méditerranéenne', *Défense nationale*, Vol. 56(2), pp.5–18.
Cheysson, C. (1996), 'Il y faut l'Impulsion de la France', *Law and European Affairs - Revue des Affaires Européennes*, Vol. 6(4), pp.309–11.
Chikh, S. (1999), 'La Sécurité et la Coopération en Méditerranée: Position de la Rive Sud', in Stradermed (ed.), *Les Actes de Milan. Deuxième Cycle d'Études Stradermed pour Décideurs de l'Union Européenne et des Pays Partenaires Méditerranéens*, Stradermed, Toulon, pp. 1–11.
Chopra, J. (1997), 'A Chance for Peace in Western Sahara', *Survival*, Vol. 39(3), pp. 51–65.
Chourou, B. (2000), 'Security Partnership and Democratisation: Perception of the Activities of Northern Security Institutions in the South', in H.G. Brauch, A. Marquina and A. Biad (eds.), *Euro-Mediterranean Partnership for the 21st Century*, Macmillan, London, pp. 163–88.
Chourou, B. (2001), 'The (Ir)Relevance of Security Issues in Euro-Mediterranean Relations', in F. Tanner (ed.), *The European Union as a Security Actor in the Mediterranean. ESDP,*

Soft Power and Peacemaking in Euro-Mediterranean Relations, Zürcher Beitrag zur Sicherheitpolitik und Konfliktforschung No. 61, pp. 57–74.

Chubin, S., Green, J.D. and Larrabee, F.S. (1999), *NATO's New Strategic Concept and Peripheral Contingencies: the Middle East*, RAND, Santa Monica (Ca.).

Clairet, P. (1994), 'EC – Middle East Relations: the Peace Process and Revisions to the Community's Mediterranean Policy', in P. Ludlow (ed.), *Europe and the Mediterranean*, Brassey's, London, pp. 147–89.

Clément, S. (1998), 'WEU and South-Eastern Europe', in G. Lenzi (ed.), *WEU at Fifty*, WEU Institute for Security Studies, Paris, pp. 1–14.

Cochran, E.S. (1996), 'Deliberate Ambiguity: an Analysis of Israel's Nuclear Strategy', *The Journal of Strategic Studies*, Vol. 19(3), pp. 321–42.

Cogan, C.G. (1999), 'Coexistence Uneasy, Cohabitation Unlikely: the Arabs and the World Outside', in N.A. Stavrou. (ed.), *Mediterranean Security at the Crossroads: a Reader*, Duke University Press, Durham (N. Ca.), pp. 278–93.

Cogen, M. and François, A. (1995), 'Realizing the Right to Self-Determination of the Palestinian People. The European Union and the Peaceful Settlement of the Israeli-Palestinian Conflict', in N. Sybesma-Knol and J. Van Bellingen (eds.), *Naar een Nieuwe Interpretatie van het Recht op Zelfbeschikking?*, VUB Press, Brussel, pp. 345–82.

Coombes, D. (1995), 'The European Community and Democracy in the Eastern Mediterranean', in E. Ahiram and A. Tovias (eds.), *Whither EU-Israeli Relations? Common and Divergent Interests*, Peter Lang, Frankfurt AM, pp. 279–94.

Cordesman, A.H. (1999), *Weapons of Mass Destruction in the Middle East. Regional Trends, National Forces, Warfighting Capabilities, Delivery Options and Weapons Effects*, Center for Strategic and International Studies, Washington DC.

Cordesman, A.H. (2000), *Weapons of Mass Destruction and Arms Control in the Middle East*, Center for Strategic and International Studies, Washington DC.

Cornish, P., Van Ham, P. and Krause, J. (eds.) (1996), *Europe and the Challenge of Proliferation*, Chaillot Paper No. 24, WEU Institute for Security Studies, Paris.

Couloumbis, T.A. (1996), 'Greek Security Challenges in the 1990's', in W. Bauwens, A. Clesse and O.F. Knudsen (eds.), *Small States and the Security Challenge in the New Europe*, Brassey's, London, pp. 198–221.

Couloumbis, T.A. (1998), *The Troubled Triangle: Cyprus – Greece – Turkey*, Hellenic Foundation for European and Foreign Policy Occasional Paper No. 6.

Couloumbis, T.A. (1999), 'Turkish Challenge and European Opportunity: Greek Foreign Policy Priorities in a Post-Cold War Setting', in S.J. Blank (ed.), *Mediterranean Security into the Coming Millennium*, US Army War College, Carlisle (PA), pp. 249–62.

Coustillière, J.-F. (1999), 'Méditerranée: Quel Enjeu pour le XXIe Siècle?', *Défense Nationale*, Vol. 55(4), pp. 5–21.

Coustillière, J.-F. (2000), 'Une Autorité de Coordination en Méditerranée', *Défense Nationale*, Vol. 56(2), pp. 19–28.

Cova, C. (1990), 'Une Nouvelle Politique Méditerranéenne', *Revue du Marché Commun*, Vol. 33(337), pp. 349–50.

Cucchi, G. (1994), 'Sécurité Européenne, Sécurité Méditerranéenne', in Fondation Méditerranéenne d'Études Stratégiques (ed.), *La Méditerranée Occidentale. Quelles Stratégies pour l'Avenir?*, Publisud, Paris, pp. 187–200.

Cuccoli, R. (2000), *The Relations between the United States and Southern European Countries in the Context of NATO's Mediterranean Dialogue*, NATO Fellowship Research Report.

Daguzan, J.-F. (1994), 'La Sécurité en Méditerranée: une Approche Globale', in Fondation Méditerranéenne d'Études Stratégiques (ed.), *La Méditerranée Occidentale. Quelles Stratégies pour l'Avenir?*, Publisud, Paris, pp. 159–72.

Daguzan, J.-F. (1997), 'Pacte de Stabilité et Désarmement en Méditerranée', in A. Marquina (ed.), *Les Élites et le Processus de Changement dans la Méditerranée*, Strademed, Toulon, pp. 1–18.
Daguzan, J.-F. (1999), *La Charte Euro-Méditerranéenne pour la Paix et la Stabilité: Éléments Juridiques et Politiques*, EuroMeSCo Paper.
Daguzan, J.-F. (2000a), 'Confidence Building Measures, Disarmament and Crisis Prevention: a View from the North', H.G. Brauch, A. Marquina and A. Biad (eds.), *Euro-Mediterranean Partnership for the 21st Century*, Macmillan, London, pp. 95–111.
Daguzan, J.-F. (2000b), 'La Charte pour la Paix et la Stabilité. La Fin des Illusions de Barcelone?', *Confluences Méditerranée*, Vol. 10(35), pp. 1–5.
Daguzan, J.-F. (2001), 'La Charte pour la Paix et la Stabilité: un Socle Concret pour la "Maison Commune" Euro-Méditerranéenne', in Fondation Méditerranéenne d'Études Stratégiques (ed.), *Euro-Méditerranée 1995–1999. Premier Bilan du Partenariat. Actes du Colloque*, Publisud, Paris, pp. 111–22.
Dauderstädt, M. (1996), 'Europa und Nordafrika: Mehr Paranoia als Partnerschaft', *Friedrich Ebert Stiftung Eurokolleg*, Vol. 8(36), pp. 1–18.
David, D. (2001), 'L'Union Européenne et la Méditerrannée: Quelles Perspectives Stratégiques?', in Fondation Méditerranéenne d'Études Stratégiques (ed.), *Euro-Méditerranée 1995–1999. Premier Bilan du Partenariat. Actes du Colloque*, Publisud, Paris, pp. 67–76.
De Figueiredo Lopes, A. (1996), 'The Mediterranean Dimension of European Security', in S.A. Pappas and S. Vanhoonacker (eds.), *The European Union's Common Foreign and Security Policy. The Challenges of the Future*, European Institute of Public Administration, Maastricht, pp. 57–63.
De Langre, G. (2001), 'La Sécurité en Méditerranée: Quelle Contribution?', in Fondation Méditerranéenne d'Études Stratégiques (ed.), *Euro-Méditerranée 1995–1999. Premier Bilan du Partenariat. Actes du Colloque*, Publisud, Paris, pp. 159–65.
Della Seta, S. and Cingoli, J. (1999), *The Price of Non-Peace: the Need for a Strengthened Role for the European Union in the Middle East*, Working Paper, Political Series, POLI 116EN, European Parliament, Directorate General for Research, Luxembourg.
Del Río Luelmo, J. (1997), *Turkey's Role in the Middle East as a Member of NATO: its Importance for Atlantic External Security*, NATO Fellowship Research Paper.
Demestichas, G. (1999), 'Greek Security and Defence Policy in the Eastern Mediterranean', in N.A. Stavrou (ed.), *Mediterranean Security at the Crossroads: a Reader*, Duke University Press, Durham (N. Ca.), pp. 265–77.
Demetriou, M. (1998), 'On the Long Road to Europe and the Short Path to War: Issue-Linkage Politics and the Arms Build-Up on Cyprus', *Mediterranean Politics*, Vol. 3(3), pp. 38–51.
De Raulin, A. (2000), *La Turquie et la Méditerranée Orientale*, NATO Fellowship Research Paper.
Derisbourg, J.-P (1997), 'The Euro-Mediterranean Partnership since Barcelona', *Mediterranean Politics*, Vol. 2(1), pp. 9–11.
De Santis, N. (1998), 'The Future of NATO's Mediterranean Initiative', *NATO Review*, Vol. 46(1), pp. 32–5.
De Vasconcelos, A. (1993), 'Disintegration and Integration in the Mediterranean', *The International Spectator*, Vol. 28(3), pp. 67–78.
De Vasconcelos, A. (1998), 'Les Relations Euro-Américaines et la Méditerranée', in Groupement d'Études et de Recherche sur la Méditerranée (ed.), *L'Annuaire de la Méditerranée 1998*, Publisud, Paris, pp. 325–33.
De Vasconcelos, A. (2000a), *Intégration et Coopération Sous-Régionale en Méditerranée*, Euromesco Paper.

De Vasconcelos, A. (2001b), 'Europe's Mediterranean Strategy: the Security Dimension', in M. Marescau and E. Lannon (eds.), *The EU's Enlargement and Mediterranean Strategies. A Comparative Analysis*, Palgrave, New York, pp. 29–41.
De Vasconcelos, A. (2001b), 'La Charte de Stabilité en Méditerranée', in Defence Studies Centre (ed.), *Proceedings. La Sécurité dans l'Espace de l'Est Méditerranéen et du proche-Orient*, Royal Defence College, Brussels, pp. 31–6.
De Vasconcelos, A. (2002), *Working group III – First Year Report: European Defence – Perceptions vs. Realities*, EuroMeSCo report.
De Wilde d'Estmael, T. (1996), 'La Coopération Politique Européenne face au Conflit Israélo-Palestinien', in A. Ait-Chalaal, B. Khader and T. De Wilde d'Estmael (eds.), *Conflits et Processus de Paix au Proche-Orient*, Bruylant-Academia, Louvain-la-Neuve, pp. 231–73.
Do Céu Pinto, M. (1998), 'European and American Responses to the Algerian Crisis', in *Mediterranean Politics*, Vol. 3(3), pp. 63–80.
Dodd, C.H. (1999), 'The Cyprus Issue: Constraints on a Solution', in S. Baier-Allen (ed.), *Looking into the Future of Cyprus-EU Relations*, Nomos, Baden-Baden, pp. 23–37.
Dokos, T.P. (1998), *Proliferation of Weapons of Mass Destruction and the Threat to NATO's Southern flank: an Assessment of Options*, NATO Fellowship Research Report.
Dokos, T.P. (2000), 'The Proliferation of Weapons of Mass Destruction in the Mediterranen: the Threat to Western Security', *Mediterranean Politics*, Vol. 5(3), pp. 95–116.
Døsenrode, S. and Stubkjær, A. (2002), *The European Union and the Middle East*, Sheffield Academic Press, London.
Drevet, J.-F. (2000), *Chypre en Europe*, L'Harmattan, Paris.
Droutsas, D.P. (1997), 'The EU and the Mediterranean: the Cypriot Application for Full Membership in the Regional Context', in H.-J. Axt and H. Brey (eds.), *Cyprus and the European Union. New Chances for Solving an Old Conflict?*, Südosteuropa-Gesellschaft, München, pp. 100–124.
Dunér, B. (1999), 'Cyprus: North is North and South is South', *Security Dialogue*, Vol. 30(4), pp. 485–96.
Duval, M. (1998), 'À la Recherche d'un Secret: l'Arme Nucléaire Israélienne', *Défense Nationale*, Vol. 54(4), pp. 91–102.
Duval, M. (1999), 'L'Europe est-elle Menacée par la Prolifération?', *Défense Nationale*, Vol. 55(7), pp. 45–59.
Echeverria, C. (1997a), 'European Security and the Mediterranean', in W. Von Bredow, T. Jäger and G. Kümmel (eds.), *European Security*, Macmillan, London, pp. 54–67.
Echeverria, C. (1997b), 'Confidence and Security Building Measures in the Mediterranean. A Brief List of Proposals', in A. Marquina (ed.), *Les Élites et le Processus de Changement dans la Méditerranée*, Strademed, Toulon, pp. 1–7.
Echeverria, C. (1999a), 'Spain and the Mediterranean', in S. Stavridis, T.A. Couloumbis, T. Veremis and N. Waites (eds.), *The Foreign Policies of the European Union's Mediterranean States and Applicant Countries in the 1990s*, Macmillan, London, pp. 98–112.
Echeverria, C. (1999b), *Cooperation in Peacekeeping among the Euro-Mediterranean Armed Forces*, Chaillot Paper No. 35, WEU Institute for Security Studies, Paris.
Edis, R. (1998), 'Does the Barcelona Process Matter?', *Mediterranean Politics*, Vol. 3(3), pp. 93–105.
Edwards, G. and Philippart, E. (1997), 'The EU Mediterranean Policy: Virtue Unrewarded or…?', *Cambridge Review of International Affairs*, Vol. 11(1), pp. 185–207.
Eichinger, F. (1997), 'Cyprus and the EU from the German Point of View', H.-J. Axt and H. Brey (eds.), *Cyprus and the European Union. New Chances for Solving an Old Conflict?*, Südosteuropa-Gesellschaft, München, pp. 197–203.

El Bekri, M.A. (1996), *Vers de Nouvelles Relations entre l'Europe et le Maghreb*, Royal Defence College, Brussels.

El Kadiri, A. (1999), 'Réflexions sur le Projet d'une Charte euro-méditerranéenne', in Groupement d'Études et de Recherche sur la Méditerranée (ed.), *L'Annuaire de la Méditerranée 1999*, Publisud, Paris, pp. 229–36.

Elmas, H.B. (1997), 'L'Union Douanière avec l'Union Européenne', *Confluences Méditerranée*, Vol. 7(23), pp. 1–6.

Elmas, H.B. (1998), *Turquie – Europe. Une Relation Ambigue*, Éditions Syllepse, Paris.

Elmir, M. (1997), 'Le Commerce et la Prolifération des Armes au Moyen-Orient', in Defence Studies Centre (ed.), *Terrorisme et Prolifération: la sécurité de l'Europe Occidentale*, Royal Defence College, Brussels, pp. 1–33.

El-Sayed, M. (1995), 'Mediterraneanism: a New Dimension in Egypt's Foreign Policy', Al-Ahram Center for Political and Strategic Studies Strategic Papers, Vol. 4(27), pp. 1–21.

El-Sayed, M. (1997), 'Egypt and the Euro-Mediterranean Partnership: Strategic Choice or Adaptive Mechanism?', Mediterranean Politics, Vol. 2(1), pp. 64–90.

El-Sayed, M. (1999), 'Arab Perceptions of the European Union's Euro-Mediterranean Projects', in S.J. Blank (ed.), *Mediterranean Security into the Coming Millennium*, US Army War College, Carlisle (PA), pp. 143–57.

El-Sayed, M. (2000a), 'Towards a New WMD Agenda in the Euro-Mediterranean Partnership: an Arab Perspective', *Mediterranean Politics*, Vol. 5(1), pp. 133–57.

El-Sayed, M. (2000b), 'Southern Mediterranean Perceptions of Security Cooperation and the Role of NATO', in H.G. Brauch, A. Marquina and A. Biad (eds.), *Euro-Mediterranean Partnership for the 21st Century*, Macmillan, London, pp. 129–46.

El Shoubasy, C. (2001), 'La Sécurité de la Méditerranée avec des Populations Riveraines du Sud et de l'Est', in Fondation Méditerranéenne d'Études Stratégiques (ed.), *Euro-Méditerranée 1995–1999. Premier bilan du Partenariat. Actes du Colloque*, Publisud, Paris, pp. 152–7.

Emiliou, N. (1997), 'Knocking on the Door of the European Union: Cyprus' Strategy for Accession', in H.-J. Axt and H. Brey (eds.), *Cyprus and the European Union. New Chances for Solving an Old Conflict?*, Südosteuropa-Gesellschaft, München, pp. 125–36.

Eralp, A. (1993), 'Turkey and the European Community in the Changing Post-War International System', in C. Balkir and A.M. Williams (eds.), *Turkey and Europe*, Pinter, 1993, pp. 24–44.

Erdogdu, E. (2002), 'Turkey and Europe: Undivided but not United', *Middle East Review of International Affairs*, Vol. 6(2), pp. 1–12.

Ergil, D. (1999), 'A Synopsis of the Kurdish Problem', *The International Spectator*, Vol. 34(1), pp. 19–22.

Ergil, D. (2001), 'Aspects of the Kurdish Problem in Turkey', in D. Lovatt (ed.), *Turkey since 1970. Politics, Economics and Society*, Palgrave, New York, pp. 161–93.

Erguvenc, S. (1997), 'Turkey in the New European Security Context. Turkey's Role and Expectations in the Transatlantic Partnership', *Foreign Policy*, Vol. 21(1–2), pp. 1–7.

Ewing, R.C. and Ramjoué, C. (1997), 'NATO and Mediterranean Security', *Bulletin of the Atlantic Council of the United States*, Vol. 8(4), pp. 1–5.

Faria, F. (1999), 'The Making of Portugal's Mediterranean policy', in S. Stavridis, T.A. Couloumbis, T. Veremis and N. Waites (eds.), *The Foreign Policies of the European Union's Mediterranean States and Applicant Countries in the 1990s*, Macmillan, London, pp. 113–39.

Faria, F. and De Vasconcelos, A. (1996), *Security in Northern Africa: Ambiguity and Reality*, Chaillot Paper No. 25, WEU Institute for Security Studies, Paris.

Farrar-Hockley, D. (1994), 'Future Instability in the Mediterranean Basin', *European Security*, Vol. 3(1), pp. 58–81.

Fenech, D. (1997), 'The Relevance of European Security Structures to the Mediterranean (and Vice Versa)', *Mediterranean Politics*, Vol. 2(1), pp. 149–76.

Fernández-Ordóñez, F. (1990), 'The Mediterranean – a Developing Security Structure', *NATO Review*, Vol. 38(5), pp. 7–11.

Figueroa, C.F. (1997), 'Conferencia Euromediterránea en La Valeta: ¿Falta de Voluntad Política de sus Actores?', *Revista de Estudios Europeos*, Vol. 11(43–44), pp. 56–67.

Fröhlich, S. (2000), 'Der Mittelmeerraum im Geostrategischen Interessenkalkül der Vereinigten Staaten', in A. Jacobs and C. Masala (eds.), *Hannibal ante Portas? Analysen zur Sicherheit an der Südflanke Europas*, Nomos, Baden-Baden, pp. 51–70.

Fuller, G.E. (1995), 'Interests in the Middle East', in J.W. Holmes (ed.), *Maelstrom. The United States, Southern Europe and the Challenges of the Mediterranean*, The World Peace Foundation, Cambridge (MA), pp. 85–101.

Galletti, M. (1999), 'The Kurdish Issue in Turkey', *The International Spectator*, Vol. 34(1), pp. 123–34.

Gallino, D. (1991), 'Security Challenges as Perceived in the Mediterranean NATO Member Countries', in M. Jopp, R. Rummel and P. Schmidt (eds.), *Integration and Security in Western Europe. Inside the European Pillar*, Westview Press, Oxford, pp. 95–114.

Garçon, J. (1995), 'L'Algérie, si Loin de Washington...', *Politique étrangère*, Vol. 60(2), pp. 427–34.

Gaudissart, M.-A. (1996), 'Cyprus and the European Union. The Long Road to Accession', *The Cyprus Review*, Vol. 8(1), pp. 1–31.

Gaudissart, M.-A. (2001), 'Cinq Ans après Barcelone. État et Perspectives du Partenariat Euro-Méditerranéen', in M. Dumoulin and G. Duchenne (eds.), *L'Europe et la Méditerranée. Actes de la VIe Chaire Glaverbel d'Études Européennes 2000–2001*, PIE – Peter Lang, Brussels, pp. 133–47.

Gautron, J.-C. (1997), 'La Politique Méditerranéenne de l'Union Européenne (Vetera et Nova)', *The European Union Review*, Vol. 2(2), pp. 25–42.

Gerges, F.A. (1999), 'The Decline of Revolution: Islam in Algeria and Egypt', *Survival*, Vol. 41(1), pp. 113–25.

Gerges, F.A. (2000), *The American Component in Europe's Middle East Policy*, Hintergrundberichte November, Friedrich-Ebert-Stiftung, North Africa and Middle East Office.

Gillespie, R. (1997a), 'Spanish Protagonismo and the Euro-Med Partnership Initiative', *Mediterranean Politics*, Vol. 2(1), pp. 33–48.

Gillespie, R. (1997b), 'Northern European Perceptions of the Barcelona process', *Revista CIDOB d'Afers Internacionals*, Vol. 16(37), pp. 1–9.

Gillespie, R. (1997c), 'The Euro-Mediterranean Partnership Initiative', *Mediterranean Politics*, Vol. 2(1), pp. 1–5.

Ginsberg, R.H. (2001), *The European Union in International Politics. Baptism by Fire*, Rowman & Littlefield, Boston.

Giro, M. (1998), 'The Community of Saint Egidio and its Peacemaking Activities', *The International Spectator*, Vol. 33(3), 3, pp. 85–100.

Gomez, R. (1998), 'The EU's Mediterranean Policy. Common Foreign Policy by the Back Door?', in J. Peterson and H. Sjursen (eds.), *A Common Foreign Policy for Europe? Competing Visions of the CFSP*, Routledge, London, pp. 133–51.

Gordon, P.H. (1998), *The Transatlantic Allies and the Changing Middle East*, Adelphi Paper No. 322, International Institute for Strategic Studies, London.

Grand, C. (2000), *The European Union and the Non-Proliferation of Nuclear Weapons*, Chaillot Paper No. 37, WEU Institute for Security Studies, Paris.

Green, J.D. (2001), 'US Middle East Policy: Restrictions and Promises for the Future', in Defence Studies Centre (ed.), *Proceedings. La Sécurité dans l'Espace de l'Est Méditerranéen et du proche-Orient*, Royal Defence College, Brussels, pp. 75–80.

Greilsammer, I. (1984), 'The Impact of Enlargement: Spain, Portugal and the Arab-Israeli Conflict', in D. Allen and A. Pijpers (eds.), *European Foreign Policy-Making and the Arab-Israeli Conflict*, Martinus Nijhoff, Den Haag, pp. 224–39.

Greilsammer, I. and Weiler, J. (1984), 'European Political Cooperation and the Palestinian-Israeli Conflict: an Israeli Perspective', in D. Allen and A. Pijpers (eds.), *European Foreign Policy-Making and the Arab-Israeli Conflict*, Martinus Nijhoff, Den Haag, pp. 121–60.

Grimaud, N. (1996), 'Le Maghreb et le Partenariat Euro-Méditerranéen', *Law and European Affairs - Revue des Affaires Européennes*, Vol. 6(4), pp. 341–9.

Grimmet, R. (1993), 'The United States and NATO in the Mediterranean: an American Perspective of the Post-Cold War Era', *The International Spectator*, Vol. 28(3), pp. 79–86.

Grønbech-Jensen, C. (1999), 'The European Union and the Case of South Lebanon', *Mediterranean Politics*, Vol. 4(3), pp. 1–22.

Guazzone, L. (1993), 'The Politics of Mediterranean Naval Security', *The International Spectator*, Vol. 28(4), pp. 11–38.

Guazzone, L. (1996), 'The Evolving Framework of Arab Security Perceptions: the Impact of Cultural Factors', *The International Spectator*, Vol. 31(4), pp. 63–74.

Gumpel, W. (1997), 'Economic Performance and Competitiveness in the Turkish Republic of Northern Cyprus', in H.-J. Axt and H. Brey (eds.), *Cyprus and the European Union. New Chances for Solving an Old Conflict?*, Südosteuropa-Gesellschaft, München, pp. 63–73.

Gundoglu, A. (2001), 'Identities in Question: Greek-Turkish Relations in a Period of Transformation?', *Middle East Review of International Affairs*, Vol. 5(1), pp. 106–17.

Güney, A. (2001), 'Turkey: Beyond the Customs Union?', in F. Attina and S. Stavridis (eds.), *The Barcelona Process and Euro-Mediterranean Issues from Stuttgart to Marseille*, Giuffrè, Milan, pp. 201–26.

Gürel, S.S. (1993), 'Turkey and Greece: a Difficult Aegean Relationship', in C. Balkir and A.M. Williams (eds.), *Turkey and Europe*, Pinter, London, pp. 161–90.

Haddadi, S. (1999), *The Western Mediterranean as a Security Complex: a Liaison between the European Union and the Middle East?*, Jean Monnet Working Paper in Comparative and International Politics No. 24.

Hadjipavlou-Trigeorgis, M. (1997), 'Little Confidence in Confidence Building? Conflict Resolution in the Context of the United Nations', in H.-J. Axt and H. Brey (eds.), *Cyprus and the European Union. New Chances for Solving an Old Conflict?*, Südosteuropa-Gesellschaft, München, pp. 36–54.

Hafidi, A. (1995), 'Islamisme Algérien et Champ Politico-Religieux au Maroc', *Politique étrangère*, Vol. 60(2), pp. 377–87.

Hakura, F.S. (1997), 'The Euro-Mediterranean Policy: the Implications of the Barcelona Declaration', *Common Market Law Review*, Vol. 34(2), pp. 337–66.

Hamdouni, S. (1992), 'Les Tentatives d'Intégration des Pays du Maghreb face à l'Élargissement de la Communauté Économique Européenne', *Études internationales*, Vol. 23(2), pp. 319–48.

Hancock, J. (1998), 'Lebanon and the West: UK, EU and US', *Mediterranean Politics*, Vol. 3(1), pp. 163–9.

Hansen, L. (1994), 'CSBMs: the Ugly Duckling Remains a Duck – but a Pretty Good One', in F. Tanner (ed.), *Arms Control, Confidence Building and Security Cooperation in the Mediterranean, North Africa and the Middle East*, Mediterranean Academy of Diplomatic Studies, Malta, pp. 1–8.

Heller, M.A. (1997), *Nuclear Weapons in the Middle East. An Israeli Perspective*, Jaffee Centre for Strategic Studies Occasional Paper.
Heller, M.A. (2000), 'Weapons of Mass Destruction and Euro-Mediterranean Policies of Arms Control: an Israeli Perspective', *Mediterranean Politics*, Vol. 5(1), pp. 158–66.
Heller, M.A. (2001a), 'Reassessing Barcelona', in F. Tanner (ed.), *The European Union as a Security Actor in the Mediterranean. ESDP, Soft Power and Peacemaking in Euro-Mediterranean Relations*, Zürcher Beitrag zur Sicherheitpolitik und Konfliktforschung No. 61.
Heller, M.A. (2001b), 'An Israeli Perception', in Defence Studies Centre (ed.), *Proceedings. La Sécurité dans l'Espace de l'Est Méditerranéen et du proche-Orient*, Royal Defence College, Brussels, pp. 49–54.
Henry, J.-R. (1999), 'L'Europe et sa Frontière Méditerranéenne: une Politique à Risques', in H. Elsenhans (ed.), *A Balanced European Architecture. Enlargement of the European Union to Central Europe and the Mediterranean*, Publisud, Paris, pp. 121–30.
Hickok, R. (1998), 'The Imia/Kardak Affair, 1995–96: a Case of Inadvertent Conflict', *European security*, Vol. 7(4), pp. 118–36.
Hoch, M. (1995), 'Konflikte im Nahen/Mittleren Osten und die Westliche Politik', *Aussenpolitik*, Vol. 46(3), pp. 280–88.
Hollis, R. (1997), 'Europe and the Middle East: Power by Stealth?', *International Affairs*, Vol. 73(1), pp. 15–29.
Hollis, R. (2000), 'Barcelona's First Pillar: an Appropriate Concept for Security Relations?', in S. Behrendt and C.P. Hanelt (eds.), *Bound to Cooperate – Europe and the Middle East*, Bertelsmann, Gütersloh, pp. 107–132.
Holm, U. (1998), 'Algeria: France's Untenable Engagement', *Mediterranean Politics*, Vol. 3(2), pp. 104–114.
Holmes, J.W. (1995), 'US Interests and Policy Options', in J.W. Holmes (ed.), *Maelstrom. The United States, Southern Europe and the Challenges of the Mediterranean*, The World Peace Foundation, Cambridge (MA), pp. 213–35.
Houfaidi, J. (1999), 'L'Euro-Méditerranée, une Dimension Nécessaire à l'Élargissement de l'UE', in Groupement d'Études et de Recherche sur la Méditerranée (ed.), *L'Annuaire de la Méditerranée 1999*, Publisud, Paris, pp. 265–74.
Hourani, A.H. (1997), *A History of the Arab Peoples*, MJF Books, New York.
Hunter, S. (1999), 'Bridge or Frontier? Turkey's Post-Cold War Geopolitical Posture', *The International Spectator*, Vol. 34(1), pp. 63–78.
Hutchence, J. (2001), 'The Middle East Peace Process and the Barcelona Process', in F. Attina and S. Stavridis (eds.), *The Barcelona Process and Euro-Mediterranean Issues from Stuttgart to Marseille*, Giuffrè, Milan, pp. 171–200.
Ibrahim, S.E. (1996), 'The Changing Face of Egypt's Islamic Activism', in R. Aliboni, G. Joffé and T. Niblock (eds.), *Security Challenges in the Mediterranean Region*, Frank Cass, London, pp. 27–40.
Inbar, E. (2000), 'Regional Implications of the Israeli-Turkish Strategic Partnership', *Middle East Review of International Affairs*, Vol. 5(2), pp. 48–65.
Instituto Español de Estudios Estratégicos (2001), *Diálogo Mediterráneo. Percepción Española*, Cuadernos de Estrategia No. 133, Ministerio de Defensa, Madrid.
International Institute for Strategic Studies (2000), *The Military Balance 2000–2001*, IISS, London.
Jacobs, A. (2000), 'Sicherheit durch Kooperation? Die Euro-Mediterrane Partnerschaft', in A. Jacobs and C. Masala (eds.), *Hannibal ante Portas? Analysen zur Sicherheit an der Südflanke Europas*, Nomos, Baden-Baden, pp. 178–200.
James, R.K. (1996), *The Islamist Challenge in the Middle East and North Africa*, USAF Air War College Research Report.

Jean, C. (1999), 'Security in the Mediterranean and Italy's Role', in N.A. Stavrou (ed.), *Mediterranean Security at the Crossroads: a Reader*, Duke University Press, Durham (N. Ca.), pp. 153–69.

Jiménez-Ugarte, J. (2001), 'The Barcelona Process: Past, Present and Future', in I. Bourloyannis-Tsangaridis (ed.), *Development of Euro-Mediterranean Relations. Perspectives and Problems*, Hellenic Foundation for European and Foreign Policy Occasional Paper No. 1, pp. 8–20.

Jobert, M. (1996), 'À la Recherche d'un Interlocuteur', *Law and European Affairs - Revue des Affaires Européennes*, Vol. 6(4), pp. 312–4.

Joffé, G. (1994), 'The European Union and the Maghreb', in R. Gillespie (ed.), *Mediterranean Politics*, Pinter, London, pp. 22–45.

Joffé, G. (1996a), 'The Economic Factor in Mediterranean Security', *The International Spectator*, Vol. 31(4), pp. 75–87.

Joffé, G. (1996b), 'Low-Level Violence and Terrorism', in R. Aliboni, G. Joffé and T. Niblock (eds.), *Security Challenges in the Mediterranean Region*, Frank Cass, London, pp. 139–60.

Joffé, G. (1997), 'Southern Attitudes towards an Integrated Mediterranean Region', *Mediterranean Politics*, Vol. 2(1), pp. 12–29.

Joffé, G. (1998a), 'Relations between the Middle East and the West. The View from the South', in B.A. Roberson (ed.), *The Middle East and Europe. The Power Deficit*, Routledge, London, pp. 45–73.

Joffé, G. (1998b), *The Euro-Mediterranean Partnership: Two Years after Barcelona*, The Royal Institute of International Affairs Briefing Papers No. 44.

Joffé, G. (1998c), *Algeria in Crisis*, The Royal Institute of International Affairs Briefing Paper No. 48.

Joffé, G. (2000), *International Implications of Domestic Security*, Euromesco Paper.

Joffé, G. (2001a), 'European Union and the Mediterranean', in M. Teló (ed.), *European Union and New Regionalism. Regional Activities and Global Governance in a Post-Hegemonic Area*, Ashgate, Aldershot, pp. 207–25.

Joffé, G. (2001b), 'European Multilateralism and Soft Power Projection in the Mediterranean', in F. Tanner (ed.), *The European Union as a Security Actor in the Mediterranean. ESDP, Soft Power and Peacemaking in Euro-Mediterranean Relations*, Zürcher Beitrag zur Sicherheitpolitik und Konfliktforschung No. 61.

Jones, P. (1994), 'Maritime Confidence Building Measures in the Middle East', in F. Tanner (ed.), *Arms Control, Confidence Building and Security Cooperation in the Mediterranean, North Africa and the Middle East*, Mediterranean Academy of Diplomatic Studies, Malta, pp. 1–5.

Joseph J.S. (1997), 'Searching for a Solution to the Cyprus Problem: Can the European Union be More Succesful than the United Nations?', in H.-J. Axt and H. Brey (eds.), *Cyprus and the European Union. New Chances for Solving an Old Conflict?*, Südosteuropa-Gesellschaft, München, pp. 74–88.

Joseph J.S. (1999), 'Learning from the Past to Build a Better Future', in S. Baier-Allen (ed.), *Looking into the Future of Cyprus-EU Relations*, Nomos, Baden-Baden, pp. 127–47.

Joxe, A. (1997), 'Construction de l'État et Risques de Destruction de l'État en Méditerranée', *Revista CIDOB d'Afers Internacionals*, Vol. 16(37), pp. 1–8.

Jünemann, A. (1998), 'Europe's Interrrelations wit North Africa in the New Framework of Euro-Mediterranean Partnership – a Provisional Assesment of the 'Barcelona concept', in European Community Studies Association (ed.), *Third ECSA World Conference. The European Union in a Changing world. Brussels, 19–20 September 1996. A Selection of Conference Papers*, Office for Official Publications of the European Communities, Luxembourg, pp. 365–84.

Jünemann, A. (1999), 'Europas Mittelmeerpolitik im Regionalen und Globalen Wandel: Interessen und Zielkonflikte', in W. Zippel (ed.), *Die Mittelmeerpolitik der EU*, Nomos, Baden-Baden, pp. 29–63.
Kadry Said, M. (1999), *The Euro-Mediterranean Charter and Confidence Building Measures: a Practical Approach*, EuroMeSCo Paper.
Kadry Said, M. (2001), 'An Arab Perception', in Defence Studies Centre (ed.), *Proceedings. La Sécurité dans l'Espace de l'Est Méditerranéen et du proche-Orient*, Royal Defence College, Brussels, pp. 55–74.
Kaminaris, S.C. (1999), 'Greece and the Middle East', *Middle East Review of International Affairs*, Vol. 3(2), pp. 1–10.
Karamanlis, K. (2000), 'Greece: the EU's Anchor of Stability in a Troubled Region', *The Washington Quarterly*, Vol. 23(2), pp. 7–11.
Karaosmanoglu, A.L. (1999), 'NATO Enlargement and the South. A Turkish Perspective', *Security Dialogue*, Vol. 30(2), pp. 213–24.
Karsh, E. and Sayigh, Y. (1994), 'A Cooperative Approach to Arab-Israeli Security', *Survival*, Vol. 36(1), pp. 114–25.
Kasoulides, I. (1999), *Cyprus and its Accession to the European Union*, ZEI Discussion Paper No. 47.
Keramane, A. (2000), 'Energy Cooperation and Stability in the Mediterranean', A. Marquina and H.G. Brauch (eds.), *Political Stability and Energy Cooperation in the Mediterranean*, UNISCI – AFES-PRESS, Madrid – Mosbach, pp. 59–70.
Kerdoun, A. (1995), *La Sécurité en Méditerranée. Défis et Stratégies*, Publisud, Paris.
Keridis, D. (1999), *Greek-Turkish Relations in the Era of European Integration and Globalization*, NATO Fellowship Research Paper.
Kessedjian, B. (2001), 'France and the Mediterranean', in I. Bourloyannis-Tsangaridis (ed.), *Development of Euro-Mediterranean Relations. Perspectives and Problems*, Hellenic Foundation for European and Foreign Policy Ocasional Paper No. 1, pp. 2–8.
Khader, B. (1984), 'Europe and the Arab-Israeli Conflict 1973–1983: an Arab Perspective', in D. Allen and A. Pijpers (eds.), *European Foreign Policy-Making and the Arab-Israeli Conflict*, Martinus Nijhoff, Den Haag, pp. 161–86.
Khader, B. (1992a), *Le Grand Maghreb et l'Europe. Enjeux et Perspectives*, Publisud, Paris.
Khader, B. (1992b), *L'Europe et le Monde Arabe. Cousins, Voisins*, Publisud, Paris.
Khader, B. (1996a), 'Le Partenariat Euro-Méditerranéen: une Approche Singulière pour une Méditerranée Plurielle', in Defence Studies Centre (ed.), *Proceedings. La Coopération Euro-Méditerranéenne: Hypothèses de Base et Résultats. Colloque, 21 février 1996*, Royal Defence College, Brussels, pp. 1–24.
Khader, B. (1996b), *La Conférence Euro-Méditerranéenne: un An après Barcelone*, Centre for Euro-Mediterranean Studies Research Paper No. 3, University of Reading.
Khader, B. (1997a), 'Les Relations Économiques Euro-Arabes. Bilan d'un Quart de Siècle: 1973–1997', *Revista CIDOB d'Afers Internacionals*, Vol. 16(37), pp. 1–20.
Khader, B. (1997b), *Le Partenariat Euro-Méditerranéen après la Conférence de Barcelone*, l'Harmattan, Paris.
Khader, B. (1999), *L'Europe et la Palestine: des Croisades à Nos Jours*, L'Harmattan, Paris.
Khader, B. (2001), 'L'Europe et le Proche-Orient – l'Impératig Géopolitique', in Defence Studies Centre (ed.), *Proceedings. La Sécurité dans l'Espace de l'Est Méditerranéen et du proche-Orient*, Royal Defence College, Brussels, pp. 1–22.
Khalilzad, Z., Lesser, I.O. and Larrabee, S.F. (2000), *The Future of Turkish-Western Relations: Toward a Strategic Plan*, Rand, Santa Monica (Ca.).
Khouri, R.G. (1998), 'The Arab-Israeli Peace Process: Lessons from the Five Years since Oslo', *Security Dialogue*, Vol. 29(3), pp. 333–44.

Kienle, E. (1998), 'Destabilization through Partnership? Euro-Mediterranean Relations after the Barcelona Declaration', *Mediterranean Politics*, Vol. 3(2), pp. 1–20.
Kirisci, K. (1999), 'Turkey and the Mediterranean', in S. Stavridis, T.A. Couloumbis, T. Veremis and N. Waites (eds.), *The Foreign Policies of the European Union's Mediterranean States and Applicant Countries in the 1990s*, Macmillan, London, pp. 250–94.
Kizilyürek, N. and Hadjipavlou-Trigeorgis, M. (1997), 'An Analysis of the Cyprus Conflict: its Structure and Causes', in H.-J. Axt and H. Brey (eds.), *Cyprus and the European Union. New Chances for Solving an Old Conflict?*, Südosteuropa-Gesellschaft, München, pp. 10–23.
Köhler, M. (1996), 'Stability in Algeria, Morocco and Tunisia', in J. Janning and D. Rumberg (eds.), *Peace and Stability in the Middle East and North Africa*, Bertelsmann, Gütersloh, pp. 111–20.
Köhler, M. (1998), *Die Mittelmeerpolitik im Anschluß an die Konferenz von Barcelona*, Working Paper, Political Series, POLI 103DE, European Parliament, Directorate General for Research, Luxembourg.
Kollias, C.G. (1996), 'The Greek-Turkish Conflict and Greek Military Expenditure 1960–92', *Journal of Peace Research*, Vol. 33(2), pp. 217–28.
Korany, B. (1994), 'Un Dualisme Dérangeant', in Centre d'Études et de Recherches Internationales et Communautaires (ed.), *La Méditerranée: Espace de Coopération?*, Economica, Paris, pp. 107–22.
Koulaimah Gabriel, A. (1995), *Raison d'État ou Droit des Peuples? Le Dilemme de l'Union Européenne dans ses Rapports avec le Maroc et Israël*, Document de Travail No. 9 du Collège d'Europe, Presses interuniversitaires européennes, Brussels.
Kramer, H. (1996), 'Turkey and the European Union: a Multi-Dimensional Relationship with Hazy Perspectives', in V. Mastny and R.C. Nation (eds.), *Turkey between East and West. New Challenges for a Rising Regional Power*, Westview Press, Oxford, pp. 203–32.
Kramer, H. (1997), 'The Cyprus Problem and European Security', *Survival*, Vol. 39(3), pp. 16–32.
Kubicek, P. (2000), 'The Earthquake, Europe and Prospects for Political Change in Turkey', *Middle East Review of International Affairs*, Vol. 5(2), pp. 34–47.
Kuniholm, B. (1991), 'Turkey and the West', *Foreign Affairs*, Vol. 70(2), pp. 34–48.
Kuniholm, B. (1996), 'Sovereignty, Democracy and Identity: Turkey's Kurdish Problem and the West's Turkish Problem', *Mediterranean Politics*, Vol. 1(3), pp. 353–70.
Kyriacou, A.P. (2000), 'A "Just and Lasting" Solution to the Cyprus Problem: in Search of Institutional Viability', *Mediterranean Politics*, Vol. (3), pp. 54–75.
Lacoste, P. (1994), 'Une Nouvelle Donne Géostratégique', in Fondation Méditerranéenne d'Études Stratégiques (ed.), *La Méditerranée Occidentale. Quelles Stratégies pour l'Avenir?*, Publisud, Paris, pp. 155–8.
Lalor, P. (1999), 'Whither the Arab-Israeli Peace Process?', *Security Dialogue*, Vol. 30(3), pp. 353–64.
Lamchichi, A. (1998), 'Islam-Occident, Islam-Europe: Choc des Civilisations ou Coexistence des Cultures?', in T. Cao-Huy and A. Fenet (eds.), *La Coexistence, Enjeu Européen*, Presses Universitaires Françaises, Paris, pp. 261–86.
Lannon, E. (1996), 'La Déclaration Interministérielle de Barcelone, Acte Fondateur du Partenariat Euro-Méditerranéen', *Revue du Marché Commun et de l'Union Européenne*, Vol. 39(398), pp. 358–68.
Lannon, E. (1997), 'L'Accord d'Association Intérimaire Communauté Européenne - OLP: l'Institutionalisation Progressive des Relations Euro-Palestiniennes', *Law and European Affairs – Revue des Affaires Européennes*, Vol. 7(2), pp. 169–90.

Lannon, E. (1999), 'La PESC et le Processus de Paix au Moyen-Orient: Bilan et Perspectives Offertes par le Traité d'Amsterdam', in M. Dony (ed.), *L'Union Européenne et le Monde après Amsterdam*, Éditions de l'ULB, Brussels, pp. 259–90.

Lannon, E., Inglis, K. and Haenebalcke, T. (2001), 'The Many Faces of EU Conditionality in Pan-Euro-Mediterranean Relations', in M. Marescau and E. Lannon (eds.), *The EU's Enlargement and Mediterranean Strategies. A Comparative Analysis*, Palgrave, New York, pp. 97–138.

Larrabee, F.S. (1998), 'The EU Needs to Rethink its Cyprus Policy', *Survival*, Vol. 40(3), pp. 25–9.

Larrabee, F.S. (1999), 'US Policy toward Cyprus and the Eastern Mediterranean: Changing Strategic Perspectives after the Cold War', in S. Baier-Allen (ed.), *Looking into the Future of Cyprus-EU Relations*, Nomos, Baden-Baden, pp. 231–47.

Larrabee, F.S., Green, J., Lesser, I.O. and Zanini, M. (1998), *NATO's Mediterranean Initiative. Policy Issues and Dilemmas*, Rand Corporation, Santa Monica (Ca.).

Larrabee, F.S. and Thorson, C. (1996), *Mediterranean Security. New Issues and Challenges*, Rand Corporation, Santa Monica (Ca.).

Latter, R. (1991), *Mediterranean Security*, Wilton Park Paper No. 48., HMSO, London.

Latter, R. (1995), *The Mediterranean Security Crisis*, Wilton Park Paper No. 103, HMSO, London.

Leenders, R. (1999), 'Algeria. Civilians Trampled in a State of Turmoil', in European Platform for Conflict Prevention and Transformation (ed.), *Searching for Peace in Africa. An Overview of Conflict Prevention and Management Activities*, EPCPT, pp. 8–16.

Leenders, R. (1999), 'Western Sahara. Africa's Last Colony', in European Platform for Conflict Prevention and Transformation (ed.), *Searching for Peace in Africa. An Overview of Conflict Prevention and Management Activities*, EPCPT, pp. 1–7.

Lemke, H.-D. (2000), 'Rüstungskontrolle für den Mittelmeerraum: Chance oder Utopie?', in A. Jacobs and C. Masala (eds.), *Hannibal ante Portas? Analysen zur Sicherheit an der Südflanke Europas*, Nomos, Baden-Baden, pp. 96–121.

Le Morzellec, J. (1998), 'Sécurité Régionale: l'Exemple du Bassin Méditerranéen', *Les Cahiers du CREMOC*, September, pp. 1–14.

Leonard, S. (2001), 'La Stratégie Commune de l'Union Européenne à l'égard de la Région Méditerranéenne', in M. Dumoulin and G. Duchenne (eds.), *L'Europe et la Méditerranée. Actes de la VIe Chaire Glaverbel d'Études Européennes 2000–2001*, PIE – Peter Lang, Brussels, pp. 281–300.

Leray, R. (2001), 'L'Élargissement du Rôle Politique de l'Europe', in Fondation Méditerranéenne d'Études Stratégiques (ed.), *Euro-Méditerranée 1995–1999. Premier Bilan du Partenariat. Actes du Colloque*, Publisud, Paris, pp. 77–80.

Lesser, I.O. (1995), 'Growth and Change in Southern Europe', in J.W. Holmes (ed.), *Maelstrom. The United States, Southern Europe and the Challenges of the Mediterranean*, The World Peace Foundation, Cambridge (MA), pp. 11–28.

Lesser, I.O. (1997), 'Unresolved Issues: Assignments for the North and South', *Revista CIDOB d'Afers Internacionals*, Vol. 16(38–39), pp. 1–3.

Lesser, I.O. (1999a), 'The Changing Mediterranean Security Environment: a Transatlantic Perspective', in G. Joffé (ed.), *Perspectives on Development. The Euro-Mediterranean Partnership*, Frank Cass, London, pp.212–27.

Lesser, I.O. (1999b), 'Turkey's Strategic Options', *The International Spectator*, Vol. 34(1), pp. 79–87.

Lesser, I.O. (2000a), 'Turkey in a Changing Security Environment', *Journal of International Affairs*, Vol. 54(1), pp. 183–98.

Lesser, I.O. (2000b), *NATO Looks South: New Challenges and New Strategies in the Mediterranean*, Rand Corporation, Santa Monica (Ca.).

Lesser, I.O. (2000c), 'Geopolítica del Mediterráneo Occidental', *Política Exterior*, Vol. 75(Mayo/Junio), pp. 73–83.
Lesser, I.O., Green, J., Larrabee, F.S. and Zanini, M. (2000), *The Future of NATO's Mediterranean Initiative: Evolution and Next Steps*, Rand Corporation, Santa Monica (Ca.).
Lesser, I.O. and Tellis, A.J. (1996), *Strategic Exposure. Proliferation around the Mediterranean*, Rand Corporation, Santa Monica (Ca.).
Leveau, R. (1992), *Algeria: Adversaries in Search of Uncertain Compromises*, Chaillot Paper No. 4, WEU Institute for Security Studies, Paris.
Leveau, R. (1996), 'The Future of the Maghreb', in J. Janning and D. Rumberg (eds.), *Peace and Stability in the Middle East and North Africa*, Bertelsmann, Gütersloh, pp. 93–110.
Leveau, R. (1999), 'Vers une Coopération Euro-Américaine à la Stabilisation du Maghreb?', in P. Cross and G. Rasamoelina (eds.), *Conflict Prevention Policy of the European Union. Recent Engagements, Future Instruments*, Nomos, Baden-Baden, pp. 48–54.
Levite, A.E. and Landau, E.B. (1997), 'Confidence and Security Building Measures in the Middle East', *The Journal of Strategic Studies*, Vol. 20(1), pp. 143–71.
Lewis, B. (2002), *What Went Wrong? Western Impact and Middle Eastern Response*, Oxford University Press, Oxford.
Lewis, W.H. (1999), 'Policy Challenges – Past, Present and Future', in N.A. Stavrou (ed.), *Mediterranean Security at the Crossroads: a Reader*, Duke University Press, Durham (N. Ca.), pp. 57–68.
Liguori, C. (2001), *Europa e Maghreb: Ipotesi per Nuove Forme di Cooperazione nel Quadro del Partenariato Euro-Mediterraneo*, Italian Chair Working Papers in Euro-Mediterranean Relations and Politics No. 2.
López Aguirrebengoa, P. (1998), 'Transatlantic Coordination and the Middle East Peace Process', in J. Monar (ed.), *The New Transatlantic Agenda and the Future of EU-US Relations*, Kluwer Law International, London, pp. 33–47.
Lorca Corrons, A.V. (1996), 'The EU and the Mediterranean: Is an "Us" versus "Them" Situation Inevitable?', *The International Spectator*, Vol. 31(3), pp. 51–69.
Lorca Corrons, A.V., Almansa Maroto, A. and Jerch, M. (1996), 'La Compatibilité des Frontières "Sud versus Est"', *Law and European Affairs - Revue des Affaires Européennes*, Vol. 6(4), pp. 324–35.
Luft, G. (1999), 'The Palestinian Security Services: Between Police and Army', *Middle East Review of International Affairs*, Vol. 3(2), pp. 47–63.
Maoz, Z. (1997), 'Regional Security in the Middle East: Past Trends, Present Realities and Future Challenges', *The Journal of Strategic Studies*, Vol. 20(1), pp. 1–45.
Marks, J. (1996), 'High Hopes and Low Motives: the New Euro-Mediterranean Partnership Initiative', *Mediterranean Politics*, Vol. 1(1), pp. 1–24.
Marquina, A. (1997a), 'Seguridad y Estabilidad Política en el Mediterráneo', *Revista CIDOB d'Afers Internacionals*, Vol. 16(37), pp. 1–11.
Marquina, A. (1997b), 'Security and Political Stability in the Mediterranean', in A. Marquina (ed.), *Les Élites et le Processus de Changement dans la Méditerranée*, Stradimed, Toulon, pp. 1–9.
Marquina, A. (2000a), 'Review of Initiatives on CBMs and CSBMs in the Mediterranean', in H.G. Brauch, A. Marquina and A. Biad (eds.), *Euro-Mediterranean Partnership for the 21st Century*, Macmillan, London, pp. 61–76.
Marquina, A. (2000b), 'Short Term Proposals for Partnership Building Measures and Conflict Prevention', in H.G. Brauch, A. Marquina and A. Biad (eds.), *Euro-Mediterranean Partnership for the 21st Century*, Macmillan, London, pp. 245–58.

Marquina, A. (2001), 'Confidence Building Measures in the Mediterranean', in Fondation Méditerranéenne d'Études Stratégiques (ed.), *Euro-Méditerranée 1995-1999*. Premier Bilan du Partenariat. Actes du Colloque, Publisud, Paris, pp. 141-51.

Marr, P. (1998), 'The United States, Europe and the Middle East. Cooperation, Cooptation or Confrontation?', in B.A. Roberson (ed.), *The Middle East and Europe. The Power Deficit*, Routledge, London, pp. 74-103.

Marr, P. (1999), Swords into Plowshares: the Middle East Economic Challenge', in N.A. Stavrou (ed.), *Mediterranean Security at the Crossroads: a Reader*, Duke University Press, Durham (N. Ca.), pp. 222-43.

Martín Díaz, A. (1999), *The Middle East Peace Process and the European Union*, Working Paper, Political Series, POLI 115EN, European Parliament, Directorate General for Research, Luxembourg.

Martin-Muñoz, G. (1995), 'Egypte et Algérie: Convergences et Divergences', *Politique étrangère*, Vol. 60(2), pp. 403-14.

Martin-Muñoz, G. (2000), 'Political Reform and Social Change in the Maghreb', in A. De Vasconcelos and G. Joffé (eds.), *The Barcelona Process. Building a Euro-Mediterranean Regional Community*, Frank Cass, London, pp. 96-130.

Masala, C. (2000a), 'Semper Idem? Strukturen und Prozesse Transatlantischer Sicherheitspolitik nach dem Ende des Ost-West-Konflikts', in A. Jacobs and C. Masala (eds.), *Hannibal ante Portas? Analysen zur Sicherheit an der Südflanke Europas*, Nomos, Baden-Baden, pp. 11-35.

Masala, C. (2000b), 'Ein Meer voller Dialoge. Die Mittelmeerinitiativen von OSZE, WEU und NATO', in A. Jacobs and C. Masala (eds.), *Hannibal ante Portas? Analysen zur Sicherheit an der Südflanke Europas*, Nomos, Baden-Baden, pp. 161-77.

Masala, C. (2000c), *Die Euro-Mediterrane Partnerschaft. Geschichte – Struktur – Prozeß*, ZEI Discussion Paper No. 68.

Méndez Alemán, R. (2000), '*La Sécurité Méditerranéenne. L'OTAN est-elle la Solution?*', NATO Fellowship Research Report.

Menotti, R. (1999), *NATO's Mediterranean Dialogue Initiative: Italian Positions, Interests, Perceptions and the Implications for Italy-US Relations*, NATO Fellowship Research Report.

Mey, H.H. (2000), 'Möglichkeiten und Grenzen einer Non- und Counterproliferationspolitik für den Mittelmeerraum', in A. Jacobs and C. Masala (eds.), *Hannibal ante Portas? Analysen zur Sicherheit an der Südflanke Europas*, Nomos, Baden-Baden, pp. 71-95.

Meyrede, L. (1999), 'France's Foreign Policy in the Mediterranean', in S. Stavridis, T.A. Couloumbis, T. Veremis and N. Waites (eds.), *The Foreign Policies of the European Union's Mediterranean States and Applicant Countries in the 1990s*, Macmillan, London, pp. 40-72.

Miskel, J.F. (1998), 'The Future of the US Military Presence in the Mediterranean', *Mediterranean Politics*, Vol. 3(2), pp. 93-103.

Mitterrand, D. (1999), 'Europe and the Kurds', *The International Spectator*, Vol. 34(1), pp. 23-5.

Moghadam, A. (2001), 'Diplomacy and Force in the Middle East Crisis: Israeli Crisis Management Strategies, September – December 2000', *Middle East Review of International Affairs*, Vol. 5(1), pp. 90-105.

Mohsen-Finan, Kh. (1996), 'Sahara Occidental: de la Prolongation du Conflit à la Nécessité de son Règlement', *Politique étrangère*, Vol. 61(3), pp. 665-75.

Molina Del Pozo, C.F. (1996), 'L'Espagne et l'Espace Méditerranéen Rénové', *Law and European Affairs - Revue des Affairs Européennes*, Vol. 6(4), pp. 358-60.

Monar, J. (1998), 'Institutional Constraints of the European Union's Mediterranean Policy', *Mediterranean Politics*, Vol. 3(2), pp. 39-60.

Monar, J. (1999), 'Die Interne Dimension der Mittelmeerpolitik der Europäischen Union: Institutionelle und Verfahrensmäßige Probleme', in W. Zippel (ed.), *Die Mittelmeerpolitik der EU*, Nomos, Baden-Baden, pp. 65–90.

Monar, J. (2000), 'Institutional Constraints of the European Union's Middle Eastern and North African Policy', in S. Behrendt and C.-P. Hanelt (eds.), *Bound to Cooperate – Europe and the Middle East*, Bertelsmann, pp. 209–43.

Moratinos, M.A. (1998a), *The Role of the EU in the Middle East Peace Process*, speech, Barcelona, 31 March.

Moratinos, M.A. (1998b), *Palestine and the European Union: a Partnership for Peace and Economic Development in the Middle East*, speech, Ramallah, 2 October.

Morisse-Schilbach, M. (1999), *L'Europe et la Question Algérienne. Vers une Européanisation de la Politique Algérienne de la France?'*, Presses Universitaires de France, Paris.

Mortimer, E. (1994), 'Europe and the Mediterranean: the Security Dimension', in P. Ludlow (ed.), *Europe and the Mediterranean*, Brassey's, London, pp. 105–26.

Moss, K.B. (2000), 'Europe, the Mediterranean and the Middle East', *Middle East Review of International Affairs*, Vol. 4(1), pp. 1–11.

Müller, H. (2001), 'Middle Eastern Threats to the Atlantic Community', Internationale Politik und Gesellschaft, No. 4, pp. 1–18.

Nachmani, A. (2000), 'Scant Resources: the Problem of Water in Cyprus', *Mediterranean Politics*, Vol. 5(3), pp. 76–94.

Naïr, S. (1995), 'Del Nacionalismo Árabe al Islamismo', *Anuario Internacional CIDOB*, Vol. 7, pp. 1–7.

Nathan, J. (1997), 'Turkey on Edge', *International Relations*, Vol. 13(5), pp. 15–25.

Nation, R.C. (1999), 'Greek-Turkish Rivalry and the Mediterranean Security Dilemma', in S.J. Blank (ed.), *Mediterranean Security into the Coming Millennium*, US Army War College, Carlisle (PA), pp. 281–315.

Neuwahl, N. (2000), *Cyprus, Which Way? In Pursuit of a Confederal Solution in Europe*, Jean Monnet Working Paper No. 4.

Niblock, T. (1996), 'North-South Socio-Economic Relations in the Mediterranean', in R. Aliboni, G. Joffé and T. Niblock (eds.), *Security Challenges in the Mediterranean Region*, Frank Cass, London, pp. 115–36.

Nicolaïdis, K. (1998), 'Exploring Second-Best Solutions for Cyprus', *Survival*, Vol. 40(3), pp. 30–34.

Nimetz, M. (1999), 'Mediterranean Security after the Cold War', in N.A. Stavrou (ed.), *Mediterranean Security at the Crossroads: a Reader*, Duke University Press, Durham (N. Ca.), pp. 45–56.

Nordam, J. (1997), 'The Mediterranean Dialogue: Dispelling Misconceptions and Building Confidence', *NATO Review*, Vol. 45(4), pp. 26–9.

Norton, A.R. and Wright, R. (1994), 'The Post-Peace Crisis in the Middle East', *Survival*, Vol. 36(4), pp. 7–20.

Nugent, N. (1997), 'Cyprus and the European Union: a Particularly Difficult Membership Application', *Mediterranean Politics*, Vol. 2(3), pp. 53–75.

Nugent, N. (1998), 'EU Enlargement and "the Cyprus Problem"', *Journal of Common Market Studies*, Vol. 38(1), pp. 131–50.

Olgun, E. (1998), 'Recognizing Two States in Cyprus would Facilitate Co-Existence and Stability', *Survival*, Vol. 40(3), pp. 35–42.

Olgun, E. (1999), 'Possible Scenarios for Cyprus and their Implications', in S. Baier-Allen (ed.), *Looking into the Future of Cyprus-EU Relations*, Nomos, Baden-Baden, pp. 161–9.

Onis, Z. (1999), 'Turkey, Europe and Paradoxes of Identity: Perspectives on the International Context of Democratization', *Mediterranean Quarterly*, Vol. 10(3), pp. 107–36.

Ormanci, E.Y.B. (2000), *Mediterranean Security Concerns and NATO's Mediterranean Dialogue*, NATO Fellowship Research Paper.
Ortega, A. (1995), 'Relations with the Maghreb', in J.W. Holmes (ed.), *Maelstrom. The United States, Southern Europe and the Challenges of the Mediterranean*, The World Peace Foundation, Cambridge (Ma.), pp. 31–57.
Ortega, A. (1999a), 'Dialogue Méditerranéen de l'Union de l'Europe Occidentale: Évolutions Récentes', in Stradermed (ed.), *Les Actes de Milan. Deuxième Cycle d'Études Stradermed pour Décideurs de l'Union Européenne et des Pays Partenaires Méditerranéens*, Stradermed, Toulon, pp. 1–2.
Ortega, A. (1999b), *Military Dialogue in the Euro-Mediterranean Charter: an Unjustified Absence*, EuroMeSCo Paper.
Ortega, A. (2000), *The Future of the Euro-Mediterranean Security Dialogue*, Occasional Paper No. 14, WEU Institute for Security Studies, Paris.
OSCE (2000), *Handbook*, OSCE, Vienna.
Ounais, A. (1994), 'Security Trends in the Mediterranean', in F. Tanner (ed.), *Arms Control, Confidence Building and Security Cooperation in the Mediterranean, North Africa and the Middle East*, Mediterranean Academy of Diplomatic Studies, Malta, pp. 1–7.
Pace, R. (1998), 'The Domestic and International Politics of the Next Mediterranean Enlargement of the European Union', *The European Union Review*, Vol. 3(1), pp. 77–102.
Pace, R. (1999), 'Malta's Foreign Policy in the 1990s', in S. Stavridis, T.A. Couloumbis, T. Veremis and N. Waites (eds.), *The Foreign Policies of the European Union's Mediterranean States and Applicant Countries in the 1990s*, Macmillan, London, pp. 195–249.
Park, W. (2000), 'Turkey's European Union Candidacy: from Luxembourg to Helsinki – to Ankara?', *Mediterranean Politics*, Vol. 5(3), pp. 31–53.
Peresso, E.M. (1998), 'Euro-Mediterranean Cultural Cooperation', *European Foreign Affairs Review*, Vol. 3(1), pp. 135–56.
Perroni, F. (1997), 'Le Processus de Paix au Proche-Orient et l'Union Européenne', *Revue du Marché Commun et de l'Union Européenne*, Vol. 40(413), pp. 656–61.
Perthes, V. (1996), 'Security Perceptions and Cooperation in the Middle East: the Political Dimension', *The International Spectator*, Vol. 31(4), pp. 53–62.
Perthes, V. (1998), *Germany and the Euro-Mediterranean Partnership. Gradually Becoming a Mediterranean State*, Euromesco Paper.
Perthes, V. (1999a), 'Der Mittelmeerraum, der Nahöstliche Friedensprozeß und die Europäische Union: Die Suche nach einer Politischen Rolle', in W. Zippel (ed.), *Die Mittelmeerpolitik der EU*, Nomos, Baden-Baden, pp. 173–84.
Perthes, V. (1999b), 'Cooperation and Security in the Euro-Mediterranean Region', in Stradermed (ed.), *Les Actes de Milan. Deuxième Cycle d'Études Stradermed pour Décideurs de l'Union Européenne et des Pays Partenaires Méditerranéens*, Stradermed, Toulon, pp. 1–22.
Peters, J. (1996a), *Pathways to Peace: the Multilateral Arab-Israeli Talks*, Royal Institute of International Affairs, London.
Peters, J. (1996b), 'The Multilateral Dimension of the Middle East Peace Process', in R. Gillespie (ed.), *Mediterranean Politics. Volume 2*, Pinter, London, pp. 26–40.
Peters, J. (1997), *Europe and the Middle East Peace Process: Emerging from the Sidelines*, Centre for Euro-Mediterranean Studies Research Paper, University of Reading.
Peters, J. (1998), 'The Arab-Israeli Multilateral Peace Talks and the Barcelona Process: Competition or Convergence?', *The International Spectator*, Vol. 33(4), pp. 63–76.
Peters, J. (1999a), 'Can the Multilateral Middle East Talks be Revived?', *Middle East Review of International Affairs*, Vol. 3(4), pp. 1–14.

Peters, J. (1999b), 'Europe and the Arab-Israeli Peace Process: the Declaration of Berlin and Beyond', in S. Behrendt and C. Hanelt (eds.), *Security in the Middle East*, Centre for Applied Policy Research, Munich, pp. 1–14.

Peters, J. (1999c), 'Europe and the Middle East Peace Process: Emerging from the Sidelines, in S. Stavridis, T.A. Couloumbis, T. Veremis and N. Waites (eds.), *The Foreign Policies of the European Union's Mediterranean States and Applicant Countries in the 1990s*, Macmillan, London, pp. 295–316.

Piening, C. (1997), *Global Europe. The European Union in World Affairs*, Lynne Rienner Publications, London.

Pierros, F., Meunier, J. and Abrams, S. (1999), *Bridges and Barriers. The European Union's Mediterranean Policy, 1961–1998*, Ashgate,.

Pisano, V.S. (1997), 'Contemporary Terrorism and the West. A Continuing Challenge', in Defence Studies Centre (ed.), *Terrorisme et Prolifération: la Sécurité de l'Europe Occidentale*, Royal Defence Academy, Brussels, pp. 125–37.

Plattner, H. (1999), *Die Türkei. Eine Herausforderung für Europa*, Herbig, München.

Politi, A. (1999), 'Transnational Security Challenges in the Mediterranean', in S.J. Blank (ed.), *Mediterranean Security into the Coming Millennium*, US Army War College, Carlisle (PA), pp. 35–91.

Primor, A. (1998), *Der Friedensprozeß im Nahen Osten und die Rolle der Europäischen Union*, ZEI Discussion Paper No. 25.

Promodou, E.H. (1998), 'Reintegrating Cyprus: the Need for a New Approach', *Survival*, Vol. 40(3), pp. 5–24.

Pugh, M. (1997), 'Maritime Peace Support Operations in the Mediterranean', *Mediterranean Politics*, Vol. 2(3), pp. 1–19.

Pugh, M. (2000), *Europe's Boat People: Maritime Cooperation in the Mediterranean*, Chaillot Paper No. 41, WEU Institute for Security Studies, Paris.

Ragionieri, R. (1999), 'Europe, the Mediterranean and the Middle East', in S.J. Blank (ed.), *Mediterranean Security into the Coming Millennium*, US Army War College, Carlisle (PA), pp. 419–44.

Ravenel, B. (1991), 'Mer Commune, Sécurité Commune', *Confluences Méditerranée*, Vol. 1(2), pp. 1–10.

Ravenel, B. (1995), *Méditerranée. L'Impossible Mur*, L'Harmattan, Paris.

Ravenel, B. (2000), *Vers une Sécurité Commune en Méditerranée. Démilitariser le Concept de Sécurité*, Damoclès, Lyon.

Redmond, J. (1995), 'Security Implications of the Accession of Cyprus to the European Union', *The International Spectator*, Vol. 30(3), pp. 27–38.

Redmond, J. (1996), 'Mediterranean Enlargement of the European Union', in P.G. Xuereb and R. Pace (eds.), *The European Union, the IGC and the Mediterranean. State of the European Union Conference 1996*, University of Malta, Malta, pp. 186–204.

Redmond, J. (1997), 'From Association towards the Application for Full Membership: Cyprus' Relations with the European Union', in H.-J. Axt and H. Brey (eds.), *Cyprus and the European Union. New Chances for Solving an Old Conflict?*, Südosteuropa-Gesellschaft, München, pp. 89–99.

Regelsberger, E. (1997), 'The European Union Still a Capable International Actor? Consequences of the Mediterranean and the Eastern Enlargement', in H.-J. Axt and H. Brey (eds.), *Cyprus and the European Union. New Chances for Solving an Old Conflict?*, Südosteuropa-Gesellschaft, München, pp. 204–12.

Reissner, J. (1999), 'Christliches Abendland und Islamischer Orient: Probleme des Dialogs zwischen den Kulturen', in W. Zippel (ed.), *Die Mittelmeerpolitik der EU*, Nomos, Baden-Baden, pp. 11–27.

Remacle, E. (2001), 'La Nouvelle Architecture Européenne de Sécurité et sa Signification pour la Méditerranée et le Proche-Orient', in Defence Studies Centre (ed.), *Proceedings. La Sécurité dans l'Espace de l'Est Méditerranéen et du proche-Orient*, Royal Defence College, Brussels, pp. 23–30.

Research group on European Affairs (1998), *Europe, the Middle East and North Africa: the Barcelona Process in Danger?*, Universität München, München.

Reuter, J. (2000), *Reshaping Greek-Turkish Relations: Developments before and after the EU-Summit in Helsinki*, Hellenic Foundation for European and Foreign Policy Occasional Paper No. 1.

Rhein, E. (1995), 'Common and Conflicting Interests of Israel and Europe in the Middle East and the Mediterranean', in E. Ahiram and A. Tovias (eds.), *Whither EU-Israeli Relations? Common and Divergent Interests*, Peter Lang, Frankfurt AM, pp. 23–7.

Rhein, E. (1996), 'Europe and the Mediterranean: a Newly Emerging Geopolitical Area?', *European Foreign Affairs Review*, Vol. 1, pp. 79–86.

Rhein, E. (2000a), *The Role of the European Union in the Current Crisis of the Middle East Peace Process and Beyond*, Hintergrundberichte, Friedrich-Ebert-Stiftung, North Africa and Middle East Office,.

Rhein, E. (2000b), 'Searching for a Sustainable Peace Settlement between Israel and its Neighbours', in S. Behrendt and C.-P. Hanelt (eds.), *Bound to Cooperate – Europe and the Middle East*, Bertelsmann, Gütersloh, pp. 133–49.

Rhein, E. (2001), 'Peacemaking in the Middle East: Mission Possible', in F. Tanner (ed.), *The European Union as a Security Actor in the Mediterranean. ESDP, Soft Power and Peacemaking in Euro-Mediterranean Relations*, Zürcher Beitrag zur Sicherheitpolitik und Konfliktforschung No. 61, pp. 83–97.

Rich, P.B. (1998), 'The Algerian Crisis and the Failure of International Mediation', *Cambridge Review of International Affairs*, Vol. 11(2), pp. 134–51.

Rich, P.B. (2000), 'European Security and the Resurgence of Radical Islam: the Issue of the Maghreb and Algeria', in L. Aggestan and A. Hyde-Price (eds.), *Security and Identity in Europe. Exploring the New Agenda*, Macmillan, London, pp. 216–33.

Richmond, O. (1998), Broadening Concepts of Security in the Post-Cold War Era: Implications for the EU and the Mediterranean, Centre for Euro-Mediterranean Studies Research Paper No. 4, University of Reading.

Richmond, O. (1999), 'The Cyprus Conflict, Changing Norms of International Society and Regional Disjunctures', *Cambridge Review of International Affairs*, Vol. 13(1), pp. 239–53.

Richter, H.A. (1999), 'Ursachen und Perspektiven des Zypernkonflikts vor dem Hintergrund Regionaler Interessengegensätze sowie Möglicher Beiträge der EU zur Überwindung des Zypernproblems', in W. Zippel (ed.), *Die Mittelmeerpolitik der EU*, Nomos, Baden-Baden, pp. 133–56.

Richter, H.A. (2000), 'Cyprus – the Perennial Conflict', in H.G. Brauch, A. Marquina and A. Biad (eds.), *Euro-Mediterranean Partnership for the 21st Century*, Macmillan, London, pp. 225–41.

Roberson, B.A. (1998a), 'The Challenges to Lebanon in the Future Middle East', *Mediterranean Politics*, Vol. 3(1), pp. 1–9.

Roberson, B.A. (1998b), 'Islam and Europe. An Enigma or a Myth?', in B.A. Roberson (ed.), *The Middle East and Europe. The Power Deficit*, Routledge, London, pp. 104–29.

Robins, P. (1998), 'Turkey. Europe in the Middle East, or the Middle East in Europe?', in B.A. Roberson (ed.), *The Middle East and Europe. The Power Deficit*, Routledge, London, pp. 151–69.

Romeo, I. (1998), 'The European Union and North Africa: Keeping the Mediterranean "Safe" for Europe', *Mediterranean Politics*, Vol. 3(2), pp. 21–38.

Roper, J. (1999), 'The West and Turkey: Varying Roles, Common Interests', *The International Spectator*, Vol. 34(1), pp. 89–102.
Roy, P. (2001), 'La Coopération dans le Domaine Maritime en Méditerranée', in Fondation Méditerranéenne d'Études Stratégiques (ed.), *Euro-Méditerranée 1995–1999. Premier Bilan du Partenariat. Actes du Colloque*, Publisud, Paris, pp. 133–9.
Rühl, L. (1999), 'Implications on the Regional and European Security Architecture', in S. Baier-Allen (ed.), *Looking into the Future of Cyprus-EU Relations*, Nomos, Baden-Baden, pp. 63–69.
Rühl, L. (2000), 'Strategische Partnerschaften im Mittelmeerraum', in A. Jacobs and C. Masala (eds.), *Hannibal ante Portas? Analysen zur Sicherheit an der Südflanke Europas*, Nomos, Baden-Baden, pp. 36–50.
Rupérez, I. (1995), 'Turquía, un Nuevo Líder para un Mundo Diferente', *Anuario Internacional CIDOB*, Vol. 7, pp. 1–6.
Safir, N. (1993), 'Question Migratoire, Sécurité et Coopération en Méditerranée Occidentale', *Études internationales*, Vol. 24(1), pp. 79–102.
Said, A.M. (2000), 'From Geopolitics to Geo-Economics: Collective Security in the Middle East and North Africa', in S. Behrendt and C.-P. Hanelt (eds.), *Bound to Cooperate – Europe and the Middle East*, Bertelsmann, Gütersloh, pp. 35–54.
Said, A.M., and Mahmoud, A.I. (1995), 'Conventional Arms Control in the Middle East', Al-Ahram Center for Political and Strategic Studies Strategic Papers Vol. 4(29), pp. 1–28.
Salam, M.A. (1999), 'The Proliferation of Nuclear Capabilities in the Middle East: Strategic Dimensions', Al-Ahram Center for Political and Strategic Studies Strategic Papers, Vol. 8(76), pp. 1–29.
Salamé, G. (1998), 'Torn between the Atlantic and the Mediterranean. Europe and the Middle East in the Post-Cold War Era', in B.A. Roberson (ed.), *The Middle East and Europe. The Power Deficit*, Routledge, London, pp. 19–44.
Sánchez Mateos, E. (2000), *The Antipersonnel Landmines Issue in the Mediterranean*, Euromesco Paper.
Sanges d'Abadie, D. (1998), 'The EU after Amsterdam: Still towards the Mediterranean?', *Mediterranean Politics*, Vol. 3(3), pp. 81–92.
Schilling, W. (2000), 'Stabilität im Mittelmeerraum: Aufgabe Europäischer Politik', *Europäische Sicherheit Online*, No. 11, pp. 1–4.
Sefiani, N. (2001), 'Developments on the Euro-Mediterranean Relations – the Point of View of Morocco', in I. Bourloyannis-Tsangaridis (ed.), *Development of Euro-Mediterranean Relations. Perspectives and Problems*, Hellenic Foundation for European and Foreign Policy Occasional Paper No. 1, pp. 21–7.
Sehimi, M. (2001), 'Prévention des Crises et Règlement des Conflits: Quelle Vision de son Rôle par le Sud?', in Fondation Méditerranéenne d'Études Stratégiques (ed.), *Euro-Méditerranée 1995–1999. Premier Bilan du Partenariat. Actes du Colloque*, Publisud, Paris, pp. 89–97.
Sezer, D. (1999), 'Turkish Security Challenges in the 1990s', in S.J. Blank (ed.), *Mediterranean Security into the Coming Millennium*, US Army War College, Carlisle (PA), pp. 263–79.
Shalev, A. (1994), 'Trends and Risks of Security in the Middle East', in F. Tanner (ed.), *Arms Control, Confidence Building and Security Cooperation in the Mediterranean, North Africa and the Middle East*, Mediterranean Academy of Diplomatic Studies, Malta, pp. 1–2.
Shpiro, S. (2000), 'Terrorism, Media and Intelligence Cooperation', in A. Jacobs and C. Masala (eds.), *Hannibal ante Portas? Analysen zur Sicherheit an der Südflanke Europas*, Nomos, Baden-Baden, pp. 143–60.

Snyder, J.C. (1996), 'Arms and Security in the Mediterranean Region', in R. Aliboni, G. Joffé and T. Niblock (eds.), *Security Challenges in the Mediterranean Region*, Frank Cass, London, pp. 161-85.
Soffer, A. (1998), *Natural Resources in the Middle East*, Hellenic Foundation for European and Foreign Policy Occasional Paper No. 2.
Solana, J. (1999), 'NATO and the Mediterranean', in N.A. Stavrou (ed.), *Mediterranean Security at the Crossroads: a Reader*, Duke University Press, Durham (N. Ca.), pp. 35-44.
Soltan, G.A.G. (1997), 'State Building, Modernization and Political Islam. The Search for Political Community in the Middle East', *Revista CIDOB d'Afers Internacionals*, Vol. 16(37), pp. 1-8.
Soltan, G.A.G. and Aly, A.M.S. (1999), 'The Middle East Experience with Conflict Prevention', *The International Spectator*, Vol. 34(2), pp. 87-108.
Sonyel, S.R. (1997), 'Reactions in the Turkish Republic of Northern Cyprus to the Application by the Greek Cypriot Administration of South Cyprus for Membership of the European Union', in H.-J. Axt and H. Brey (eds.), *Cyprus and the European Union. New Chances for Solving an Old Conflict?*, Südosteuropa-Gesellschaft, München, pp. 151-8.
Sonyel, S.R. (1999), 'The EU as an International Actor in Conflict Resolution?', in S. Baier-Allen (ed.), *Looking into the Future of Cyprus-EU Relations*, Nomos, Baden-Baden, pp. 189-211.
Soysal, M. (1999), 'The Kurdish Issue: a Turkish Point of View', *The International Spectator*, Vol. 34(1), pp. 11-17.
Spencer, C. (1994), 'Algeria in Crisis', Survival, Vol. 36(2), pp. 149-63.
Spencer, C. (1996), 'Islamism and European Reactions: the Case of Algeria', in R. Gillespie (ed.), *Mediterranean Politics. Volume 2*, Pinter, London, pp. 121-40.
Spencer, C. (1997), 'Building Confidence in the Mediterranean', *Mediterranean Politics*, Vol. 2(2), pp. 23-48.
Spencer, C. (1998a), *Algeria: a New European Approach?*, Centre for Euro-Mediterranean Studies Research Paper No. 3, University of Reading.
Spencer, C. (1998b), 'Algeria. France's Disarray and Europe's Conundrum', in B.A. Roberson (ed.), *The Middle East and Europe. The Power Deficit*, Routledge, London, pp. 170-83.
Spencer, C. (1999a), 'Security Implications of the EMPI for Europe', in G. Joffé (ed.), *Perspectives on Development. The Euro-Mediterranean Partnership*, Frank Cass, London, pp. 202-11.
Spencer, C. (1999b), 'Partnership-Building in the Mediterranean', *The International Spectator*, Vol. 34(4), pp. 59-74.
Spencer, C. (1999c), CBMs and CSBMs and Partnership Building Measures in the Euro-Mediterranean Charter, EuroMeSCo Paper.
Spencer, C. (2001a), 'The EU as a Security Actor in the Mediterranean: Problems and Prospects', in F. Tanner (ed.), *The European Union as a Security Actor in the Mediterranean. ESDP, Soft Power and Peacemaking in Euro-Mediterranean Relations*, Zürcher Beitrag zur Sicherheitpolitik und Konfliktforschung No. 61, pp. 9-30.
Spencer, C. (2001b), 'The EU and Common Strategies: the Revealing Case of the Mediterranean', *European Foreign Affairs Review*, Vol. 6(1), pp. 31-51.
Stavridis, S. (1999), 'Double Standards, Ethics and Democratic Principles in Foreign Policy: the European Union and the Cyprus problem', *Mediterranean Politics*, Vol. 4(1), pp. 95-112.
Stavridis, S. (2001), 'The Euro-Mediterranean Partnership in perspective', in F. Attina and S. Stavridis (eds.), *The Barcelona Process and Euro-Mediterranean Issues from Stuttgart to Marseille*, Giuffrè, Milan, pp. 1-16.
Stavridis, S. and Hutchence, J. (2000), 'Mediterranean Challenges to the EU's Foreign Policy', *European Foreign Affairs Review*, Vol. 5(1), pp. 35-62.

Stefanova, R. (1999), *Early Warning in the Euro-Mediterranean Context: Conceptual Questions, Procedures and Instruments*, Euromesco Paper.
Stein, K.W. (1995), 'Politische Instabilitäten im Nahen Osten', *Internationale Politik*, Vol. 50(3), pp. 25–32.
Steinbach, U (2000), 'Der EU-Beitritt der Türkei', *Internationale Politik*, Vol. 55(3), pp. 55–61.
Steinberg, G.M. (1994), 'Middle East Arms Control and Regional Security', *Survival*, Vol. 36(1), pp. 126–41.
Steinberg, G.M. (1996a), 'The Arab-Israeli Security Dilemma and the Peace Process', *The International Spectator*, Vol. 31(4), pp. 89–103.
Steinberg, G.M. (1996b), 'European Security and the Middle East Peace Process: Lessons from the OSCE', *Mediterranean Quarterly*, Vol. 7(1), pp. 1–9.
Steinberg, G.M. (1999), 'The European Union and the Middle East Peace Process', *Jerusalem Letter*, No. 418, pp. 1–13.
Stivachis, Y.A. (1999), *European Union's Mediterranean Security Policy. An Assessment*, Hellenic Foundation for European and Foreign Policy Occasional Paper No. 1.
Stora, B. (1995), 'Conflits et Champs Politiques en Algérie', *Politique étrangère*, Vol. 60(2), pp. 329–42.
Sturmer, M. (1996), 'Security in the Mediterranean: Evolution in North Africa and Impact on the Whole Region', in Defence Studies Centre (ed.), *Proceedings. La Coopération Euro-Méditerranéenne: Hypothèses de base et Résultats. Colloque, 21 février 1996*, Royal Defence College, Brussels, pp. 55–9.
Tahiroglu, M. (1999), 'Cyprus-EU Negotiations: Potential Implications and Consequences for the Economy of Northern Cyprus', in S. Baier-Allen (ed.), *Looking into the Future of Cyprus-EU Relations*, Nomos, Baden-Baden, pp. 115–23.
Tank, G.P. (1998), 'Security Issues Emanating from the Mediterranean Basin', in K.A. Eliassen (ed.), *Foreign and Security Policy in the European Union*, Sage, London, pp. 161–83.
Tanner, F. (1996a), 'An Emerging Security Agenda for the Mediterranean', *Mediterranean Politics*, Vol. 1(3), pp. 279–94.
Tanner, F. (1996b), 'The Mediterranean Pact: a Framework for Soft Security Cooperation', *Journal of International Affairs*, Vol. 1(4) pp. 1–6.
Tanner, F. (1997), 'The Euro-Med Partnership: Prospects for Arms Limitations and Confidence Building after Malta', *The International Spectator*, Vol. 32(2), pp. 3–25.
Tanner, F. (1999a), 'Joint Actions for Peace-Building in the Mediterranean', *The International Spectator*, Vol. 34(4), pp. 75–90.
Tanner, F. (1999b), *Euro-Mediterranean Joint Actions in Support of Peace-Building and Good Governance: Prospects and Limits*, EuroMeSCo Paper.
Tanner, F. (2000a), *The Role of the EU in Peace-Building in the Mediterranean*, Geneva Centre for Security Policy Occasional Paper.
Tanner, F. (2000b), 'The Euro-Mediterranean Security Partnership: Prospects for Arms Limitation and Confidence Building', *Mediterranean Politics*, Vol. 5(1), pp. 189–206.
Tayfur, F. (2000), *Turkish Perceptions of the Mediterranean*, Euromesco Paper.
Tenet, G.J. (2000), 'Weapons of Mass Destruction: a New Dimension of US Middle East Policy', *Middle East Review of International Affairs*, Vol. 4(2), pp. 54–64.
Terpstra, R.W. (1997), 'The Mediterranean Basin as a New Playing Field for European Security Organisations', *Helsinki Monitor*, Vol. 8(1), pp. 1–8.
Theophanous, A. (1999), 'The European Union and Cyprus: Accession Negotiations and Prospects for a Solution of the Cyprus Problem', in S. Baier-Allen (ed.), *Looking into the Future of Cyprus-EU Relations*, Nomos, Baden-Baden, pp. 149–59.

Theophanous, A. (2001), 'Cyprus, Greece, Turkey and the European Union', in F. Attina and S. Stavridis (eds.), *The Barcelona Process and Euro-Mediterranean Issues from Stuttgart to Marseille*, Giuffrè, Milan, pp. 227–48.

Tibi, B. (2000), 'Politisierung der Religion. Sicherheitspolitik im Zeichen des Islamischen Fundamentalismus', *Internationale Politik*, Vol. 55(2), pp. 27–34.

Toukan, A. (1997), *Un Plan pour une Prévention Euro-Méditerranée des Conflits*, Philip Morris Institute Discussion Paper No. 14.

Tovias, A. (1997), 'Les Tribulations de la Politique Méditerranéenne de l'Union Européenne', in G. Benhayoun, M. Catin and H. Regnault (eds.), *L'Europe et la Méditerranée: Intégration Économique et Libre-Échange*, l'Harmattan, Paris, pp. 23–39.

Tovias, A. (1998), *Israel and the Barcelona Process*, Euromesco Paper.

Tovias, A. (2001), *EU Membership and Partnership as Anchors to Economic and Political Reforms in Europe's (Mediterranean) Periphery*, paper presented at the 4th Pan-European International Relations Conference, Canterbury, 8–10 September.

Tsardanidis, C. (1994), 'European Community Members and Third World States in the Mediterranean', in W. Goldstein (ed.), *Security in Europe. The Role of NATO after the Cold War*, Brassey's, London, pp. 79–89.

Tsardanidis, C. (1995), 'Common and Conflicting Interests of Mediterranean EU Member States and Third Mediterranean Countries', in E. Ahiram and A. Tovias (eds.), *Whither EU-Israeli Relations? Common and Divergent Interests*, Peter Lang, Frankfurt AM, pp. 29–44.

Tsardanidis, C. and Nicolau, Y. (1999), 'Cyprus Foreign and Security Policy: Options and Challenges', in S. Stavridis, T.A. Couloumbis, T. Veremis and N. Waites (eds.), *The Foreign Policies of the European Union's Mediterranean States and Applicant Countries in the 1990s*, Macmillan, London, pp. 171–94.

Turan, I. (1998), 'Mediterranean Security in the Light of Turkish Concerns', *Journal of International Affairs*, Vol. 3(2), pp. 1–7.

Tuschl, R.H. (1997), *Mare Nostrum Limes. Der Umgang Europäischer Sicherheitsinstitutionen mit Peripheren Konfliktformationen*, Friedenszentrum Burg Schlaining, Schlaining.

Tuygan, A. (2001), 'Developments on the Euro-Mediterranean Relations: a View from Turkey', in I. Bourloyannis-Tsangaridis (ed.), *Development of Euro-Mediterranean Relations. Perspectives and Problems*, Hellenic Foundation for European and Foreign Policy Occasional Paper No. 1 pp. 35–40.

Tzschaschel, J. (1994), 'Algerien im Widerstreit zwischen Fundamentalismus und Demokratie', *Aussenpolitik*, Vol. 44(1), pp. 23–33.

Ugboaja Ohaegbulam, F. (2000), 'US Measures against Libya since the Explosion of Pan Am Flight 103', *Mediterranean Quarterly*, Vol. 11(1), pp. 111–35.

Ünal, H. (1999), 'Implications on the EU-Turkey Relationship', in S. Baier-Allen (ed.), *Looking into the Future of Cyprus-EU Relations*, Nomos, Baden-Baden, pp. 83–89.

Valinakis, Y.G. (1994), 'La Grèce dans la Nouvelle Europe', *Politique Étrangère*, Vol. 59(1), pp. 223–32.

Valinakis, Y.G. (1999), 'Implications on the Greek-Turkish Relationship', in S. Baier-Allen (ed.), *Looking into the Future of Cyprus-EU Relations*, Nomos, Baden-Baden, pp. 71–81.

Vandewalle, D. (1994), 'The Middle East Peace Process and Regional Economic Integration', *Survival*, Vol. 36(4), pp. 21–34.

Vaner, S. (1996), 'Chypre et l'Union Européenne', *Politique Étrangère*, Vol. 61(3), pp. 651–64.

Vaner S. (2001), 'Une Perception Turque', in Defence Studies Centre (ed.), *Proceedings. La Sécurité dans l'Espace de l'Est Méditerranéen et du proche-Orient*, Royal Defence College, Brussels, pp. 37–48.

Van Leeuwen, M. (1999), *EU and US - Security Relations and the New Transatlantic Agenda. Two Case Studies*, Nederlands Instituut voor Internationale Betrekkingen Clingendael, Den Haag.
Van Westerling, J. (2000), 'Conditionality and EU Membership: the Cases of Turkey and Cyprus', *European Foreign Affairs Review*, Vol. 5(1), pp. 95–118.
Vella, G. (1999), 'Mediterranean Security in the Context of Malta's Foreign Policy', N.A. Stavrou (ed.), *Mediterranean Security at the Crossroads: a Reader*, Duke University Press, Durham (N. Ca.), pp. 145–52.
Velo, D. (1996), 'Europe's Mediterranean Policy between Variable Geometry and Single Market', *The European Union Review*, Vol. 1(1), pp. 25–40.
Venturoni, G. (1993), 'Naval Arms Control and Maritime Security in the Mediterranean', *The International Spectator*, Vol. 28(4), pp. 7–9.
Viorst, M. (1997), 'Algeria's Long Night', *Foreign Affairs*, Vol. 76(6), pp. 86–99.
Wæver, O. and Buzan, B. (2000), 'An Inter-Regional Analysis: NATO's New Strategic Concept and the Theory of Security Complexes', in S. Behrendt and C.-P. Hanelt (eds.), *Bound to Cooperate – Europe and the Middle East*, Bertelsmann, Gütersloh, pp. 55–106.
Waites, N. and Stavridis, S. (1999), 'The European Union and the Mediterranean', in S. Stavridis, T.A. Couloumbis, T. Veremis and N. Waites (eds.), *The Foreign Policies of the European Union's Mediterranean States and Applicant Countries in the 1990s*, Macmillan, London, pp. 22–39.
Watzal, L. (1995), 'Hilfreiche Konkurrenz? Die Nahost-Politik der USA und der EU im Vergleich', *Internationale Politik*, Vol. 50(7), pp. 37–42.
Webb, M. (1999), 'Regional Cooperation in the Euro-Mediterranean Partnership', in Stradedem (ed.), *Les Actes de Milan. Deuxième Cycle d'Études Stradedem pour Décideurs de l'Union Européenne et des Pays Partenaires Méditerranéens*, Stradedem, Toulon, pp. 1–15.
Weidenfeld, W. (1995), 'Europa und der Nahe Osten. Auf dem Weg zu einer Neuen Ordnung', *Internationale Politik*, Vol. 50(7), pp. 31–6.
Weidenfeld, W., Janning, J. and Behrendt, S. (1997), *Transformation im Nahen Osten und Nordafrika. Herausforderung und Potentiale für Europa und seine Partner*, Bertelsmann Stiftung, Gütersloh.
Weinrod, W.B. (1999), 'The US, NATO and the Mediterranean Region in the Twenty-First Century', in N.A. Stavrou (ed.), *Mediterranean Security at the Crossroads: a Reader*, Duke University Press, Durham (N. Ca.), pp. 89–104.
Whitman, R.G. (1999), *Securing Europe's Southern flank? A Comparison of NATO, EU and WEU Policies and Objectives*, NATO Fellowship Research Report.
Whitman, R.G. (2001), *Five Years of the EU's Euro-Mediterranean Partnership: Progress without Partnership?*, paper presented at the ISA conference, Chicago, 20–24 February.
Wilkinson, P. (1997), 'The Changing International Terrorist Threat', in Defence Studies Centre (ed.), *Proceedings. Terrorisme et Prolifération: la Sécurité de l'Europe Occidentale. Colloque, 5 mars 1997*, Royal Defence College, Brussels, pp. 25–38.
Willa, P. (1999), *La Méditerranée comme Espace Inventée*, Jean Monnet Working Paper in Comparative and International Politics No. 25.
Willis, M. (1996), 'The Islamist Movements of North Africa', in R. Aliboni, G. Joffé and T. Niblock (eds.), *Security Challenges in the Mediterranean Region*, Frank Cass, London, pp. 3–26.
Winrow, G.M. (1996), 'A Threat from the South? NATO and the Mediterranean', *Mediterranean Politics*, Vol. 1(1), pp. 43–59.
Winrow, G.M. (1998), *NATO and the Mediterranean: an Emerging Security Dialogue*, NATO Fellowship Research Report.

Winrow, G.M. (2000), *Dialogue with the Mediterranean. The Role of NATO's Mediterranean Initiative*, Garland, London.
Wohlfeld, M. and Abela, E. (2000), 'The Mediterranean Dimension of the OSCE: Confidence-Building in the Euro-Mediterranean Region', in H.G. Brauch, A. Marquina and A. Biad (eds.), *Euro-Mediterranean Partnership for the 21st Century*, Macmillan, London, pp. 77–93.
Xenakis, D.K. (1998), *The Barcelona Process: Some Lessons from Helsinki*, Jean Monnet Working Paper in Comparative and International Politics No. 17.
Xenakis, D.K. (1999a), Mediterranean Complexities, Cyprus and the EU's Enlargement, Centre for Euro-Mediterranean Studies Research Papers No. 2, University of Reading.
Xenakis, D.K. (1999b), 'From Policy to Regime: Trends in Euro-Mediterranean Governance', *Cambridge Review of International Affairs*, Vol. 13(1), pp. 254–70.
Xenakis, D.K. (2000), 'Order and Change in the Euro-Mediterranean System', *Mediterranean Quarterly*, Vol. 11(1), pp. 75–90.
Xenakis, D.K. and Chryssochoou, D.N. (2000), 'The New Framework for Euro-Mediterranean Cooperation', *Adriatico*, Vol. 1(2), pp. 1–5.
Xenakis, D.K. and Chryssochoou, D.N. (2001), *The Emerging Euro-Mediterranean System*, Manchester University Press, Manchester.
Yaffe, M.D. (1994), 'An Overview of the Middle East Peace Process. The Working Group on Arms Control and Regional Security', in F. Tanner (ed.), *Arms Control, Confidence Building and Security Cooperation in the Mediterranean, North Africa and the Middle East*, Mediterranean Academy of Diplomatic Studies, Malta, pp. 1–4.
Yata, F. (1998), 'La Perception Marocaine de la Sécurité en Méditerranée: ni Alibi, ni Placébo', in A. Marquina (ed.), *Perceptions Mutuelles dans la Méditerranée. Unité et Diversité*, Publisud, Paris, pp. 249–54.
Yilmaz, B. (1994), 'Die Neue Rolle der Türkei in der Internationalen Politik', *Aussenpolitik*, Vol. 45(1), pp. 90–98.
Yilmaz, B. (1995), 'Regionalmacht Türkei. Hat sie ihre Führungsrolle Verpaßt?', *Internationale Politik*, Vol. 50(5), pp. 37–42.
Younessi, B. (1995), 'L'Islamisme Algérien: Nébuleuse ou Mouvement Social?', *Politique Étrangère*, Vol. 60(2), pp. 365–76.
Youngs, R. (1999), 'The Barcelona Process after the UK Presidency: the Need for Prioritization', Mediterranean Politics, Vol. 4(1), pp. 1–24.
Youngs, R. (2001), *The European Union and the Promotion of Democracy. Europe's Mediterranean and Asian Policies*, Oxford University Press, Oxford.
Zaim, F. (1998), 'La Deuxième Conférence Euro-Méditerranéenne de Malte. Lenteurs et Vicissitudes du Processus Euro-Méditerranéen', in Groupement d'Études et de Recherches sur la Méditerranée (ed.), *L'Annuaire de la Méditerranée 1998*, Publisud, Paris, pp. 32–43.
Zaoual, H. (1996), 'Aspects Culturels, Islam et Fondamentalisme: Influences sur la Pratique Régionale', in Defence Studies Centre (ed.), *Proceedings. La Coopération Euro-Méditerranéenne: Hypothèses de Base et Résultats. Colloque, 21 février 1996*, Royal Defence College, Brussels, pp. 29–34.
Zervakis, P. (1997), 'The Accession of Cyprus to the EU: the Greek Viewpoint', in H.-J. Axt and H. Brey (eds.), *Cyprus and the European Union. New Chances for Solving an Old Conflict?*, Südosteuropa-Gesellschaft, München, pp. 137–50.
Zoubir, Y.H. and Bouandel, Y. (1998), 'Islamism and the Algerian Political Crisis: International Responses', *Cambridge Review of International Affairs*, Vol. 11(2), pp. 117–33.
Zucconi, M. (1999), 'NATO in the Mediterranean', in S.J. Blank (ed.), *Mediterranean Security into the Coming Millennium*, US Army War College, Carlisle (PA), pp. 111–23.

Index

'11 September' 15, 47, 50, 57, 58, 59, 62, 67, 69, 72, 79, 82, 92, 96, 103, 114, 118, 124
'5+5' Dialogue 27–8, 29

African Union, *see* Organization of African Unity
Algeria
    EMP 37, 42, 49, 54–5, 89, 123
    EU conflict resolution 76–9, 89–93, 114, 124–6
    tensions with Morocco, *see* Morocco
AMU, *see* Arab Maghreb Union
Arab League 3–4, 32, 43, 113
Arab Maghreb Union 4, 29, 31, 32, 43, 48, 80, 113
arms control
    agreements 8–10, 39, 44, 108–9
    measures 26, 33, 36, 55–6, 107–10, 115

CFSP, *see* Common Foreign and Security Policy
Cold War period 2–3, 51
    end of 25, 31–2, 34, 81–2, 120
Common Foreign and Security Policy
    Common Strategy on the Mediterranean 38, 43–6, 55, 62, 71, 113
    credibility of 19, 89, 114, 117
    EU periphery 18–19, 20–21, 30, 31, 34, 44, 73–5, 76, 79, 88–9, 91, 112–5
    objectives 18, 29, 35, 59
    organization 40, 45–6, 51, 58–9, 60, 102, 114
Common Strategy, *see* CFSP
Conference on Security and Cooperation in the Mediterranean 26–7, 28, 29, 34
CSCE, see Organization for Security and Cooperation in Europe
CSCM, *see* Conference on Security and Cooperation in the Mediterranean

Cyprus
    conflict 1, 51, 118
    EMP 37–9, 54–5, 88, 89, 123
    EU conflict resolution 82–3, 84–5, 86–8, 88–9, 89–92, 114, 124–5
    EU membership 1, 86–7

defence expenditure 5–6
democratization 11, 18, 20, 32, 59, 61, 76–7, 111–2, 114, 118, 126
disarmament, *see* arms control

ecologic issues 2, 18
    water 2
economic and financial partnership 33–4, 37, 77; *see also* socio-economic issues
EMP, *see* Euro-Mediterranean Partnership
EPC, *see* European Political Cooperation
ESDP, *see* European Security and Defence Policy
EU, *see* European Union
Euro-Arab Dialogue 24–5
EUROFOR, *see* Western European Union
EUROMARFOR, *see* Western European Union
Euro-Mediterranean Partnership
    Algeria, *see* Algeria
    Barcelona Declaration
        objectives 33–7, 70, 118
        implementation 42, 43, 44, 47, 54–62, 62–3, 79–80, 90, 109, 121
    confidence and security building measures 21, 37, 38, 39–40, 41, 42, 43–4, 46–7, 50, 54, 56–7, 62–3, 71, 96, 97–8, 99, 100, 101, 102–4, 107, 108–10, 111, 112, 115, 120, 125–8
    conflict prevention 21, 35, 40, 43, 62–3, 100, 115, 120, 125–6

conflict resolution 35, 37, 40, 43, 44, 54–5, 62–3, 70–71, 89–92, 115, 120, 122, 123, 124–5
crisis management 21, 43, 44, 46, 62–3, 89, 99, 105–6, 115, 120, 125–8
Cyprus, *see* Cyprus
Euro-Mediterranean Association Agreements 35, 37, 61, 66–7, 68, 71, 77, 79
Euro-Mediterranean Charter for Peace and Stability 33, 36, 38, 40, 42, 43, 46–7, 50, 62–3, 72, 97, 98, 101–102, 104, 110, 120
Euro-Mediterranean Ministerial Conferences
    Brussels 47–50, 55, 72–3
    Malta 39–41
    Marseilles 46–7, 52, 55
    Palermo 41–2
    Stuttgart 42–3, 81
    Valencia 50–51, 55, 73, 77
    institutions 34, 37–9, 42, 50–51, 60–62, 90, 98–102, 110–12, 112–113, 125–8
    Libya, *see* Libya
    MEDA 39, 60, 61
    Middle East peace process, *see* Middle East peace process
    origins 31–3
    political and security dialogue 33, 35, 36, 38, 42, 43, 46, 62–3, 98–102
    security concept, *see* security
    terrorism, *see* terrorism
    Turkey, *see* Turkey
    Western Sahara, *see* Western Sahara
European Political Cooperation 24, 29, 31, 35
European Security and Defence Policy
    EMP 44, 46, 50, 56, 57–8, 58–9, 60, 95–102, 105–7, 114, 115, 123, 125–6
    EU periphery 18–19, 20–21, 34, 82, 83–4
    objectives and organization 18, 94, 97, 117, 119
    Political and Security Committee 18, 105

European Union
    CFSP, *see* Common Foreign and Security Policy
    conflict resolution
        Algerian crisis, *see* Algeria
        Cyprus issue, *see* Cyprus
        Greek-Turkish tensions, *see* Turkey
        Kurdish issue, *see* Kurds, the
        Middle East, *see* Middle East peace process
        Western Sahara, *see* Western Sahara
    ESDP, *see* European Security and Defence Policy
    periphery, *see* Common Foreign and Security Policy

Global Mediterranean Policy 24–5

human rights 11, 18, 20, 32, 59, 61, 76–7, 86, 111–2, 114, 118, 126

islamism 2, 10–11, 14–5, 51, 58, 78, 79, 117–8

Kurds, the 1, 82–3, 84–5, 86, 88–9, 89–93

Libya
    EMP 36, 43, 44, 46–7, 48, 80–81
    tensions with neighbours 2, 4
    tensions with the West 8, 24, 28, 29, 30, 32, 80–81
    WMD 6–7, 13; *see also* proliferation

Mediterranean Council 29
Mediterranean Forum 28–9, 48
Middle East peace process
    EMP 27, 33, 36, 39, 40–41, 41–2, 44–5, 46, 49–50, 51, 54–6, 70–73, 81, 89, 90, 112, 121
    EU conflict resolution policy 68–70. 73–6
    Euro-Mediterranean security 1–2, 3. 30, 32, 51, 65–76, 79, 102, 107–8
    Oslo framework 1, 70, 122

Morocco
　tensions with Algeria 2, 28
　tensions with Spain 2
　Western Sahara, *see* Western Sahara

nationalism
　foreign policy 2, 3
　islamism 10–11
　proliferation 7
NATO, *see* North Atlantic Treaty Organization non-proliferation, *see* arms control
North Atlantic Treaty Organization
　Euro-Mediterranean security 2–3, 6, 14, 15, 51, 56, 57, 92, 106
　Mediterranean Dialogue 52, 78, 100, 103–4, 107
　member states 1, 23, 82, 83–4, 85, 96, 98, 100, 125

OAU, *see* Organization of African Unity
Organization for Security and Cooperation in Europe
　EMP 34, 35, 42, 100, 101
　Mediterranean dimension 26, 100
Organization of African Unity 4–5
OSCE, *see* Organization for Security and Cooperation in Europe

proliferation 6–10, 12–4, 31, 33, 51, 55–6, 57, 107–10, 118

regional integration 3–5, 26, 31, 35, 37, 61, 112, 118
Renovated or Redirected Mediterranean Policy 25–6

security
　comprehensive 20, 31, 32, 34, 35, 59, 61–2, 62–3, 111–114, 119, 121, 122
　cooperative 35, 59, 62–3, 96–7, 114, 121, 126
　'hard' 20–21, 24, 32, 34, 35, 37, 44, 54, 59, 62–3, 85, 111, 112, 117, 119, 121, 122, 126
　politico-military dimension of 20–21, 24, 32, 34, 35, 37, 44, 54, 59, 62–3, 85, 111, 112, 117, 119, 121, 122, 126

socio-economic issues 11–12, 16–18, 20, 24, 25, 26, 32, 57, 59, 77, 111–2, 114, 118, 119, 126
South-South integration, *see* regional integration

terrorism
　threat of 11, 15–6, 31, 51
　EMP 33, 36, 38, 39, 42, 44, 46, 48–9, 50, 58, 62, 63, 66, 74, 78, 103, 118–9
Turkey
　Cyprus issue, *see* Cyprus
　EMP 56, 84
　EU membership 82–4, 84–5
　Greece, tensions with 82–3, 84–5, 85–6, 88–9, 89–92, 123, 124–5
　Kurds, *see* Kurds, the

UN, *see* United Nations
United Nations
　arms control 9; *see also* arms control
　conflict resolution 89–92, 125
　Cyprus 82, 86–8, 125; *see also* Cyprus
　Libya 28, 43, 80; *see also* Libya
　Middle East peace process: 66, 69, 75; *see also* Middle East peace process
　terrorism 49; see *also* terrorism
United States
　Algeria 78
　Euro-Mediterranean security 19, 27, 32, 92, 118–9
　Libya 80–81
　Middle East peace process 36, 66, 67, 68–70, 74, 124
　Turkey 83–4, 86
US, *see* United States

weapons of mass destruction, *see* proliferation
Western European Union
Euro-Mediterranean security 29, 51–2, 96
　EUROFOR 53–4, 57, 106, 123
　EUROMARFOR 53–4, 57, 106, 123
　forces 53–4
Western Sahara
　dispute 2, 4, 28, 30
　EMP 89, 123

EU conflict resolution 79–80, 89–92, 114, 124–5
Morocco 79–80

WMD, *see* proliferation
WEU, *see* Western European Union